AF839754

Tokenisation Applied

Tokenisation is the new champion of digital transformation: a revolution that strikes at the heart of industry and commerce by elevating the humble ledger to global scale.

While other technologies stole the headlines, tokenisation quietly and steadily got to work, becoming the engine room that is now powering a wave of innovation across sectors. It is driving out inefficiency, eliminating friction, mobilising data, and enabling distributed processes built on the principles of transparency, equitable access, and trust.

From theory to practice, this clear and compelling guide explores the foundations and applications of tokenisation. Starting from such blockchain essentials as cryptographic keys, wallets and transactions, it moves into the truly transformational world of smart contracts, distributed databases and interoperability before analysing real-world applications in trade finance, healthcare, wealth management, and real estate.

Wherever you look, tokenisation is turning bold ideas into operational reality. This isn't theory; it's infrastructure. And it's here.

Whether you are a curious newcomer or a seasoned technologist, *Tokenisation Applied* looks beyond the hype to demonstrate where and why this technology matters.

Part primer, part playbook, it is an essential roadmap to the Web3 future.

Tokenisation Applied

A Business Leader's Guide to Blockchain, Smart Contracts, and Unlocking Web3

Kevin Wooldridge and Stephen Ashurst

Routledge
Taylor & Francis Group
A PRODUCTIVITY PRESS BOOK

Designed cover image: Shutterstock

First published 2026
by Routledge
605 Third Avenue, New York, NY 10158

and by Routledge
4 Park Square, Milton Park, Abingdon, Oxon, OX14 4RN

Routledge is an imprint of the Taylor & Francis Group, an informa business

ISBN: 9781032945620 (hbk)
ISBN: 9781032939643 (pbk)
ISBN: 9781003571421 (ebk)

DOI: 10.4324/9781003571421

Typeset in Garamond
by Newgen Publishing UK

Kevin Wooldridge:
For my beloved family and their unwavering support.

Stephen Ashurst:
For Anthony and Isabella forever.

Contents

Foreword

In my many years at the forefront of institutional financial services, most recently in my role as CEO of BNY Asset Servicing for EMEA, I have witnessed any number of transformative shifts across the global investment ecosystem. Few innovations, however, carry the disruptive potential and systemic promise of tokenisation.

Tokenisation is not merely a technical innovation; it represents a structural evolution in the way financial assets can be created, transferred, stored, and reconciled. For institutional investors and their service providers, the implications are profound. We are entering an era where the foundations of asset issuance, distribution and governance are being redefined.

Tokenisation Applied arrives at a critical inflection point. Market infrastructure, regulatory frameworks, and investor appetites are aligning in ways that signal a paradigm shift. Yet, understanding how to practically harness tokenisation remains a challenge. That is where this book is of most value.

This is not a book of theory. It is a practical, thoughtful, and timely guide for decision-makers who must navigate complex legacy systems while preparing for a digital future. It demystifies the technology, but more importantly, it lays out concrete use cases, operational considerations, and strategic frameworks which bridge the gap between concept and implementation.

The authors bring a unique blend of technical fluency and acumen. They understand the language of CIOs, COOs, risk officers, and regulators. Their insights will resonate with anyone tasked with future-proofing their technology and operational infrastructure.

I commend this book to all stakeholders who recognise that the time to engage with tokenisation is now.

Daron Pearce
Former CEO, BNY Asset Servicing, EMEA
Chairman, Tokenbridge (June, 2025)

Acknowledgements

As always, we are indebted to all of those who (directly or indirectly) have done the heavy lifting before us and provided a wealth of information in books, articles, blogs, websites, and videos. We couldn't have done this without you. If we've forgotten to mention you, that's on us – keep doing what you do.

We're also very grateful for the technologists, reviewers and idea-bouncers whom we have been lucky enough to be able to call on during the course of writing. Again, if what we've written is somehow not what you told us, that's all down to us.

We'd like to acknowledge contributions from Andrew Cook and Allison Fromm, as well as Tabish Mazhar for the cover art. Also a special thank you to Daron Pearce for his kind words.

We're extremely grateful to D2 Legal Technology and in particular Professor Sarah Green (Head of Digital Assets and Trade Finance, D2LT and Professor of Private Law at the University of Bristol) and Emma Wooldridge (Managing Consultant, D2LT) for their insightful perspectives into the legal status of tokens and some of the practical legal aspects of tokenisation in industry contexts.

Special thanks are also due to Igor Natanzon (courtesy of Franklin Templeton), who was able to share with us the insight he has gained from his groundbreaking work in the field of asset tokenisation during the development and launch of Franklin Templeton's tokenised money market fund FOBXX (Franklin OnChain U.S. Government Money Fund, also known as the BENJI).

And, as always, our thanks to Kris Mednansky at Taylor & Francis for her support and encouragement throughout the process.

If you're interested in a dynamic searchable repository of knowledge on blockchains and smart contracts, you could do a lot worse than taking a look at the Ethereum website (ethereum.org). Under the banner "Learn," there's a wealth of information to follow and to discover. Many of the other blockchain networks provide a similar educational service, so it's worth also visiting solana.com, cardano.org, polkadot.com, cosmos.network, tezos.com, avax.network, and algorand.co.

About the Authors

Kevin Wooldridge

After a mostly enthusiastic (and mostly successful) tilt at an Astrophysics degree, Kevin rather wandered into a career in financial technology (long before it was interesting enough to be branded as fintech). Initially cutting code in the languages of the day, he found his sweet spot as an interpreter between the worlds of business and technology, spending most of his career drawing blobs and arrows on paper and screens and explaining them to a largely sceptical audience. Latterly, Kevin has embraced the potential of tokenisation, serving as Chief Architect at Tokenbridge, a token aggregator.

A keen rambler, board gamer and self-confessed foodie, Kevin fills his spare time trying to escape London for the distant idyllic hills and woodlands of the countryside (but always comes back for the food).

This is Kevin 's third book.

Technology Applied, A Business Leader's Guide to Software, Systems and IT Projects (also with Stephen Ashurst; Routledge, 2024) is a guide for business stakeholders unfamiliar with IT projects.

The Wise Business Analyst (self-published, 2024) is a companion for business analysts at any stage in their careers.

Stephen Ashurst

By day, Stephen Ashurst is an independent software writer and wealth tech consultant. By night, he is a fintech entrepreneur. Stephen did manage to get an undergraduate degree in PPE, but failed Bar School miserably. Seeing the light, he quit law and turned his attentions to the IT industry – a good move, for all concerned.

A resident of London, Stephen travels constantly for pleasure and work. But home is where the heart is. And so are family, friends, dogs and 3,000 books. Sadly, so is his kitchen, the site of varyingly successful cooking experiments.

Introduction

What does it feel like to be in the middle of a revolution?

If there was a major technology revolution going on, you'd probably expect to have noticed.

Well, something very profound is changing right now. But you might be surprised to learn that this disruptive innovation is not in the storied fields of artificial intelligence, vaccine technology, CGI or space flight. It concerns instead the somewhat dry and dusty world of *ledgers*.

"Ledgers?" you ask. "History's most boring revolution?"

Well, ledgers are about to become exciting. Very exciting. Distributed ledger technology (aka blockchain) is already threatening to rewrite the rules of finance through the *enfant terrible* that is Bitcoin and its fellow cryptocurrencies.

But while Bitcoin has been busy grabbing all the headlines, the building blocks that support the transparent exchange of financial data in a trustless peer-to-peer network have quietly and surely become foundational to a new type of global financial solution: tokenisation.

If blockchain is the distributed motorway network of the nation, Bitcoin and its chums are the flashy sports cars weaving in and out of traffic: getting there fast but causing mayhem on the way. Tokens, on the other hand, are the trucks of heavy industry: calmly plying their trade up and down the network, delivering value (and lots of it) to all parts of the supply chain.

Ledgers (distributed or otherwise), blockchains, tokens: it's all a bit confusing to the uninitiated. What are they? Why are things changing, and why now?

That's where we can help.

Let's start with the humble *ledger*.

The Oxford English Dictionary (OED)[1] defines *ledger*, a noun that found a home in the language from 1588 CE onwards, as "...A book that lies permanently in some place... The principal book of the 'set of books' ordinarily employed recording mercantile transactions".

The good dictionary goes on in more detail: "[The ledger's] distinctive feature is that its contents consist of 'debtor-and-creditor accounts'. Usually each person (or firm) with whom the trader has business relations has an account in the ledger, headed with his or her name, and showing the sums charged to his or her debit on the left page or half-page, and on the right those credited to him or her. In the system of 'double entry' the ledger includes other accounts of similar form to these, but headed with the designations of certain branches or subdivisions of the trader's own business."

Humans have had ledgers since the first nocks were carved in sticks in prehistoric times, or the first cuneiform marks were gouged into clay tablets in ancient Egypt and Mesopotamia. In Europe in the 16th Century, the big step forwards was the implementation of the double-sided ledger, as the OED records. It literally transformed human society and government: banks were invented, finance, trade, legal contracts ... all of that and more.

Hundreds of years later, in 1970, the ledger went 3D with the invention of the relational database, presaging a huge leap forward in software design.

And then, with the invention of Bitcoin in 2009, a new type of ledger was born: *distributed ledger technology*, also known as a *blockchain*.

But that's not quite the whole story.

Because humans have used plenty of distributed ledgers for millennia, and in countless different cultures and societies.

Take the calendar, for example. No one person owns or controls the calendar. We all have equal access to it. The calendar is transparent and each new "block" of time, whether a day or week or month or year, contains all the history that's ever gone before – unless a majority of us agree to change that. We don't (these days) have to reconcile the day or date in a calendar: we all implicitly trust it.

Distributed ledgers are, in fact, an ancient concept. It's only the technology that's new.

So, where do tokens fit in?

Well, tokens are actually like cloakroom tickets, or chips in a game of poker or at the roulette wheel. The word comes to us from the Old English for a sign, symbol or mark. A token refers to something else – like an address on a distributed ledger. Or an entry in a calendar.

Let's imagine that Kevin and Stephen have agreed to meet for a beer in a popular spot in London's Highgate. Having agreed on the date and the time, they each write an entry in their copy of the distributed ledger (aka in the calendar app in their phones).

"*Beer at The Flask, Highgate, 7pm Sunday 13th July 2025*".

The entry itself has no value: it is not the table at which the two friends will sit nor is it the beer they will drink. It is just data: the details of when and where those things will happen. Data that's stored on the distributed ledger that is the calendar.

It's a *token.*

We might call it a "meeting token" and it shares many of the properties of the tokens you'll read about in this book. It is not owned by one party or the other.

It can be accessed by everyone involved. It is transparent and, once agreed and accepted by both parties, they can trust that the meeting will take place.

In the real world, things can get a bit more complicated than in our simple calendar and meeting example. Blockchain networks need to be established and managed. Participants and token issuers need to worry about more than simply adding entries to a calendar app on their phones. The issue of trust (as we shall see) is pivotal: in our example above, both friends implicitly trust that the other will show up (and the worst outcome is that one of them sits for a while sipping on a beer, scrutinising his phone while projecting the air of one who enjoys solitude). In business, when vast sums of money are potentially on the line, trust and security are paramount.

But this very complexity is what makes real-world tokens (and tokenisation) potentially so transformative. It's what sets them apart from our simple calendar entry. For example, what if the meeting token was programmable?

Imagine that not only do Kevin and Stephen have an app on their phone, but that access to the app is also given to the proprietor of the pub and to the local transport authority, among others. Imagine that the token in the app could be so conceived that it could be updated by any of these parties to record a delay, or the table availability, or any one of a number of logistical aspects: all in one place, on a medium that everyone trusts. What if each of the friends had recorded their beer preferences in tokenised form, and that this information was available on the app for the landlord to read? A perfect pint waiting for you as you step into the pub? Every time? Now that's transformative!

Now you might think that some (or indeed all) of this information is available on the web. We have calendars. We have maps. We have train timetables. But here's the thing: these are all through different apps, each updated (and the data owned and managed) by a separate party.

Where blockchains and tokens collide: that's where the magic happens.

That's the heart of Web3.

Chris Dixon's work, *Read, Write, Own*[2] is a seminal text on the power of blockchains, much loved by the authors of this book. In it, Dixon notes that the internet and World Wide Web have moved through three distinct phases:

- Web1 – "Read" – the early internet user was typically looking for data written or recorded by someone else – characterised by early online directories such as Yahoo! Or centrally-published material
- Web2 – "Write" – the web opened up to content creators through YouTube and social media channels (although the material is increasingly owned by the mega corporations that run these platforms)
- Web3 – "Own" – through blockchain (specifically), data is democratised and can be owned by content creators.

As we'll see through the rest of this book, tokens and tokenisation build on the ownership capabilities enabled by the blockchain networks to facilitate trustless processes and data that is fully owned by the participants.

This book is in two parts.

Part 1 is a "how to" guide. Starting (necessarily) from blockchain and the components that make up the distributed ledger, we move through the features that separate tokenisation from the mechanics of the cryptocurrencies and promise genuine opportunities for change.

In Part 2, we get a bit more practical. Expanding on some of the case studies introduced in our sister volume *Blockchain Applied*,[3] we explore how tokenisation can add value to the core processes in a range of industries by removing friction, sharing data and building trustless, efficient automated processes.

By the end, we hope that even if you're not directly participating in the tokenisation revolution, you'll at least have a good grasp of why it's happening and where it's going.

Notes

1 Oxford University Press. (n.d.). *Oxford English Dictionary* (3rd ed., continuously updated; update June 2025).

2 Dixon, Chris. (2025). *Read Write Own: Building the Next Era of the Internet*. London: Penguin Random House (UK) / Cornerstone Press.

3 Ashurst, S., & Tempesta, S. (2021). *Blockchain Applied: Practical Technology and Use Cases of Enterprise Blockchain for the Real World*. Abingdon, UK / New York, NY: Routledge (Taylor & Francis).

TOKENISATION MECHANICS

I

In Part I of this book, we explore and explain the inner workings of tokenisation.

Starting with a general overview of blockchain technology, we move on to explore how data and applications are deployed onto the blockchain, how identity can be managed and how tokenised applications and data can interoperate across and within networks. We'll also examine the risks from a technology, business and legal perspective.

This isn't a technical book, so we'll stop short of anything that's too detailed. Our goal is to provide a broad understanding of the technological foundations of a transformative business proposition.

DOI: 10.4324/9781003571421-1

Chapter 1

The Case for Tokenisation

Blockchain technology is still relatively young. Bitcoin, the original distributed ledger, is barely sixteen years old.[1]

Tokenisation (the representation of real-world assets or data on a blockchain) is even younger. The Ethereum network heralded the arrival of the tokenisation toolset as recently as July 2015.[2]

That's just over a decade ago.

By way of comparison, the World Wide Web launched in 1991. It was another seven years before Google arrived on the scene; six more for Facebook.

By that yardstick, tokenisation is about to take off.

Tokenisation offers so much: "a new model of digital asset ownership that enhances transparency, efficiency and accessibility";[3] not just a way to automate existing manual processes, but to enhance them through new capabilities. Multi-stage processes can become smoother with more efficient hand-offs between parties and data that is visible to all. Dispute-resolution will become a simple matter of consulting the shared ledger: one source of truth, accepted and acknowledged by everyone. Friction is reduced; control is increased. Costs and risks are avoided.

And yet there still seems to be a degree of inertia, even reticence, within the industries it could transform. Distributed ledger technology is still viewed in many quarters as a solution looking for a problem.

DOI: 10.4324/9781003571421-2

It's true that there are still some barriers that need to be overcome. The global regulatory landscape remains uneven with different jurisdictions treating tokens in inconsistent and sometimes contradictory ways. While some countries have embraced the innovation, others continue to apply outdated pre-tokenisation frameworks. On the technology side, the infrastructure is still evolving, and most organisations are yet to get to grips with the technology and collaborative mindset that tokenisation requires. Hurdles such as identity management and security of both interfaces and data remain.

Public trust is also an issue. Blockchain is invariably tarnished by its relationship with cryptocurrencies, their scandals, their wild fluctuations in value and their links to nefarious activities.

But blockchain is not crypto. Blockchain is *more than* crypto.

Think of blockchain as a network of highways, an infrastructure capable of delivering enormous value to those who use it. Cryptocurrencies, then, are the flashy sports cars, racing up and down, weaving from lane to lane, craving all the attention. Look at me! Tokenisation represents the heavy goods vehicles of industry and the white vans of entrepreneurship: putting the highways to good use, delivering value to commerce and enabling new industries to flourish.

So how should one evaluate whether a process or business function is ripe for tokenisation? We propose three key criteria:

- Transparency
- Equitable access
- Trust.

Transparency is fundamental. If a process benefits from a shared, immutable ledger where auditability and traceability are important, then blockchain becomes a natural fit. This is evident in areas like supply chain management, where knowing the provenance and movement of goods is critical, or in public record-keeping, where tamper-proof data is vital.

Equitable access is the second criterion. Traditional systems often rely on centralised parties to mediate access to data or resources. If a process involves multiple actors who require shared visibility and where no single party should own the process or the data, then tokenisation creates a neutral, accessible infrastructure. This makes it ideal for consortium-based industries or collaborative ecosystems where power needs to be balanced across participants.

And finally, *trust*. Specifically, where trust is required for the adequate execution of the process but is not to be placed in the hands of a specific party. Instead of trusting a central authority or intermediary, participants can trust in the underlying code and consensus mechanisms that govern a tokenised system. This shift can be transformative, particularly in sectors where intermediaries add cost, complexity, or where their impartiality is in question.

There are other factors.

High-frequency or high-volume processes, or complex processes requiring point-of-execution logic will benefit from the automation that tokenisation brings. The fragmentation of high-value assets may act as a gateway to the democratisation of such assets by making them available to the person in the street. But many of these benefits would also accrue from a non-tokenised but well-automated system.

Not every process should be tokenised. Sometimes, the existing solution may simply need to be upgraded or replaced with better engineering. Simple, bilateral exchanges or highly centralised systems may not benefit from the added complexity of tokenisation. Sometimes, a trusted authority has a role to play in an ecosystem. Tokenisation should not be a hammer looking for a nail.

There are risks, too. Legal and regulatory concerns may have an impact on the pace (or even possibility) of tokenisation, depending on the industry. When trust is replaced (or federated) by a tokenised solution, there may need to be controls on who can deploy solutions and how they are audited. For more multi-party solutions, the orchestration and sequencing of activities may become complex. And there will continue to be a robust debate over the use of public or private blockchain networks in finding the balance between security and transparency.

This is not about evangelising a technology for its own sake. Any decision to tokenise must be grounded in genuine need and demonstrable advantage.

Start with the problem. Ask where the pain points lie. Identify where data is siloed, access is inequitable, or trust is in short supply. If transparency, equitable access, and trust are not just desirable but necessary, then the case for tokenisation becomes not just clear but compelling.

In the rest of this book, we explore how these principles play out in the real world. From tokenised equity to digital identity, from logistics to intellectual property, we will trace the contours of this new economy.

Notes

1 Nakamoto, S. (2008, October 31). *Bitcoin: A Peer-to-Peer Electronic Cash System.* Retrieved from https://www.bitcoin.org/bitcoin.pdf

2 Buterin, V. (2014). *Ethereum White Paper: A Next-Generation Smart Contract & Decentralized Application Platform.* Retrieved from https://ethereum.org/whitepaper/

3 World Economic Forum & Accenture. (2025, May). *Asset Tokenization in Financial Markets: The Next Generation of Value Exchange.* Geneva: World Economic Forum. Retrieved from https://www.weforum.org/publications/asset-tokenization-in-financial-markets-the-next-generation-of-value-exchange/

Chapter 2

Tokenisation: The Basics

Tokenisation is the process by which real-world assets or services are converted into digital tokens on a distributed ledger. The digital token becomes an on-chain representation of the real-world asset and can be managed by participants who have access to the distributed ledger as part of a blockchain network.

After a potted history of blockchain and tokenisation, in this chapter we'll look at what blockchains are and how they work. We will also start to look at the tokenisation process and how it builds on the opportunities and capabilities provided by blockchain, before starting to think about the practical aspects of tokenisation.

2.1 Tokenisation: A Short History

Digitising real-world assets is nothing new. High street banks have been digitising money for well over half a century.

Initially, records were held internally. We would only get to know our account balance if we went into a branch to ask or received a paper statement in the post. Let's call that Web0.

The arrival of the internet (Web1) allowed us to see our bank balance on screen any time we wanted through the bank's own applications. Web2 and initiatives

DOI: 10.4324/9781003571421-3

such as open banking made this data available to non-proprietary applications. We could see and use the data through whichever medium we chose, but the data still belonged to the bank.

Which brings us to Web3, blockchain, and tokenisation. Tokenisation allows real-world assets to be represented on a network, capable of being owned and managed by the individual. It is this ownership and transparency that sets the world of tokenisation apart from the versions that have gone before.

In October 2008, following the global economic crash, the hitherto unknown name of Satoshi Nakamoto was associated with an extraordinary paper *Bitcoin: A Peer-to-Peer Electronic Cash System*,[1] which was posted to an obscure cryptography mailing list. Not only did the paper set out the proposed mechanics for a cryptographic distributed currency, it also railed against the iniquities of the traditional banking system and "the inherent weaknesses of the trust based model."

Satoshi put forward a solution for an "electronic payment system based on cryptographic proof instead of trust, allowing any two willing parties to transact directly with each other without the need for a trusted third party.[2]"

In January 2009, Bitcoin was launched and the first cryptocurrency transaction took place. Other coins followed, mostly cloned from the original Bitcoin source code. Over the next few years, cryptocurrencies grew from being niche and obscure to mainstream news with stories about their dramatic rise in value. Relatively few people, however, took the time to look behind the news stories at the mechanism that powered cryptocurrencies – blockchain.

It was the launch of the Ethereum network in 2015 that transformed blockchain from being purely a cryptocurrency mechanism into a truly innovative business infrastructure. Ethereum's founders saw the vast potential of blockchain and realised that Bitcoin and its derivatives were too constrained by the original source code to realise that potential. So rather than copying Bitcoin, they built a new network – Ethereum – that would create a distributed virtual machine through executable code implemented as transactions on the blockchain. Instead of centrally creating a solution for each business case in turn, these "smart contracts" would allow the community of users to solve their own business cases however they chose by building software (implementing a "Turing-complete programming language[3]") that could be distributed to every node. Instead of just democratising currencies, it was now possible to democratise any security, be it stocks and bonds, mutual funds, real estate, or even business functions like supply chains.

In the decade since Ethereum's launch, blockchain networks have continued to evolve. Ethereum itself has significantly changed some of its key operational parameters while new entrants such as Cardano and Polkadot propose alternative architectures that address lingering concerns over scalability, security and decentralisation (the so-called "blockchain trilemma").

The blockchain community and well-funded research and development teams have enhanced the capabilities of blockchain that were evident to Ethereum's founders in 2015. There are now thousands of different blockchain networks, capable of supporting the tokenisation needs of almost any industry.

Much of the press and public attention is still given to coins and their valuations. Even when people talk about tokens, they are often referring to coin-like pseudo-investments (with recent unprecedented interest in "fan" tokens, "meme coins" and more infamous "shit coins"). Tokenisation and the true potential of blockchain to bring efficiency and scale to global industries sits very much in the background.

But, as we shall see, designing and delivering a tokenised solution to an industry problem is not a simple task. An entire new discipline has been created and even the most forward-thinking organisations are only just beginning to scratch the surface.

2.2 Tokenisation: An Overview

This section provides an overview of tokenisation and the distributed ledger (blockchain) technology behind it: an "elevator pitch" if you will, or "tokenisation for dummies". Don't worry if some of the terminology seems strange or obscure – the rest of this chapter will expand and demystify most of it (we hope).

Distributed Ledger Technology (DLT), in the form of blockchains, may sound complicated, but in truth it's very simple. A number of computers, connected to each other by the public internet, share a program that allows them to collectively manage transactions and data. The trusted data (the "ledger") is then shared equally and transparently ("distributed") to and by all of the network of computers (the "technology").

At its core, blockchain technology is about *trust* without intermediaries. Traditional financial transactions require a trusted third party, such as a bank, to verify and process payments. Blockchain eliminates this need by using cryptographic hashing proofs and consensus mechanisms to secure a distributed, tamper-proof ledger. Each block of transactions is cryptographically linked to the previous one, ensuring that once data is recorded, it cannot be altered.

Cryptography plays a central role in securing blockchain networks. Public-Key Cryptography (PKC) generates secure key pairs, allowing users to sign transactions without exposing their private keys. Elliptic Curve Cryptography (ECC) ensures that a *public key* can be derived from a *private key*, but not vice versa. Meanwhile, hashing algorithms such as SHA-256 create unique digital fingerprints of transaction data to prevent or detect tampering.

A *blockchain network* is composed of *nodes*: computers running the blockchain's software (the *node program*). Nodes connect to other nodes to form the network, as well as validating and storing transactions. Full nodes store the entire blockchain history, while light nodes may store only part of it. Verification is performed by validator or mining nodes.

A blockchain's node program defines its key operating parameters, as well as its governance rules. Public networks, like Bitcoin and Ethereum, are open to all participants, whereas private blockchains restrict access to selected members. Hybrid models, like Polkadot and Cosmos, allow for interoperability between different blockchains. Some governance models involve using the features of the blockchain itself for voting and decision-making, to create a Decentralised Autonomous Organisation (DAO).

Nodes submit and verify *transactions*, which alter the state of the data within the network. *Consensus* mechanisms, such as Proof of Work (PoW) and Proof of Stake (PoS), ensure that only legitimate transactions are added to the blockchain. *Network security* is ensured because attackers would need to control over 50% of the network's resources to manipulate the system, which is prohibitively expensive.

Most networks support a native *coin* (such as Bitcoin or Ether). *Gas* fees, paid in the network's native coin, incentivise nodes to process transactions.

Smart contracts are programs that can be deployed on some blockchain networks. They are invoked by transactions, allowing the manipulation of data and the management of *tokens* which represent digital or real-world assets or services (Figure 2.1).

2.3 Tokenisation: The Components

Let's unpick that overview, term by term.

To help to illustrate some of the concepts (and uses) of blockchain and tokenisation, we're going to use the example of the "Blockchain Book Club."

The Blockchain Book Club comprises five (previously six) members who make regular contributions to a kitty which is then spent on table reservations and supplies for club meetings.

The members of the club are Kai, Alexis, Jo, Rene, and Kiran. Following some bouts of theft from the kitty by the previous treasurer, Sam, the club members have decided to operate using some of the concepts of blockchain for additional security.

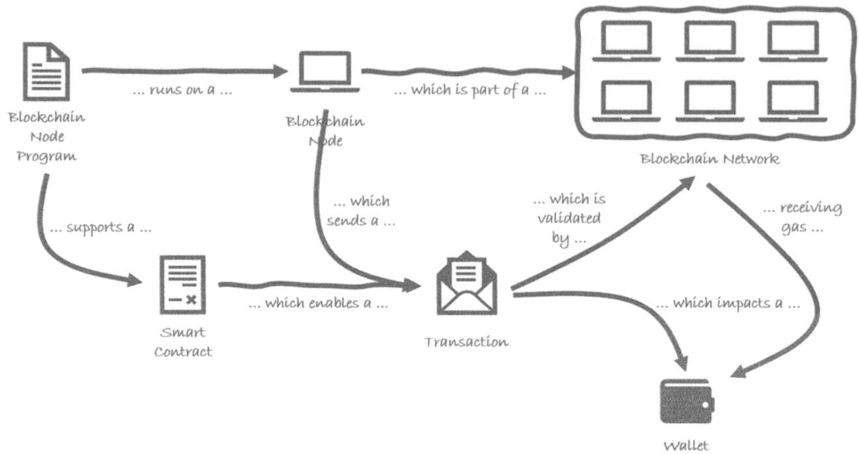

Figure 2.1 Tokenisation Basics.

They have each purchased a laptop on which they all run the same spreadsheet software. On the spreadsheet they record every contribution to the kitty made by members of the club which then creates a balance for each member. They use a messaging application to stay in touch with each other and to regularly check the contents of every cell in all copies of the spreadsheet. The five copies of the spreadsheet should always be in step – and this is the distributed ledger.

2.3.1 Trust

The story of blockchains is essentially one of *trust*. The first blockchain network (Bitcoin) was created by Satoshi Nakamoto as a response to the perceived need for a trusted third party in any financial transaction.

As soon as things get more complicated than a simple bilateral exchange of goods or services between two parties, somewhere in the transaction there is a third party on whom both the buyer and seller rely to facilitate the exchange. In the case of fiat currency, the trusted third party is whoever minted the coin or printed the note, giving it value. In electronic transactions, the trusted third party is invariably a regulated bank who monitors and validates transactions and balances, ensuring that the buyer has the necessary funds to pay the seller.

In a blockchain, this trust is achieved through a shared database secured by *cryptographic hashing* – a one-way conversion of data into a complex code using a *cryptographic key*. All parties know that they can trust the data in the shared database because it would be impossible, due to the mathematics required, for any one party to amend the cryptography and replicate the cryptographic signature.

Trust is fundamental to blockchains and tokenisation. The network participants must know that the data in the blockchain is reliable before they will think about using a distributed ledger to hold or transfer valuable data. Critical to this trust are two key concepts: cryptographic hashing and consensus. Together, these concepts ensure the immutability of existing data on the chain as new blocks of data are appended.

Think of a trusted third party, such as a bank. It is the bank that looks after your data. The database is secure, protected by a firewall, and you can only see it by using the bank's own applications. You completely rely on the bank to only update your data based on your authorised inputs.

In a distributed ledger, transactions are gathered together in blocks and stored sequentially on a shared database. As each new block is validated, it is appended to the end of the chain by the validating node before being replicated to all the other nodes. It is the mechanism by which these blocks are appended that allows all participants to trust the data on the chain.

The data in each block is hashed together using an algorithm defined by the blockchain. This one-way operation creates a code that can be replicated at any time by performing the same hash operation on the same data. Crucially, this code is then embedded in the next block to be written.

If a "dishonest node" sought to gain an advantage by rewriting chain history, it can't simply replace the data in a previous block as the data and the hashed code would no longer correspond.

However, a dishonest node could seek to write erroneous transactions in new blocks, such as sending non-existent money from a wallet address (so called "double spending"). The node could write the erroneous transaction, "validate" it and add it to the end of the blockchain. But this is where the consensus mechanism defends the integrity of the data. All of the other nodes in the network ("honest nodes") are working hard validating their own blocks of transactions. The honest nodes are continually checking the data in the chain and conferring with each other to agree what is the correct version of the truth. They do this essentially by agreeing to honour the longest chain of data.

Figure 2.2 shows how a dishonest node acting alone is outpaced by honest nodes adding valid blocks and forming the longest chain of blocks.

For a dishonest node (or a collection of dishonest nodes) to convince the rest of the network that their chain is the correct one would require the malicious participant to control more than 50% of the network nodes (namely, be able to add blocks on the end of the erroneous chain faster than the rest of the network is able to add blocks to the end of the genuine chain). Public blockchains take great care not to allow this to happen.

For the Blockchain Book Club, trust is clearly a key consideration, given the previous thefts by the trusted party, Sam. By regularly sharing the details held in their separate spreadsheets they ensure that each of them always has an up-to-date account of the kitty contents. To ensure that messages on the application are only sent by members of the club, they create a group within the messaging application containing only the club members.

2.3.2 Cryptography

Throughout this book, we're going to talk a lot about cryptography. We've mentioned it three times already just in this chapter. There's no getting away from it. Data in a blockchain is cryptographically hashed, cryptographically secured, cryptographically signed and so on. Cryptography is at the heart of the trust-less nature that is integral to blockchain and distributed ledgers. It has even given its name to the poster child of blockchain: cryptocurrency.

But most of us only have a vague idea of what cryptography is. Very few of us will ever really understand it well. Most of the time, the concepts and complex algorithms can stay shut away in a box. We don't need to know about them to take advantage of the opportunities that blockchain provides us.

But let's lift the lid of that box just a little.

Online dictionaries give us a range of definitions for cryptography, from "the enciphering and deciphering of messages in secret code or cipher[4]" or "the practice of creating and understanding codes that keep information secret[5]" to Wikipedia's rather insightful version: "the practice and study of techniques for secure communication in the presence of adversarial behaviour[6]".

Essentially, cryptography is about coding messages (or data) in such a way that they are readable only by the intended recipient, through the mechanism of a secret code. The word itself comes to us from the Greek *kryptós*, meaning "hidden" or "secret," and *graphein*, meaning "to write."

For our purposes, we'll consider two key concepts: *public-key cryptography* and *hashing*.

Public-Key Cryptography (PKC) is about generating public keys from private keys in a way that keeps secrets and doesn't expose the value of the private key. PKC allows messages to be sent (or data to be encrypted) using a key that is demonstrably from the sender (because it uses a public key) without compromising their security.

Public-key cryptography typically uses the mathematical properties of elliptic curves (known as Elliptic Curve Cryptography or ECC) to generate a public key

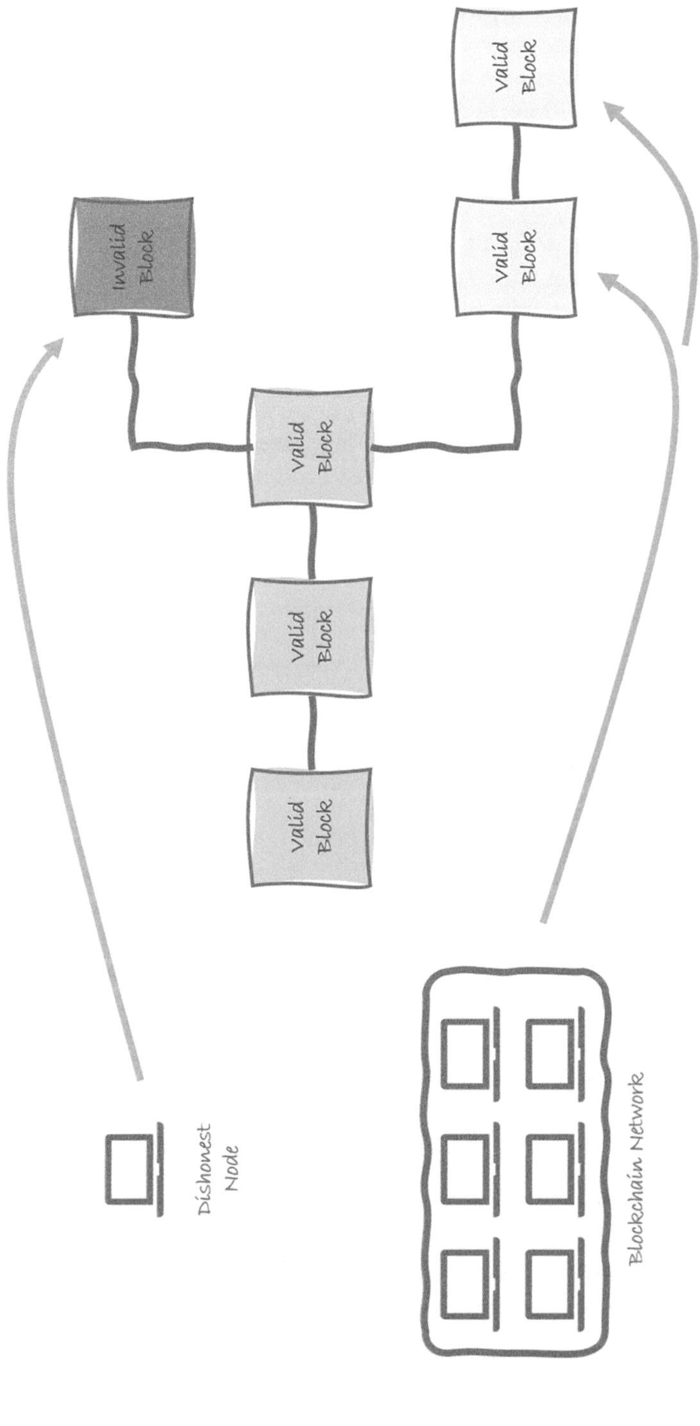

Figure 2.2 The Longest Chain Explained.

from a given private key. The process cannot be reversed to derive the private key from the public key.

Hashing is about creating a digital fingerprint of a set of data: a key that will represent that data for as long as it remains unchanged. Once a hashing algorithm has been applied to a set of data and the resulting key recorded, any tampering will be detected as the key will no longer correspond to the result of the same hashing algorithm.

The most common form of hashing is SHA-256 (Secure Hash Algorithm 256-bit), which produces a fixed-length 256-bit output.

Before we dig into public-key cryptography and hashing in more detail, it might be worth understanding how a mathematical transformation can be one way.

First, let's generate a public key from a private key.

Keeping things very simple for now, let's take a transformation where we multiply a numeric private key by a fixed random number 5678 (known to everyone) and apply a modulus 311 (meaning that any result over 310 is "wrapped around" until it falls within the range 0–310).

Starting with a private key of 1234, multiplication by 5678 gives us an interim answer of 7,006,652. Applying modulus 311 gives us a result of 133. Our public key is therefore "133". There is no way we can work backwards from 133 to get to a single originating private key.

In our simple example, it is the modulus operation that creates a one-way transformation. In reality, the elliptic curve equation is also one-way.

Now let's look at the process of hashing data to create a linked identifier. Suppose that my data is a name: "George". If I assign a value to each letter equal to its position in the alphabet and then multiply by the position that letter occupies in the data, I get $(1 \times 7) + (2 \times 5) + (3 \times 15) + (4 \times 18) + (5 \times 7) + (6 \times 5)$ for a total of 199. If I store the number 199 alongside the data "George" I can immediately tell if the data has been tampered with. If a malicious agent alters the data to "Charles", the hash value would need to be altered as well, to (in this case) 317.

Note that it is impossible to work backwards from the hash value (199) to recreate the data ("George") itself. The name could equally well be "Jason".

Now let's look a little more deeply into the mechanisms that are commonly used in blockchain. As we've seen, the most widely used form of public key cryptography is Elliptic Curve Cryptography (ECC), which uses features of elliptic curves to generate public keys, while for hashing data the most common algorithm is SHA-256 (Secure Hash Algorithm 256-bit).

Previous cryptographic methods to generate private/public key pairs typically involved multiplying large prime numbers to generate even larger results that were difficult to convert back into factors. ECC has the advantage that it can attain the same level of security using much smaller keys that are therefore much faster to transmit and easier to store.

ECC uses some very specific features of elliptic curves to generate a public key from a given private key. The coordinates of any two points on the curve can be added to generate a third point in a non-reversible conversion.

If you're really interested (and this is as deep as we're going to go here):

- The specific curve used for Bitcoin was $y^2 = x^3 + 7 \bmod p$ with a fixed starting point G.
- Given a private key k, the public key can be generated by adding G to itself a number of times equal to k (using the curve equation to generate a new result each time, constrained by modulus p).
- This specific curve is known as "secp256k1" which tells us that it has been categorised by the Standards for Efficient Cryptography (SEC), that it uses prime fields (p) for modular arithmetic, uses 256 bit length, is a Koblitz curve (k) and is variant 1.

SHA-256 (Secure Hash Algorithm 256-bit) is a cryptographic hash function that takes an input and produces a fixed-length output (256-bits). It is one-way and deterministic, which means that the same input always produces the same output. It is also important that no two inputs should produce the same output. The algorithm itself moves through the data in chunks, comparing each bit to the next, storing a 1 or a 0 depending on the relationship between the bits (cycling between rules such as XOR, AND, OR and other transformations in a fixed sequence). This creates a (nearly) unique output that will differ if just one part of the data is changed.

Let's imagine that the members of the Blockchain Book Club want to add some layers of security by using cryptography so they know they can trust each message that they receive. They agree on a very simple code. Each member of the club is assigned a code number based on the value of the letters in their name (1 to 26). Every time they send a message, they add their code number to the number of the words in the message. They tag the result to the end of the message. So, if Alexis (code 70) sends a message saying "I have paid in my contribution of ten pounds" the actual message would read: "Alexis: I have paid in my contribution of ten pounds. 79." which is calculated as 70 (Alxis code) + 9 (number of words in message).

Although this is a very simple code by comparison, it does illustrate how each recipient has everything they need to decipher the code and confirm that the message has been sent by Alexis and has not been tampered with (by adding or removing a word).

2.3.3 Public and Private Keys

The concept of keys is one of the most important concepts in blockchain. The keys are generated cryptographically, which is where we get the new word "cryptocurrency" from.

Keys are generated in pairs:

- A *private key* which is 64 characters long
- A *public key* which is 128 characters long.

As we have seen, the public key is generated directly from the private key using a one-way cryptographic process. The mathematics involved in that means it is not possible to recreate or retrocalculate the private key from the public key.

The private key and public key can be combined cryptographically ("hashed") to generate a *wallet* address (the result of the hash function is shortened to 40 characters and then prefixed with two additional characters to make a 42-character long wallet address). Note that one public key and private key pair may generate many wallet addresses this way. The terms "public key" and "wallet address" are often used interchangeably but they do technically mean different things.

Transactions (from a wallet) are signed with both the public and private key. The act of signing a transaction proves that the sender has control over the private key and is used by the blockchain to confirm that the transaction has been sent legitimately. The private key should always be kept secret and secure (preferably off-grid) as without it, transactions cannot be sent from the corresponding wallet address.

The relationship between the two keys is important. Because of the mathematical derivation of the public key from the private key, it is possible to validate that the digital signature used in the transaction was indeed derived from the sender's secret private key by using only their public key.

The private key is vital to the security of the blockchain. Each person's private key should be kept very safe and secure: many people keep it off the grid completely, written down and locked in a safe. In the early days of bitcoin-mania, there were numerous stories of lost hard drives containing the private key that would unlock millions of dollars' worth of stranded cryptocurrency.

We have already seen how public and private keys feature heavily in the security of blockchain transactions and token balances. Transactions on blockchain networks are signed with both the public and the private key. The act of signing a transaction proves that the sender has control over the private key and is used by the blockchain network to confirm that the transaction has been sent legitimately.

The relationship between private and public keys can be used in one of two ways, depending on the need. In traditional cryptography, the relationship was used to ensure only the intended recipient could decipher a message. The sender would encrypt the message using the public key. The recipient (and only person with access to the private key) would be able to decipher the message into clear text.

In blockchain, the reverse is true: the need is one of verification. That data can be sent cleanly as it is not secret, but the requirement is for the authority of the sender to be established. Do they have the right to perform the transaction (initially, the sending of coins to the recipient wallet)? The sender presents the data in clear text but creates a hash of the data as a marker. This hash value is then encrypted using the private key. The recipient (or any interested party) can decrypt the hash using the public key. They can then create their own hash of the data (using the same hashing algorithm) – if the hash value is the same as the decrypted one, they know that not only has the data not been tampered with, but that the sender has the authority to send the transaction.

Although the public key is visible to all network participants (and is used to decrypt transaction data), a wallet's private key is the single piece of data that can unlock the wallet's contents. Thus, a wallet (and all of the value associated with the tokens contained within it) is only as secure as the private key that identifies it. As we have said, but it's worth repeating, the private key should always be kept secret and secure (preferably off-grid) as without it, transactions cannot be sent from the corresponding wallet address.

If the wallet address is stored electronically, there are a number of measures that can be taken to protect it, such as ensuring it is held securely and encrypted to be readable only by the wallet's owner or controller. This is the method used by software wallet apps such as MetaMask or Trust Wallet.

If stored offline, rigorous security should be applied such as holding the wallet address in a physical hardware device kept by the wallet owner. Most wallet addresses can be codified as a number of key words in a sequence (known as a seed phrase) that allows the user to regenerate the same wallet address. These key words can be written down and stored securely. It goes without saying that physical methods of storing wallet addresses are vulnerable to physical theft while soft security measures are not.

The risk of a compromised private key varies depending on whether the key is lost or stolen. In the case of a lost key, it would no longer be possible to sign (authorise) transactions for the related wallet(s). If the key is stolen, malicious agents would be able to instruct transactions on the blockchain in respect of the affected wallet(s).

Are loss or theft the only risks? What about someone simply guessing the right combination of letters and numbers?

Let's look at that for a moment.

Each private key is a string made up of 64 characters or 256 "bits". It's hard to visualise that, so here's an entirely random example:

> 1f3a4b5c6d7e8f9021121314151617181920a1b2c3d4e5f60718293
> a4b5c6d7e

with due apologies if that turns out to be your wallet address (although as we will see below, that's quite unlikely).

The combination of letters and numbers is vast, something akin to the total number of atoms in the known universe. If you had a billion supercomputers each trying a quadrillion different keys every second, you'd still run out of time before the universe died a grisly, cold death. Even then you would have tested just the tiniest fraction of possible keys.

Even so, with an eye to the future and the possibility of practical quantum computers, blockchain networks are already researching more advance cryptographic techniques ("post-quantum cryptographic algorithms") to ensure that private keys remain undiscoverable by any means.

Human error or theft remains the most likely source of compromise.

If a key is lost (and here we mean completely lost, including any copies or seed phrases), there is no possibility to recover it. Just as it's impossible for the key to be guessed by malicious parties, it also can't be guessed by your wallet provider. This is inherent in the decentralised trust model of the blockchain.

While individuals may be happy to take the risk of storing their own key (whether in a hardware module or in some other format), this option may not be preferred for commercial or industrial users. In this case, a custodial wallet may be the solution.

2.3.4 Wallets

It is convenient to think of a digital wallet as simply an electronic representation of a physical wallet – a place where you store all of your digital assets, such as cryptocurrencies or tokenised assets like a tokenised deed to a house for example.

The reality is that there's no such thing as a wallet. There is nothing you could point at and say "there it is". A wallet address is just a code associated with a transaction. All transactions that share the same code are essentially impacting the same wallet. Add up all the transactions for a given code and you get the "balance" for that "wallet".

A wallet address can be the sender or recipient of a transaction. Transactions can only be sent by the entity with access to the private key for that wallet address. Transactions can be received from any other wallet address on the network.

We already know that a blockchain wallet doesn't store any assets but instead tracks balances via blockchain transactions.

Private (non-custodial) wallets are used most often by individuals who hold small quantities (or value) of crypto currencies.

But for professional holders of cryptocurrencies, as well as any commercial or industrial users such as businesses seeking to tokenise real world artefacts, a custodial wallet may make more sense. This is a wallet that is administered by a third party. Some include additional features such as multiple signatures for additional security or role-based approval. These wallets can also come with mechanisms to reduce the gas spent on transactions, which may be a critical consideration for businesses.

The Blockchain Book Club also use digital wallets. On each of the copies of the spreadsheet there is a line for each of the members, against which is held their kitty balance. If column A is for the member's name and column B is for the kitty balance, Kai's balance might be in cell B2. This is the wallet address – just a location where each member of the club can look on their local copy of the spreadsheet to see Kai's balance.

2.3.5 Blockchain Node Program

At its most basic level, a blockchain is a software application: a computer program. The source code for the computer program is often made freely available to a community of users.

The blockchain node program sets out the operating parameters of the blockchain network: the size of the *blocks*, what constitutes a *transaction*, the hashing *algorithm* to be used to validate blocks, and how *consensus* is to be achieved. For blockchains that support *tokenisation*, the program also defines the syntax and commands that can be used for the coding of *smart contracts*.

In many networks the blockchain source code is managed by the community. New versions of the blockchain source code can be released from time to time. The blockchain begins to behave in a different way from that point on.

Members of the community can participate by compiling and running the program on a connected computer (usually via the public internet), turning it into a *node* on the blockchain network.

The blockchain node program is like the operating system of the blockchain. It controls everything from how blocks are created and managed, to network communication, consensus rules and transaction validation. Not only does the program need to define the characteristics of the blockchain network and how it interacts with other nodes, but it also needs be robust enough to protect the network and its assets from malicious intervention.

Before the first block (the "genesis block") can be added to any blockchain network, the node program must be designed, written (in an appropriate language), tested and deployed. The developer will need to consider how the network will behave in respect of cryptography, consensus, transactions, blocks, communication, data storage, and a host of other parameters.

As with any software, the program must also be ready to operate in test mode, with a range of "testing-only" features.

Imagine a famous chef opening a range of restaurants. If all the restaurants are to serve the same food to the same quality across the country, the chef must prepare a menu with precise instructions for the executive chefs and other kitchen staff. The chef must consider every aspect of food preparation (ingredients, quantities, seasoning, method) in advance, and must consider every eventuality to enable the teams to adjust if anything goes wrong. The instructions must also include how the ingredients are to be obtained and stored, as well as how the plate must be assembled and presented to the guests. If there is the slightest variation, or the slightest weakness in the instructions that allows for errors or deviation, the chef will not have created the seamless dining experience that was envisioned.

It's the same with the blockchain node program: every aspect of blockchain operation must be anticipated and codified in the program, long before the first bit of data is stored.

Instead of a chef, it's the developer who writes the program. In the case of Bitcoin, the first blockchain, it was the mysterious Satoshi Nakamoto who wrote the 14,000 or so lines of the Bitcoin Core node program in the C++ programming language. The source code for later networks was written in a range of languages such as Go, C# and Rust. The original Bitcoin Core node program was relatively compact, delivering the capability for basic cryptocurrency transactions and mining. In contrast, the Ethereum node program, Geth, has grown to over half a million lines of code, driven by the platform's support for complex smart contracts and decentralised applications as well as security enhancements, protocol upgrades and new features.

And instead of the ingredients and cooking method of our menu above, the blockchain node program must set out the rules for all potential nodes on the network to follow. These include (but are not limited to):

- How the node interacts with other nodes, including the location of any default "boot" nodes and how to be discovered by other nodes
- How the network achieves consensus (PoW, PoS and others) including stake parameters for PoS

- The size of blocks and the frequency with which they are created
- Gas and mining parameters
- How and where data is to be stored
- How keys are generated and stored (including exactly which cryptographic and hash transformations to follow)
- How transactions are managed (such as the size of the memory pool and the maximum size of transactions)
- How smart contracts are written, deployed and operated
- Governance rules for the network (such as voting for changes).

The developer of the blockchain node program must also be a visionary and anticipate all the ways that malicious actors will try to break the security of the network. The program must include defences against every avenue of attack, including the 51% attack through the creation of false nodes or other methods of consensus manipulation, denial of service attacks, node isolation, "man in the middle" attacks that intercept messages, theft or appropriation of a private key, or exploitation of weaknesses in smart contracts.

Once it's written and launched, the node program must be maintained. In many cases for a public network, this becomes the responsibility of a foundation or a community (as is the case for Bitcoin and Ethereum), a more centralised model (such as for Ripple and most private networks) or a hybrid of the two. Some networks use on-chain governance to allow holders and validators to contribute to the evolution of the source code.

Anyone wanting to run a node simply needs to equip an adequate server (remembering that a full node will require 1–2 terabytes for data storage) and download the node program before configuring it to define network and other operational settings. The node will then execute the Initial Block Download (IBD), which stores every block locally, after which the node is ready for use.

While the Blockchain Book Club don't use a node program, they do have applications and rules that collectively define how they conduct operations: the spreadsheet and how it is laid out is one such rule, how messages are passed (and coded) is another and so on. Their "program" also defines how they make decisions and how they all agree that transactions are genuine and should be applied.

2.3.6 Blockchain Node

Any computer that is running the blockchain program and is connected to the public internet becomes a blockchain node.

The functions within the blockchain application are broadly as follows:

- Discover and communicate with other nodes on the blockchain network
- Send, receive and store blockchain data

- Execute and validate transactions
- Maintain the consensus of the blockchain
- Verify blockchain information and receive rewards.

It's important to note that each node maintains a copy of all of the data within the entire blockchain. As more blocks of data are added to the end of the chain, each node needs to hold more and more data.

One of the primary jobs for a node is to verify transactions that have been added to the network. Nodes verify transactions in different ways, depending on the rules set out in the blockchain program. Usually, verification involves solving a puzzle using the cryptographic data in the transaction. The node that solves the puzzle gets to add the data to the end of the chain and replicate it to all the other nodes in the network.

All blockchain nodes share common functions such as storing data, validating transactions and maintaining network integrity. As we've seen, the operational parameters that drive these functions differ according to the rules defined in the node program source code.

However, even nodes on the same network can differ in terms of the service they provide. Most networks allow for a range of participation levels for connected nodes.

Full nodes typically provide the full range of services to the blockchain network, including storing the entire blockchain and validating all transactions.

Lightweight nodes store only key parts of the blockchain (such as the headers), relying on full nodes for verification.

Validator nodes (also called mining nodes on some networks) only provide validation services to the network.

The Ethereum network also has the concept of archive nodes for the storage of historical data.

A full node is usually a pre-requisite for organisations that wish to provide more sophisticated services to the blockchain community such as oracles and operators of smart contracts.

Anyone running a node (of any type) is best advised to keep their node software up to date and protected behind firewalls. Communications should be secure and encrypted where possible, and node data should be backed up regularly.

For the Blockchain Book Club, each node is a laptop, running the spreadsheet and messaging applications that they use to operate their network. Note that each node contains its own local copy of the spreadsheet and uses the messaging application to ensure that all copies are in agreement.

2.3.7 Blockchain Network

A blockchain network is just a collection of blockchain nodes. Collectively, the data stored on (and shared by) the blockchain nodes is referred to as a distributed ledger.

Not all blockchain networks operate in the same way. For example, the method used by each network to verify new blocks can vary. Some networks support smart contracts. These differences are governed by the differences in the blockchain program, the source code that defines the network behaviour.

Networks also differ in how they are governed. Some are open source, operated in a collaborative way by foundations whereas others are privately owned and operated. Some are open to all participants, while others operate with a closed membership.

There are mainly three types of blockchain networks: public, private, and consortium. These types differ based on their accessibility, control, and the level of decentralisation.

Public blockchains are open and permissionless networks that allow anyone to participate as a node. They aim for a high level of decentralisation, with no single central authority controlling the network. They also provide a high level of transparency, as the transaction history and the state of the ledger are publicly visible to all participants.

Private blockchains are restricted and permissioned networks, typically used within a specific organisation or a group of trusted entities. This might be for security reasons so that data on the blockchain is not available to the general public, or simply to limit the number of participants (and hence transactions) on the network. Private blockchains offer higher control to the participating entities and are often governed by a central authority or consortium. Importantly, greater levels of privacy and data confidentiality can be achieved in private blockchains, as the participating entities have more control over the visibility of transactions and data.

Consortium networks use a model that combines some of the features of both public and private blockchains. They are accessible to a specific group of pre-approved participants who collectively govern the network. Consortium members have a higher level of trust among each other compared to public blockchain participants.

A DAO (*Decentralised Autonomous Organisation*) is a blockchain-based entity that uses smart contracts to automate decision-making and governance. Instead of a traditional hierarchy, DAOs are managed by token holders, who vote on proposals to determine the organisation's actions.

Every network operates one single database made up of a chain of transactions grouped together in blocks. This single chain of data is stored on every node in the network, wherever on the globe that node is situated: data without frontiers. But this can create its own issues as the processing of blocks is single-threaded and can take a finite amount of time.

One solution to this is to take some of the activity away from the main network into another layer, referred to as a "Layer 2" network (while the main network is referred to as "Layer 1"). Transactions are executed (and validated) on the Layer 2 network and are then rolled up onto the main network.

The roles and participants involved in running a blockchain network can vary based on the specific implementation, type and governance model chosen for the network. The roles and responsibilities can be defined through agreements, consortium membership, or technical protocols established by the participating entities.

It's probably difficult to say exactly how many different blockchain networks there are, as many are private or in development. Suffice to say there are over a thousand in existence and the number is growing all the time.

As we've seen, blockchain networks can vary significantly in their design, functionality, and governance structures. While they all share the core principles of decentralisation and the use of cryptographic mechanisms to obviate the need for a trusted party, the ways in which they achieve these goals can differ drastically.

These differences arise from variations in approach, in intended usage and even in sophistication as later networks built on the successes of their predecessors.

Some blockchains are built for speed and to cater for large volumes of transactions, others for security and immutability, while some focus on interoperability, enabling different blockchains to communicate with each other. The approach to decentralisation can differ, with some networks being controlled by a small number of validators, while others distribute power across thousands of nodes globally. Other parameters include how accounts are modelled and how blocks are created and transactions are validated.

All of these architectural parameters are defined by the node program.

Here, we take a look at a few of the more commonly-used networks.

Bitcoin was the original blockchain network, designed initially purely as a vehicle for trustless cash transactions within a peer-to-peer network. As such, some of its operational parameters are focused entirely on its single use, such as by prioritising security and stability over speed. It operates using the Proof of Work (PoW) consensus mechanism which encourages decentralisation, while its block time of approximately 10 minutes and maximum block size of around 1 megabyte both act to limit transaction throughput to about 7 transactions per second, ensuring that running a full node remains feasible for individuals. The Bitcoin network is simple and robust, but it lacks the flexibility needed for more complex applications beyond payments. Its governance is off-chain and community-driven, requiring broad consensus on any proposed upgrades introduced through "BIPs" (Bitcoin Improvement Proposals) leading to a conservative approach to change.

Other networks followed, but were largely clones (or even forks) of Bitcoin.

The game-changer was the *Ethereum* network, an entirely new take on distributed ledgers that introduced the vital concepts of smart contracts and the virtual machine. Originally launched with a PoW mechanism similar to Bitcoin, Ethereum transitioned (on 15th September 2022) to a Proof of Stake (PoS) mechanism as part of an event called "The Merge", which significantly reduced Ethereum's energy consumption and increased scalability, although it remains a relatively slow platform for transactions. One of the key issues for Ethereum is the relatively high transaction costs. Ethereum is governed by the Ethereum Foundation.

The *Cardano* network[7] was built by a dedicated blockchain research and engineering company (IOHK) which was set up by one of the founders of Ethereum. It was designed specifically to address scalability, security, and sustainability issues faced by the earlier blockchain networks and favoured a rigorous research-driven, peer-reviewed approach. The network has two discrete layers: a settlement layer for handling transactions and a computation layer for running smart contracts. Its consensus is an adapted form of PoS (called Ouroboros) and its governance model is similarly community-driven through an on-chain voting system called Project Catalyst. Its layered approach allows for faster and more scalable transactions at low cost.

Similarly, *Polkadot*[8] was designed by another of the Ethereum co-founders and sought to address another of its limitations, focusing on interoperability. Polkadot operates what is known as a heterogeneous multi-chain framework, with a central chain (the Relay Chain) coordinating consensus and security and parallel chains (called parachains) for transactions and smart contracts. Each parachain benefits from the security provided by the Relay Chain and can be tailored specifically to its own task, allowing for scalability and flexibility. Polkadot uses a Nominated Proof of Stake (NPoS) consensus model, where nominators support validators by staking tokens. Polkadot is governed through the Web3 Foundation.

Solana[9] also sought to address the limited scalability of Ethereum, but instead of using multiple layers, the designer took the approach of using one super-fast network. Solana requires higher-spec hardware to run and logs the submission time of each transaction. This PoH (or Proof of History) then allows transactions to be processed in parallel achieving extremely fast transaction processing times, again at low cost.

Cosmos (the "internet of blockchains[10]") takes a modular approach to blockchain operation, allowing multiple independent blockchains to communicate with each other while maintaining their own consensus mechanisms. This communication is achieved through its Inter-Blockchain Communication (IBC) protocol whereby the central blockchain (the Cosmos Hub) connects any number of independent but interconnected blockchains (known as zones), each of which can have its own governance and consensus rules. This flexibility allows for rapid deployment of customised blockchains. Cosmos operates its own take on PoS consensus called Tendermint, which provides fast and efficient transaction finality. Cosmos does not natively support smart contracts. It is governed on-chain through the Interchain Foundation.

Tezos[11] was designed following well-publicised hard fork events on the Bitcoin and Ethereum networks. It promotes flexibility and adaptability, allowing the network to evolve without the need for forks. Tezos achieves consensus through a Liquid Proof of Stake (LPoS) model, enabling flexible delegation of staking power without relinquishing control of tokens. Its focus on formal verification also makes it attractive for applications where security and correctness are paramount, such as in financial contracts.

Avalanche[12] is another high-volume platform, with a unique consensus mechanism that relies on sampling the validation results from multiple validators to achieve almost instant verification. This allows Avalanche to process thousands of transactions per second. Avalanche also uses multiple blockchains including the Exchange Chain (X-Chain) for asset creation, the Contract Chain (C-Chain) for smart contracts, and the Platform Chain (P-Chain) for validation.

Algorand[13] is another network that sought to solve the blockchain "trilemma" of being scalable, secure and decentralised. It uses a "pure" proof of stake where the validator is chosen randomly and has instant transaction finality with low fees. Algorand uses an on-chain governance model. Due to its low energy cost it is sometimes referred to as the "carbon-negative" blockchain.

This is just a subset of the many hundreds of public blockchain networks (not to mention the additional private networks created by organisations for their own purposes). Each network has its own characteristics that suit certain types of transactions. Any organisation or community looking to implement a blockchain solution will need to consider a range of variables before deciding which is the most suitable network for the use case in hand.

The network used by the Blockchain Book Club is arguably a private or permissioned network, as no one else has been (or will be) invited to join. The club members would be advised to set out clear rules on the governance of the network, such as how consensus is to be achieved.

2.3.8 Transactions

A transaction is an instruction to change values on the ledger. Initially, transactions were simply a means to send coins (such as Bitcoin) from one wallet to another, but following the introduction of smart contracts and tokenisation, transactions can also be used to initiate any of the smart contract's functions.

A transaction is initiated by the submitting node, and will typically include the following elements:

- A unique identifier assigned to the transaction, often represented as a hash value. This serves as a reference to the transaction and can be used to track and verify its status on the blockchain
- The wallet addresses for the sender and the recipient
- Any transaction data – the details of the transaction, which can vary depending on the blockchain network and the reason for the transaction
- A digital signature – a cryptographic signature generated by the blockchain software to verify the authenticity and integrity of the transaction.

Once a transaction has been generated, it is written to a pool (called the "mempool") and is copied to all nodes on the network. Each node will add the new transaction to the block it is currently building – once that block is complete, the node will begin to solve the cryptographic puzzle to verify the whole block.

Depending on the consensus mechanism in use for that particular network (see below), one or more nodes will attempt to verify the transactions in the block (which includes ensuring that there is a sufficient coin balance in the sending wallet's account to effect the transaction). Regardless of the consensus mechanism, one node will be successful in validating the block, and will add it to the end of the growing chain of blocks. This data is then circulated to all nodes in the network.

If any other nodes have attempted to validate a block at the same time as the successful node (possible depending on the consensus mechanism) the unvalidated blocks become orphaned and the constituent transactions are returned to the pool for inclusion in a later block.

Once verified and final, transactions are *immutable*. Because the data in the transaction (or block of transactions) has been used as part of the puzzle to generate the cryptographic signature of the block, any change to that data will invalidate the signature. It is this link between the digital signature and the data in the block that is fundamental to the security of blockchain and distributed ledger technology.

We have seen how transactions are processed, and this is broadly the same across all networks. There are small differences in the detail, such as how transactions affect accounts, how they are selected from the mempool and how the pool is managed (especially across multiple chain networks).

The main variations relate not so much to transaction behaviour but to their speed (how long it takes a given transaction to be processed), the throughput (how many transactions per second can be processed by the network) and finality.

Transaction speeds can vary from less than one second to minutes, while volumes range from a few per second to tens of thousands.

Finality is a concept worth dwelling on for a moment.

Finality refers to the point at which a blockchain transaction is considered irreversible and immutable. This is the point where it is permanently recorded on the blockchain and cannot be altered, reversed, or removed. Once a transaction achieves finality, users can be certain that the transaction is valid and that it can't be impacted by later forks in the chain.

In some chains, finality is absolute. This happens in some PoS networks. As soon as enough validators have verified the transaction, it is considered immediately final.

In most other networks, just because one node has verified the block does not mean that the new block will continue to become the longest chain. If other nodes are validating blocks more quickly, then even a transaction that has been verified by a node and written to a chain may eventually be discarded as belonging to the non-preferred, shorter chain. In this case, finality is defined as being "probabilistic". In Bitcoin, for example, a transaction can be considered to be "probably" final after six more blocks have been added, but this is not completely guaranteed. Ethereum takes checkpoints regularly (every 15 minutes or so), to confirm that all transactions prior to the checkpoint are now final and cannot be reversed.

Figure 2.3 shows how a transaction is submitted by the initiating node and then validated. Only when the conditions for finality have been achieved is the transaction considered final. Finality is vital, especially in high value financial transactions, to ensure that assets and cash swap from buyer to seller at the exact same time.

Another aspect of transactions that can vary from network to network is verification. While many of the common features of transactions are verified on all networks, some network-specific features may vary.

Common verification includes:

- That the transaction is specified in the correct format
- That the transaction was signed by the rightful owner using public-key cryptography

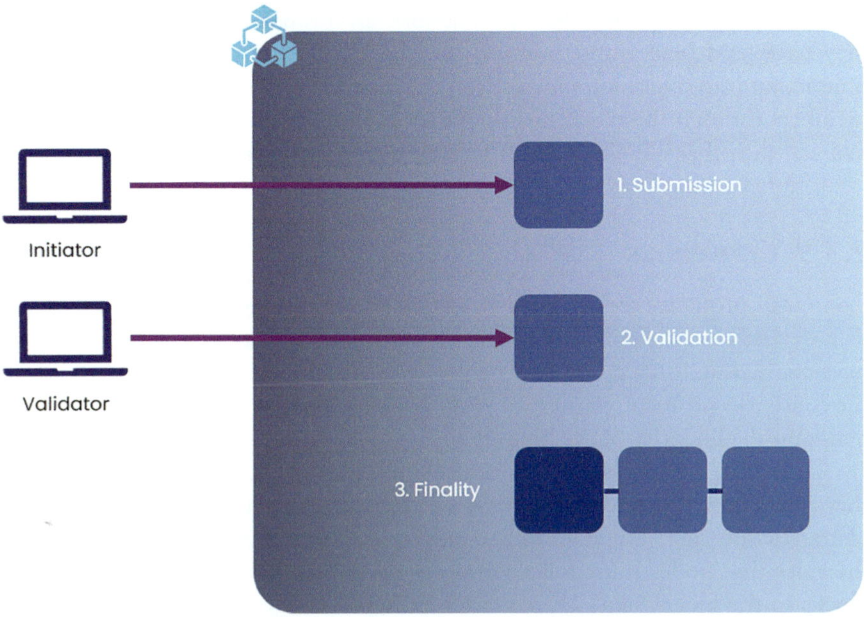

Figure 2.3 Transaction Submission, Validation and Finality.

- That the sender hasn't already spent the same funds elsewhere
- That the sender has enough funds to cover the transaction amount plus fees
- That the block's referential data such as the previous block hash is consistent and correct.

Network-specific verification may include:

- Checking that the consensus mechanism has functioned correctly (for example, that a miner has solved the puzzle correctly, or that the validator was correctly chosen for a PoS validation)
- For smart contracts, that the transaction is calling a valid smart contract deployed on the network, that a valid method is being called and that executing the function will not violate the network rules
- That the gas parameters are valid and that the sender has sufficient gas to cover the transaction costs.

In the Blockchain Book Club, transactions are proposed by the member after they have paid (real world) money into the kitty. After entering details of the transaction into their own spreadsheet, the member sends the details to the other members through the messaging application. Only when the transaction is verified will the other members add it to their own spreadsheets.

2.3.9 Consensus

Consensus protocols are designed to address the challenge of achieving consensus in a decentralised and trustless environment, where multiple participants may have conflicting interests or may be prone to malicious behaviour. By following the consensus protocol, participants can agree on a single version of the truth and maintain the integrity of the blockchain.

Consensus protocols are a critical component of blockchain technology, as they enable multiple nodes within a decentralised network to agree on the validity of transactions and the state of the ledger. The consensus protocol determines the rules that nodes must follow in order to validate transactions and add new blocks to the blockchain. There are several types of consensus protocols used in blockchain technology. Two of the most common are Proof of Work (PoW) and Proof of Stake (PoS).

Proof of Work (PoW) is a consensus protocol used in the Bitcoin blockchain network, where nodes compete to solve complex mathematical problems to validate transactions and add new blocks to the chain. The first node to solve the problem earns a reward of cryptocurrency for their effort. The data in the block is cryptographically hashed with a trial value (called the "nonce") and if the resulting string meets certain criteria (such as having a specified number of sequential zeroes at the start), then the puzzle is deemed to have been solved. The node's success in completing the puzzle is the "proof" that it has done the necessary "work".

Proof of Stake (PoS) is a consensus protocol that is used in several blockchain networks, including Ethereum. In a proof of stake system, specific nodes are selected to validate transactions and add new blocks based on the amount of cryptocurrency they hold, rather than performing computational work. The chosen node is (usually) offered a reward either from fees or in the form of newly-minted coins.

Other consensus protocols (including derivatives of PoS) exist, each applying a unique approach to reaching consensus in a trustless environment.

Consensus is a critical component of distributed ledger technology. The consensus protocol implemented by the network replaces the "trusted third party" in a more traditional relationship.

As we have seen, blockchain networks implement a range of consensus protocols. But they all seek to do the same thing: identify one or more nodes that apply a set of verified transactions to a block and add that block to the end of the chain.

In general, except for "light" nodes, every node on the blockchain network will validate every transaction. This contributes to the overall security of the decentralised ledger and helps with the identification of malicious actors. The consensus protocol is there purely to identify the node that will add any given block to the chain.

Proof of Work (PoW) is used by Bitcoin (and clones such as Litecoin). Miners compete to solve a complex mathematical puzzle. The winning node (namely, the first to solve the puzzle) gets to add a new block to the blockchain and earn a reward. It's highly secure due to the massive amount of energy and resources needed but is slow and requires huge amounts of computational power which comes at a significant cost (in terms of both hardware and energy).

As the "original" consensus mechanism, it's worth walking through the PoW calculation performed by the node (remembering that this is performed by all the mining nodes on the network). The goal of the puzzle (the "work") is to identify a special number called the nonce, such that when it is hashed (using the agreed hash mechanism such as SHA-256) with the transaction data and the previous block's hash, the resulting hash starts with a specified number of leading zeroes (the more leading zeroes are required, the harder the puzzle is to solve). Each time a node calculates the hash for a given value of the nonce and it does not meet the success criteria, it tries a different value for the nonce and calculates again. As soon as the node learns that another node has solved the puzzle, it validates the work done by that node and then records the block before starting to solve the puzzle for the next block.

Proof of Stake (PoS) is used by Ethereum. Validators stake a number of native coins to participate in block creation. The winner is chosen using an algorithm that rewards the amount of coins proven as staked. PoS is energy-efficient and has much faster transaction speeds with lower fees than PoW although there is a concentration risk in that "the rich get rich" because they are able to stake more coins than other nodes.

The mechanism behind PoS is very simple. Once the algorithm has selected a validator, that validator verifies the block and its transactions (always) and then creates the block. Only the validator does this and there are no complex calculations to perform, hence why the mechanism is both faster and cheaper than PoW.

Figure 2.4 shows how PoS achieves the same result with a lower consumption of energy than PoW (where a number of unsuccessful nodes consume energy in trying to solve the cryptographic puzzle).

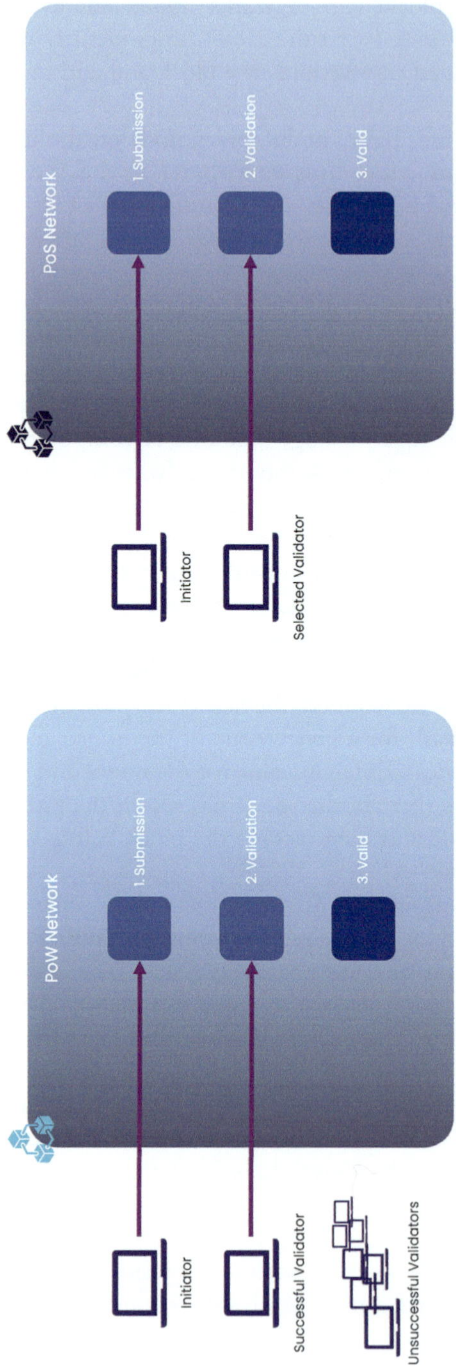

Figure 2.4 PoW and PoS Consensus.

There are a number of variants of the PoS protocol, below. In the main, they differ in respect of how the validator is chosen.

In *Nominated Proof of Stake (NPoS)*, validators and nominators work together. Both stake their coins, then nominators delegate their stake to trusted validators, contributing to the selection process. This is helpful for multi-chain networks such as Polkadot.

The *Ouroboros (PoS)* variant used by Cardano introduces some new concepts to ensure validation work is distributed. Time is divided into epochs and slots, with each slot being allocated a "slot leader" to perform the validation and block creation. This ensures a spread of validators.

Tendermint is a PoS variant used on the Cosmos network. Validators take turns proposing new blocks and a new block is only added once a proportion of validators reach consensus. This provides instant finality of transactions and is very scalable but does require a robust network of validators to maintain security.

Liquid Proof of Stake (LPoS) is used by Tezos. It is similar to PoS but uses a liquid delegation model. Users can delegate their tokens to validators (called bakers) without locking them up permanently. For self-amending blockchains like Tezos, this dynamic model supports on-chain voting on upgrades.

The Avalanche network uses **random sampling** alongside PoS. Validators randomly sample other validators to check if transactions are valid. Similarly to the Tendermint consensus model, this enables high volumes and provides immediate finality.

In the *Delegated Proof of Stake (DPoS)* model used by the EOS and Tron networks, holders vote for a small group of delegates (validators) to secure the network. This is fast but is less decentralised than other methods (and is vulnerable to collusion).

Proof of History (PoH) is used by Solana. Each transaction gets a timestamp that ensures events occur in sequence. This reduces the need for communication between nodes, resulting in faster transaction speeds.

Finally, in a *Proof of Authority (PoA)* model, a few defined, trusted validators (authorities) are able to validate transactions. This is really only possible in a private network.

The Blockchain Book Club members have decided to use a Proof of Stake protocol for their consensus model. After a member sends a transaction using the messaging application, any member is welcome to offer to verify it. In so doing, they are credited with a small reward, which is also logged in all copies of the spreadsheet.

2.3.10 Network Security

Many of the headlines relating to blockchain and cryptocurrencies focus on security. Notorious claims of huge thefts and security breaches catch the public attention. But many of these instances are due to poorly implemented security measures that would have left any organisation open to breaches of security.

It may seem that blockchain is particularly susceptible due to the transparent nature of the data, the use of consensus, and in particular the fact that the source code for the blockchain nodes is open source. This latter point means that any malicious party could take their own copy of the code, amend it and use it to interact with the network.

So, how does the network defend itself against such malicious nodes?

- Consensus rules are enforced by all nodes, so even the malicious node must follow the same rules as the rest of the network, meaning that blocks must contain valid transactions, correct cryptographic proofs, and adhere to gas limits, and transactions must have valid digital signatures and sufficient balances.
- Nodes connect to local nodes and rely on those nodes to connect to the rest of the network; any "bad" data supplied by the malicious node will not be passed on by other nodes to the rest of the network (nodes can even disconnect from misbehaving peers).
- Even a re-programmed malicious node cannot fake digital signatures based on public private key pairs, meaning that a fake node cannot simply steal assets from other nodes.
- Nodes talk to each other ("gossip protocol") and may refuse to connect to an identified malicious node (a bit like unfollowing people on social networks who send out unpleasant posts).

Another concern raised about the security of blockchain networks derives from the consensual nature of data verification and the risk that a malicious participant might seize control of that consensus to falsely verify transactions. This is known as the "51% attack threat" (as the participant would need more than 50% of the decision-making power).

If the malicious actor is able to control the consensus process, they would be able to verify their own transactions and build a longer chain than the genuine chain agreed by the other parties. At this point, the network would adopt the longer (false) chain as the true chain and the attacker's false transactions as true transactions, even if they performed illegal operations such as spending resources that don't exist or reversing genuine transactions.

The exact nature (and likelihood) of the 51% attack threat differs depending on the consensus mechanism. In most blockchain networks, however, the chances of this happening are infinitesimally small. The attacker would need to operate more than half the computing power providing consensus across the network, at a cost of billions, or own more than half the coins in circulation. Even then, should a 51% event happen, the relevant community is likely to implement a hard fork, thus rendering the false chain meaningless (representing zero reward for an astronomical financial outlay for the would-be attacker).

As we will see, although the security of public blockchain networks remains strong, some operators of tokenised solutions (such as financial institutions) may choose to implement a private blockchain network to add a definitive level of security to their service.

Let's look at that potential 51% attack in a little more detail.

First, we need to understand what it is that the attacker needs 51% of – as this differs depending on the type of consensus used. Remember that the goal of the attacker or malicious agent is to control the majority of nodes that verify transactions; only by controlling the majority can the attacker hope to begin constructing the longest chain, which is the prerequisite for creating a false version of the truth.

For a PoW (Proof of Work) consensus model, the attacker needs to control 51% of the nodes on the network. For a large network like Bitcoin, with thousands of participants running huge data centres full of racks of servers, this is prohibitively expensive.

For a PoS (Proof of Stake) consensus model, the attacker will need to be able to stake over 50% of the total value of coins on the network. Again, for a large, established network such as Ethereum, this is astronomically expensive. Furthermore, having gathered such wealth in a single form of currency, it would represent spectacularly poor planning to want to obliterate that wealth by executing a successful attack on the same network's credibility.

Having successfully executed their attack, the malicious agent could abuse their control of consensus to approve erroneous transactions (to potentially reverse debits from their own wallet and thus allow them to "double spend" coins) or to deliberately fail to validate other participant's genuine transactions. As an extreme, an attacker might execute a "deep chain reorganisation" to essentially rewrite the chain's history.

It's important to note that the attacker in this scenario would only have control of the approval of transactions. They would not acquire the capability to recode the blockchain node software to create entirely fictitious rules, amend the parameters for smart contracts, or to steal coins from other users' wallets.

In addition to the purely logistical barriers to mounting a 51% attack, blockchain networks are actively working to further mitigate the risk. Consensus and mining algorithms have been tweaked to discourage large concentrations of activity. In a PoS model, rules have been put in place to deprive malicious validators of their staked tokens ("slashing"), while the algorithms have also been adjusted to increase the random element of the selection of the validating node.

And if, in spite of these barriers and measures, a 51% attack were to be executed and detected, it is quite likely that the community for the affected network would implement a hard fork, rendering the attacker's chain worthless.

While major blockchains like Bitcoin and Ethereum have never suffered a successful 51% attack due to their size and security, some smaller blockchain networks have been successfully targeted (notably Bitcoin Gold and Ethereum Classic), often through the use of rented mining nodes. Both networks have tightened their rules (especially regarding the use of rented nodes in this way).

One aspect to bear in mind in the context of tokenisation (as opposed to cryptocurrencies) is that barriers to a 51% attack may be reduced if the value of the "real world assets" vastly exceeds the value of the coins that power the network: a malicious agent may consider staking a large value in coins to risk obtaining real world assets of greater value.

2.3.11 Coins

The first blockchains (such as Bitcoin) were created purely as mechanisms for the trustless transfer of cryptocurrencies between participants and the generation of rewards through mining for the validation of transactions. Each network supported a native coin that operated and was accepted only on that network. For many people (even today), blockchains and cryptocurrencies are synonymous.

Starting with the Ethereum network, however, blockchains became capable of supporting other tokenised assets through the use of smart contracts. Most networks still operated a native coin but this was no longer their sole (or even primary) purpose.

Coins are used in different ways by different networks, but broadly they provide the following capabilities:

- Trading and holding of cryptocurrencies
- As rewards for transaction validation (either through mining or staking)
- As payment for smart contract operations (gas)
- To support governance (where the governance model allows participants to vote).

In general, every network operates a native coin (the exceptions being some private networks and a few outliers that don't require incentivisation through a fee or reward system).

Depending on the specific network, native coins can be used for any of the following:

- As a cryptocurrency such as Bitcoin (BTC) that can be traded and held in wallets on the network by participants
- As a reward to participating nodes for good behaviour such as validating transactions
- As fees to support the execution of smart contracts
- As a means to vote on network upgrades or other governance matters.

For some networks (such as Bitcoin, Litecoin, Dogecoin or Stellar), cryptocurrency trading remains the primary focus. For others, the coin is simply the facilitator for the operation of smart contracts and distributed applications.

It's important to note the distinction between a native coin such as Bitcoin and a tokenised asset, which may in some cases also be perceived as a coin. For example, an organisation might immobilise a large quantity of real-world currency and trade tokens representing that currency on a blockchain network. This is also "money" but it is achieved through the use of smart contracts to tokenise and move the asset. This is usually what is referred to as a "stablecoin". Ironically, the smart contract operations to move the tokenised money in this way will consume native coins as gas on the network.

Cryptocurrency trading may also include the use of cryptocurrencies in e-commerce (the exchange of native coins for goods or services) as well as the holding of large portfolios of coins as "digital gold". Many speculators, particularly in Bitcoin, are determined to "Hold on for Dear Life" (HODL) in the hope that their portfolio will grow to multiple times its current value.

Most blockchain networks are community-driven and trustless. Participants need to be encouraged to lend their computing power to the network in order to validate transactions. Successful validators are usually rewarded for their work, paid in native coins. In some cases, these native coins are minted and given to the validator; in others the coins are exchanged as fees. Bitcoin's mining reward is stepped to reduce over time so that a fixed total of coins will ever be distributed. In a Proof of Stake (PoS) mechanism, the validator is rewarded with coins created by the network. Most networks have a mechanism to limit the creation of new coins such as by burning (destroying) a portion of the transaction fee to create a diminishing supply.

For networks that support smart contracts, the primary purpose of native coins is to support the execution of those smart contracts, through fees and validation rewards. In particular, some PoS consensus models favour those participants who either hold or have staked high numbers of native coins.

Some networks (such as Cardano and Polkadot) operate an on-chain governance model. Upgrades to the network or other operational changes are proposed to the community and a voting system based on native coin holdings determines the outcome.

2.3.12 Gas

For a transaction to be committed to the blockchain a transaction fee (often known as gas) must be paid to the node that validates the transaction. In the vast majority of blockchains this fee is paid using the blockchain's own native coin.

The size of the fee is determined by a number of factors, such as the computing power needed by the node to action the instruction.

To quote the Ethereum website[14], "ETH is the lifeblood of Ethereum".

Without gas (paid in ETH or Ether, the native coin of the Ethereum network), the network would simply not be able to operate. "The work validators do, and the capital they stake, keeps Ethereum secure and free of centralized control. ETH powers Ethereum."

Most networks follow this philosophy (the exceptions being typically private networks which use different transaction dynamics). We will look at how different networks take slightly different approaches to gas in a moment but first let's examine the Ethereum mechanism in a more detail to establish a framework.

Every transaction processed on the Ethereum network has a gas charge attached. The more complex the operation, the more units of gas are needed. For example, even the most simple transaction (such as sending ETH from one wallet to another) attracts a gas of 21,000 fractional parts of ETH itself. More complex transactions such as sending a token or interacting with a smart contract require a higher number of units (65,000 for a simple token operation).
The cost per unit of gas is calculated by the network and is made up of:

- A base fee for the transaction (which varies depending on the network's current load)
- An optional priority fee to incentivise node operators to process this particular transaction over others.

Gas cost per unit is usually quoted in terms of small sub-units or fractional parts of ETH itself, called "gwei". One gwei is equal to a billion "wei" (the smallest unit of currency) or a billionth of an ETH (and is the equivalent therefore of less than a thousandth of a penny).

The base fee is derived based on the size of the preceding block. In Ethereum, each block is allocated a "slot" of 12 seconds and is verified by a validator (selected by the network based on their stake). If the preceding block is larger than the average size (set at 15 million gas units) then the base fee is increased. This mechanism acts as a brake to restrict network participants from demanding too much work from the virtual machine. Subsequent base fees are further increased until volume dies down, so transactions can become very expensive indeed using this mechanism.

The priority fee is optional, but for most users it is set automatically by their wallet software. Validator nodes (again automatically) apply a sort to available transactions in the mempool so will normally select only those with a higher priority fee.

The gas fee (payable in ETH) is therefore the number of gas units for the required function multiplied by the base fee plus the priority fee. For a standard transaction this works out as a few pennies, whereas for a very large, complex operation during long periods of high activity can run into the thousands of dollars.

The process works like this:

- A node participant proposes a transaction to the network
- Based on the current network volumes, the proposer's node software calculates the base gas cost for the transaction
- The proposer's node software derives and adds a priority gas fee to encourage validation
- The transaction is assigned to the validator selected by the network for this time slot (slots last approximately 12 seconds)
- The validator's software sorts on priority fee and selects the transaction
- The validator's software verifies all transactions in the block and writes the block to the database
- The base gas fee is "burned" (destroyed) by the network
- The validator receives the priority gas fee as a tip for having performed the verification
- The network "mints" (creates) new ETH as a reward to the validator.

It's worth noting that the reward ETH minted by the network slightly overcompensates for the base fee ETH that is burned, except in cases where the base fee has been increased due to high volumes. This negative feedback loop ensures that the volume of ETH stays broadly the same, reducing slightly at times of high activity but increasing slightly at other times.

Gas is payable even if the transaction ultimately fails (in the case of a smart contract function that tries to execute too many instructions). The validator node ensures that any related state changes are rolled back, but gas fees are still deducted.

Not all networks apply the same concepts as Ethereum: Polkadot and Cardano derive fees based on complexity and size but without the same adjustment for high volumes, giving a more predictable outcome. Solana applies extremely low fixed fees to encourage high throughput.

2.3.13 Mining and Rewards

Some blockchain networks also choose to incentivise nodes to participate in transaction validation and block creation by rewarding them for their effort and commitment to the orderly running of the blockchain. This is done through the blockchain issuing its native coin as a reward.

When a node creates a block, the consensus mechanism rewards the node with coins. The value of these coins in part comes from speculation of the future growth of the blockchain but it is also a way of putting a value on the blockchain's transaction activity.

As we've seen, mining is really just one of the mechanisms by which validators are rewarded, typically under a PoW consensus protocol. Networks using PoS or similar consensus models (such as Ethereum) may also reward validators with minted native coins.

Although mining often features heavily in any public debate around Bitcoin, especially due to the large mining installations required to compete in a PoW environment, it is less relevant from a tokenisation perspective.

In the Blockchain Book Club's PoS model, the validator is rewarded with a credit. The next time the club meets, the person with the fewest rewards must buy the first round of teas and coffees.

2.3.14 Smart Contracts

Smart contracts are deployed onto blockchain networks as transactions. They contain executable functions and have the capability to store and amend data. Using smart contracts, financial and real-world assets or data can be represented on a blockchain network as tokens.

Not all blockchain networks support smart contracts. The first networks (such as Bitcoin) didn't, although there was some support for rudimentary variable logic.

The founders of the Ethereum network identified the huge potential that blockchain represented, particularly if the distributed ledger could also be used as a distributed application, by placing executable functions onto the network for anyone to use.

The code that defines how the Ethereum network operates also contains the rules for a simple programming language (called Solidity) that can be used to write such functions. The functions are coded into transactions that are deployed on the blockchain network.

These are called smart contracts.

Smart contracts can be used to tokenise assets as well as creating logical processes and business rules that can be invoked by transactions on the network. Later networks copied and adapted this concept so that most modern networks support smart contracts and tokenisation.

Smart contracts are at the heart of tokenisation.

A smart contract is a self-executing program deployed on a blockchain that can be invoked by transactions specifying the appropriate parameters, ensuring trustless, transparent, and tamper-proof execution. It is through the deployment of smart contracts onto a blockchain network that real-world assets and services can be represented as tokens available to a community of users (although they have uses far wider than tokenisation).

In order to tokenise an asset or service, the token issuer must create and deploy a smart contract to the network.

The first step is to write (and test) the code and then deploy it on the network as a transaction. Once deployed, the data components and functions of the smart contract are fixed and can be used reliably by anyone who knows the location of the contract and how to invoke the functions.

Data is stored in variables that can be in storage (where it is saved to each node on the blockchain) or memory (where it is used only during execution). There are also environment variables supplied by the blockchain network such as the time or the sender of the invoking transaction.

Functions can be public (available to everyone) or private and can be view-only or can modify the data within the smart contract. Some functions are invoked only at the time that the smart contract is deployed (to initialize variables).

Functions may also receive or emit event information to interface to either other smart contracts or, via an "oracle", with an off-chain application.

Functions are invoked by participants on the blockchain network posting transactions that contain data referencing the location of the smart contract and the required function (along with any parameters).

Although anyone can write a smart contract and could choose to implement a myriad of different functions, a number of templates, or standards, have been defined and adopted to encourage a consistent and reliable experience for participants invoking them. ERC-20 is one such standard.

There is much more on smart contracts later in this book.

Figure 2.5 shows how a smart contract is deployed onto a blockchain network. This where things get really interesting for the Blockchain Book Club. They decide that they also want to reward members for prompt payment of the monthly subscription to the kitty. Each month, whoever makes the payment to the kitty first gets an additional reward added to their kitty balance and whoever pays last must lose a reward. The club builds a function within the spreadsheet to calculate the first and last payer and to make the adjustments to the reward balances accordingly. The function must be deployed to every spreadsheet (the code is sent out over the messaging application to ensure everyone has the same contract in place). Every month, once each member notices that all payments are added to the kitty balance, they invoke the function in their own copy of the spreadsheet. This

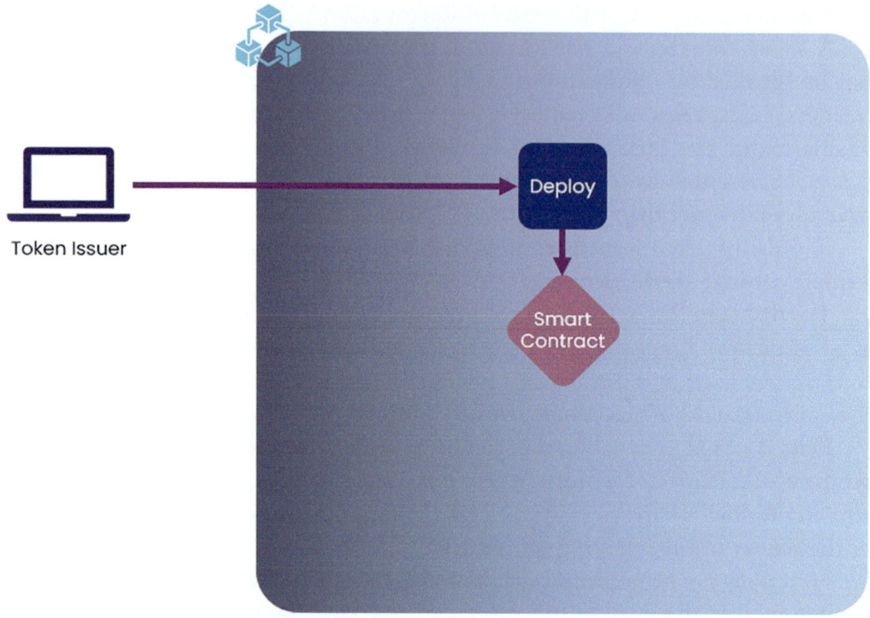

Figure 2.5 Smart Contract Deployment.

updates the reward balances locally. This example shows a critical aspect of how smart contracts interact with blockchain data – the smart contract can be run on any node and will always get to the same result.

2.3.15 Tokens

What is a token?

According to most dictionaries, in the context of information technology at least, it's a digital representation of something – either an object or a piece of data – that can be used in its place.

In the context of blockchain, a token is a representation – in the distributed database – of an asset or real-world object that is not itself on-chain.

By using smart contracts, tokens can be created on the blockchain to represent a financial asset such as a mutual fund, a bond or an equity, or a piece of digital artwork, or even real-world objects such as paintings or real estate. The act of generating a token to represent such assets is called "tokenisation".

The executable code in the smart contract governs how the off-chain asset is represented and behaves in its on-chain, tokenised form. Functions in the smart contract allow the asset to be created ("minted"), destroyed ("burnt"), transferred or impacted in some other way.

Figure 2.6 shows (in a very simplified way) how a transaction is submitted to the blockchain network to invoke the smart contract function that mints a token in the recipient's wallet.

Standards are employed to ensure tokens with the same use case can communicate with each other. The most commonly known standard is the ERC-20, a standard used to create cryptocurrency tokens. Another is ERC-721 the Non-Fungible Token (NFT) standard. These standards ensure a common set of fundamental functions for every token smart contract.

It is worth noting that the token doesn't actually exist as a separate entity on the blockchain – it is represented as data within the storage area of the smart contract. The data will identify the owner of the token (the wallet address) and any parameters relevant to the token (such as the quantity held for an asset token).

A token is an on-chain representation of a real-world (or off-chain) asset, even if that asset only exists logically, or a service.

Once generated (or "minted") through the invocation of a smart contract function, a token exists within the database of the blockchain, replicated on every full node across the network. Usually, it is linked to an owner through a wallet address.

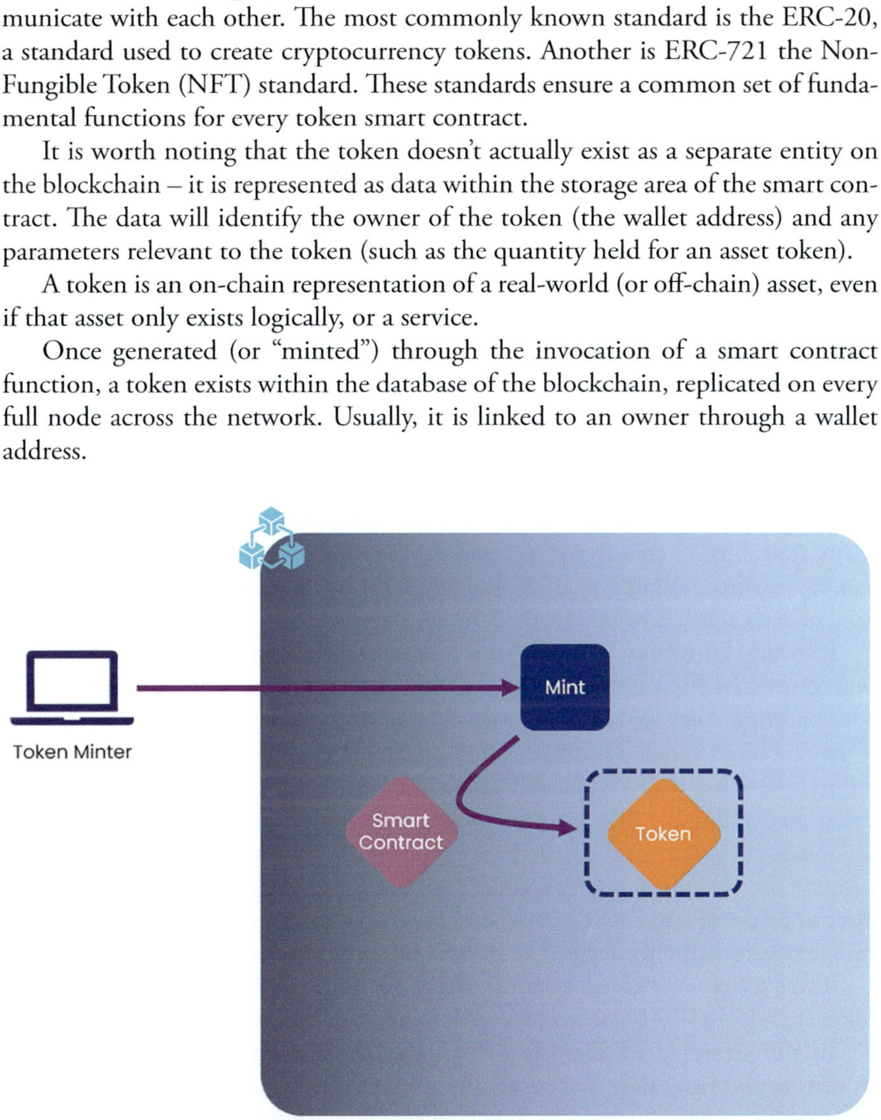

Figure 2.6 Executing a Smart Contract Function.

It is important to remember that the token, like the wallet, doesn't actually exist. In reality, both the wallet address and the token's identifier are simply linked attributes within the memory of the smart contract.

Tokens can represent real-world assets (such as a financial instrument, cash or something tangible such as a piece of art, or even a building). Tokens can also represent services such as in a loyalty scheme or a voting mechanism. These latter are referred to as utility or governance tokens.

It's important that the real-world asset (or service) is honoured by the token issuer. Just because a token has been minted on a blockchain network to represent a dollar, does not mean that it is worth a dollar to the owner. In reality, the token issuer might be expected to "lock up" the value of the real-world asset (by freezing the real-world dollars in a bank account in this example) thus ensuring that the token carries a reliable real-world value.

For a utility or governance token, the issuer of the token must be able to provide the service expected by those who interact with it. If the token represents a delivery (in supply chain management for example) then one might expect the token issuer to be the courier or the distributor of the goods. For a voting mechanism, the issuer must be able to ensure that the result of the vote is reflected in the real world.

Tokens can also be fungible or non-fungible.

Money is (generally) fungible. When someone asks you to pay them a pound for a bag of sweets, they don't (usually) mind which particular pound you give them. A grubby £1 coin from your pocket is as good as 2 fifty pence pieces, or you can pay electronically or by card. The end result is that £1 has left your fungible pool of cash and has been added to the shopkeeper's fungible pool.

Paintings are (again, generally) not fungible. You could not normally exchange one Mona Lisa for two Starry Nights. Similarly, if the shopkeeper had asked for "one painting" they would be considerably more pleased with the Mona Lisa than if they received a stick picture of "Mummy" by Bethany, aged 4.

In tokenising real-world assets, there is a difference between tokenising something that is fungible (like money) and something that is not (like artwork). This difference is evident in the functions of the smart contract that was deployed to support the tokenised asset. A smart contract for a fungible asset will allow the asset to be pooled and split (just like money) whereas a smart contract for a non-fungible asset will only allow it to be held or passed on in its entirety.

These differences are also standardised, for example in ERC-20 (for fungible tokens) and ERC-721 (for non-fungible tokens, or NFTs).

In our example of the Blockchain Book Club, the rewards awarded to validators and early payers are arguably tokens. One reward token is minted for each validator, while a reward token is burnt for the last contributor. The tokens are fungible (as one reward token is as good as any other reward token).

2.4 Tokenisation Basics Applied

We've covered a lot of basics about blockchain in this chapter. Now it's time to put some of that knowledge into practice.

How should a business (or an individual) approach the practical aspects of tokenisation? What are the questions they should be asking about their business or activities, about what technologies to use and how those technologies can be leveraged to best serve their need?

In short, how can tokenisation be applied?

We think that the following questions are appropriate:

- What's the tokenisation use case?
- What network fits the need?
- How to connect?
- What to tokenise and how?
- How will clients or customers connect?
- How to pay for activity?
- What are the risks?

2.4.1 What's the Tokenisation Use Case?

Not everything needs to be tokenised. That may seem to be a strange statement in a book about tokenisation, but it's true. Sometimes (in fact quite often) tokenisation simply isn't the right solution.

There will be some processes or requirements where centralised automation is an appropriate solution. In conversations with potential token issuers or network participants, we have frequently heard arguments in favour of tokenisation that simply don't add up. Instead, there are broken systems in the world of industry and finance: manual or poorly automated processes that would benefit from being reengineered with tokens.

A distributed ledger, tokenised or decentralised approach will only be needed where the following conditions are met:

- **Equitable access**: multiple parties need equal access to the same data
- **Transparency**: the data will be visible to anyone with the authority to view it
- **Trust**: the data needs to be reliable and trusted.

If the involved parties agree that all three conditions are met, then a tokenised solution might be the right answer. This should be a collaborative discussion. The very nature of a candidate process is one involving multiple parties with a need to share data – it's unlikely that a unilaterally designed solution will adequately address the needs of everyone involved.

In deciding whether or not the conditions are met, the involved parties must be open and honest. Is access really to be equitable? How many parties actually need to touch the data? How many simply need to view it? Is the current need to see the data based on mistrust or inefficient (current) systems? Why is there a trust issue – might a centralised model in fact be a better solution?

There are drawbacks and risks associated with a tokenised solution, but in the right circumstances, these risks can be outweighed by significant cost and efficiency savings.

2.4.2 What Network Fits the Need?

We have seen that there are many blockchain networks. Choosing the right one for the use case may not be a trivial matter. Implementations can differ dramatically from network to network, so building a solution for one network only to discover that there is an alternative that would vastly reduce costs or increase speeds may be disastrous.

Some organisations may feel that a private network is the right solution for their use case. They may be right. Private networks offer a degree of control and security not possible on a public blockchain. In the early days of software engineering, it was often assumed that the first step for a major project was to write the programming language that would be used to write the software. Eventually organisations learned to trust first the available programming languages and eventually the software products that had been written elsewhere. We might expect the same progression in the context of blockchain. As the options for public chains become more varied and as the levels of security increase, organisations may find that there is benefit in placing their distributed applications in the public domain. But there will always be a case for a private network, especially where confidentiality and security are paramount, or where there are very few parties involved.

For the rest, the nature of the non-functional requirements for the use case are most likely to provide the steer towards one blockchain network or another. Factors to consider include:

- Transaction speed
- Transaction volumes
- Finality
- Transaction costs
- Confidentiality
- Governance and community (size and nature of participants).

If the solution to the use case involves the design, build, testing and deployment of a smart contract, this is another factor that will significantly influence the choice of network, as networks have implemented a range of smart contract capabilities and use different programming languages.

2.4.3 How to Connect?

Once a network has been chosen, there is the question of the level of commitment the organisation will make to that network.

If the approach will be an entirely owned private or permissioned network, then there are significant steps required to design and launch the network. This is a massive undertaking for any organisation. Just designing the architecture (cryptographic tools, consensus mechanisms, support for smart contracts, gas and coin considerations, governance models and more) would be a complex and expensive project. Developing the core node program is a major undertaking. Launching it will require multiple test networks with all the hardware and security requirements that implies. All of this takes an enormous investment in time, people and, of course, money.

An organisation would not necessarily have to do this on its own. There is professional help available, such as from Hyperledger, Cosmos and the Ethereum Foundation, as well as communities on GitHub and other platforms.

However, depending on the choices made by the organisation, launching a private blockchain network could cost anything from $100k to $50million.

Connecting to an established network may be a simpler (and cheaper) option, but it is not without its own challenges.

The first choice is whether a direct connection is in fact warranted. If the use case solution involves a smart contract, there may be no need to directly connect to the chosen network(s) as the smart contract can be deployed through a third-party node provider. But if the organisation wants a more direct and secure link to the network, it should consider running a blockchain node. This might be a full node (which stores the full blockchain database) or a light node depending on the need. Unless validation of transactions is part of the solution, there is likely not to be a need to become a validator node, unless that brings governance benefits for additional security and control of the blockchain environment.

Once these decisions have been made, any hardware required (or cloud capability) needs to be purchased and the blockchain node program executed to initiate the node.

A step-by-step guide to running an Ethereum node:

1. Decide on your node type
2. Choose and install your hardware

3. Choose which version of Ethereum to run (there are several versions written in different languages, all executing the fundamental rules of the network); the most popular version (Geth) is written in a language called Go
4. Download the software (from https://geth.ethereum.org/); a pre-compiled version is available for most operating systems
5. Install and run the node; the first thing it will do is synchronise with the network (which may take a long time – there's a big database to download)
6. Keep your node running 24/7.

2.4.4 What to Tokenise and How?

Even if it is clear that the use case needs a tokenised solution, it may not be apparent exactly what needs to be tokenised. For real-world assets such as financial assets or even artwork, it may be conceptually simple. But where the use case involves data such as personal or logistics data, it may not be so easy. It is also important to be definitive about the characteristics of the token: will it be fungible or is each instance unique? Can the token be bought and sold, or transferred? Or is it unique to an individual and must always belong to them?

Once the scope of the token and its characteristics have been defined, it's time to create the smart contract (or contracts) that will govern the tokens on the network.

Just as with any technology project, the implementation of a smart contract requires careful planning, design, iterative development and testing, and finally deployment before it can be used. However, there are some specific aspects of smart contracts that need to be considered over and above "normal" software products:

- **Use of "standards"**: it might be possible to use one of the existing standards or templates (such as ERC-20 or ERC-721) as a start point for the token
- **Data and operation efficiency**: on-chain activities are expensive compared to off-chain so the design should build as much data storage and calculation off-chain as possible
- **Immutability**: once the smart contract is deployed it cannot be amended, so any future upgrades need to be planned and "hooks" built into the original design
- **Community and access**: a smart contract deployed on a public blockchain network can in theory be accessed by anyone, so security and access controls are paramount

See Chapter 3 for more information on data and Chapter 4 for more on smart contracts and decentralised applications.

2.4.5 How will Clients or Customers Connect?

As well as the sponsoring organisation, it's likely that other parties will need to connect to the network in order for the use case solution to operate (and if not, this may not be a use case where a tokenised solution is warranted). What role does each party play in the solution and what implication does that have in terms of their need (or otherwise) to connect to the network?

For a Business-to-Business (B2B) application, it's likely that each organisation will want to be a fully-committed party on the network, through a full node. If individual clients or customers are involved, their point of access may be a web or phone application.

These considerations need to be built into the design for the end-to-end solution for the use case.

2.4.6 How to Pay for Activity?

Activity on the blockchain costs gas. As we have seen, in some cases it can cost a lot of gas with substantial sums of real money changing hands for a single transaction (if it is complex and the network is busy).

There are ways to minimise or offset these costs, such as:

- Transaction sponsoring whereby a third party pays for the transactions rather than the initiator
- Roll-ups where many transactions on one chain are rolled up into a single transaction on the main chain, thus significantly reducing the costs per transaction
- Reducing the complexity of the on-chain operation or scheduling away from peak network usage.

Regardless of the solution (unless it's on a gas-free private network), attention must be paid to the funding of transactions in on-chain native coin. A suitable reserve must be maintained for this purpose and the solution's economics must take this into account.

2.4.7 What are the Risks?

There are always risks in launching an automated solution.

Blockchains and smart contracts introduce a few additional risks, but these can be managed with sufficient preparation and attention.

One of the most significant new risks is that smart contracts (like any transaction on the blockchain) are immutable. This means that if a smart contract is deployed that includes a logic error or other software bug it is far more difficult to correct. Instead of being able to apply a "hot fix" to the in-situ code, the original contract must be disabled and a new contract deployed.

Operations across chains (from one network to another) are complex and carry an inherent risk. Solutions should be designed with a minimum of cross-chain operation.

Another risk that is unique to blockchains and tokenised solutions is the risk that the private key is exposed, either for a wallet or for the smart contract itself. Security of the key must be paramount in the organisation's planning: the key should be held off-chain, preferable offline using a non-perishable physical medium or hardware module.

Notes

1 Nakamoto, S. (2008, October 31). *Bitcoin: A Peer-to-Peer Electronic Cash System.* Retrieved from https://www.bitcoin.org/bitcoin.pdf
2 Nakamoto, S. (2008, October 31). *Bitcoin: A Peer-to-Peer Electronic Cash System.* Retrieved from https://www.bitcoin.org/bitcoin.pdf
3 Buterin, V. (2014). Ethereum White Paper: A Next-Generation Smart Contract & Decentralized Application Platform. Retrieved from https://ethereum.org/whitepaper/
4 https://merriam-webster.com/
5 https://dictionary.cambridge.org/
6 Cryptography. In Wikipedia. Retrieved June 2025, from https://en.wikipedia.org/wiki/Cryptography. Last edited: Nov. 2, 2025.
7 https://cardano.org/
8 https://polkadot.com/
9 https://solana.com/
10 https://cosmos.network/
11 https://tezos.com/
12 https://avax.network/
13 https://algorand.co/
14 https://ethereum.org/

Chapter 3

Distributed Data

3.1 Introduction

Blockchain is often referred to as a Distributed Ledger Technology or DLT. One could argue that there are two-components to ledger-keeping: the ledger itself (the data) and the process of "keeping" it or amending the data.

As we saw in the previous chapter, in the distributed ledger data is no longer held centrally or curated by a trusted third party. Instead, it is shared freely across a network, visible to anyone who has the right authorisation and knows where to look.

In this chapter we'll take a closer look at the data aspect of a distributed ledger and how the technology of blockchain enables equitable access to data for all parties.

3.2 Distributed Data: An Overview

Data in blockchains is organised into *chains of blocks*. Each block contains a header and a number of transactions; the number of transactions per block varies from network to network based on its rules. Everything that happens on the blockchain does so through the execution of a transaction which changes data from one state to another in one or more wallets.

DOI: 10.4324/9781003571421-4

Transactions and blocks are protected from tampering through *data hashing*. The transaction data is hashed together so that no single transaction can be amended without invalidating the hash value. This provides a hash value for the block which is propagated to the next block in the chain. If any data in a previous block is tampered with, the chain is broken.

The way that transactions impact data varies from network to network. Some networks operate a very simple *accounting mechanism* where the balance of a fungible asset always adds up to the total of the inbound and outbound transactions (called UTXO, or the Unspent Transaction Output model) whereas other networks have the concept of an account balance, which is more easily adapted to smart contracts.

The chain of blocks (each containing multiple transactions) along with any balance data is *physically stored* on every full node in the network. Blocks are being continually added to the end of the chain. Blockchain networks apply various techniques to prevent indefinite *data growth* which would impact scalability or even viability of the solution. These techniques include archiving of old data, full and light nodes, compression of data and *off-chain* storage as well as financial disincentives to discourage "verbose" data.

Data on a blockchain is visible to anyone who can access the network. Commonly available apps called explorers allow almost anyone to view data on a public network. Data on private networks is typically more restricted to public view. For more privacy, or for larger items of data, off-chain storage is needed. It's fundamental to blockchain operations that any node on the system can perform the same calculation on its locally-stored version of the blockchain data and reach the same result as any other node. This is not true as soon as any data used in the calculation is off-chain, so a mechanism is needed to bring necessary data on-chain for the duration of the calculation. These mechanisms are called *oracles*.

3.3 Distributed Data – The Components

3.3.1 Chains of Blocks

On a blockchain network, every activity is carried out through the processing of a transaction.

Each transaction is made up of data: enough for the activity to be executed. A transaction that moves native coin from one wallet to another must specify the identities of the two wallets involved and the quantity of coin to be sent. For a more complex transaction invoking a smart contract, the transaction data must additionally include the operational parameters expected by the smart contract.

As we have seen in Chapter 2, transactions are then gathered into blocks by the validator nodes. Blocks also have data, such as the block identifier and

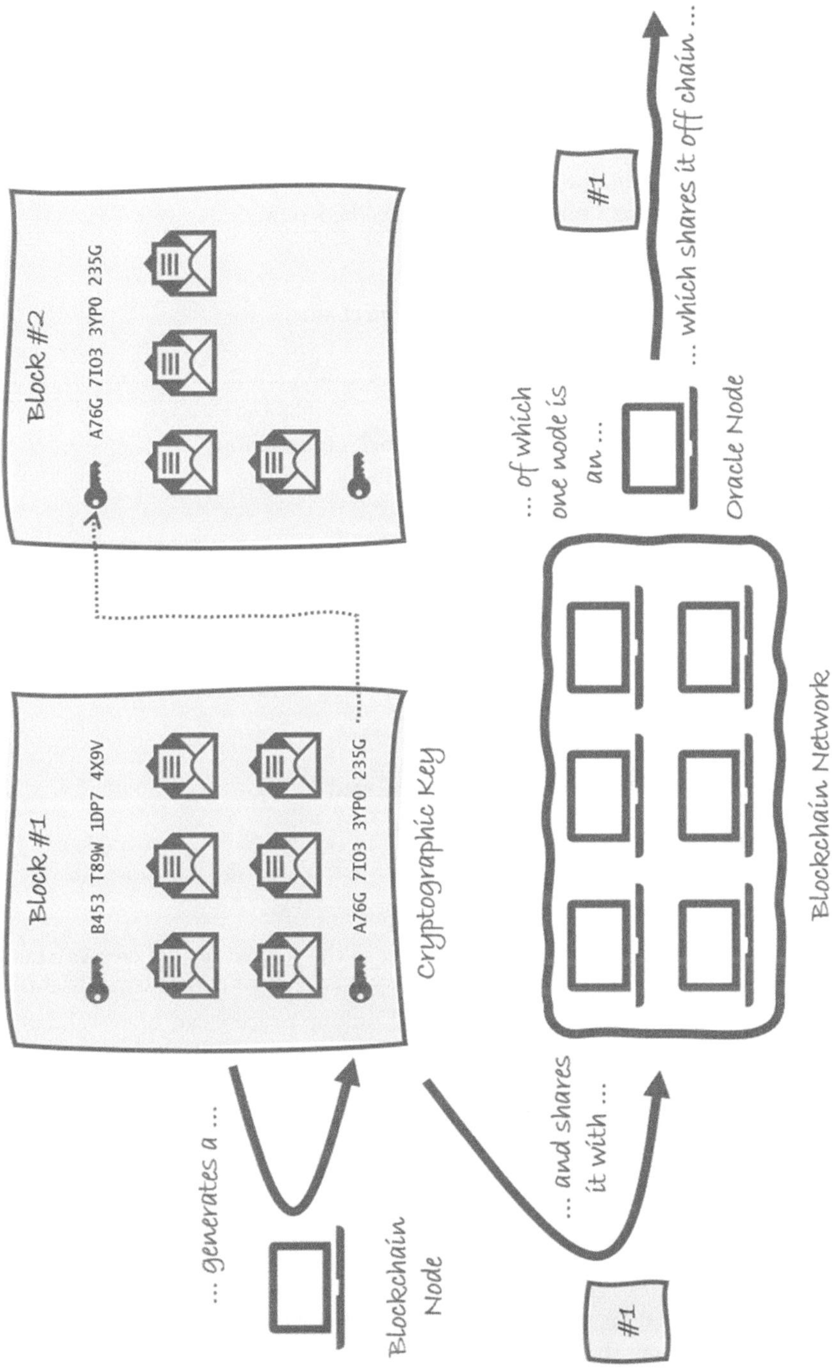

Figure 3.1 Distributed Data.

information about the transactions in the block. Some networks also require a block trailer.

All this data (transactional data, block data, wallet addresses, quantities, smart contract functions, parameters) are stored in the blockchain network's database (which, as we know, is replicated across all full nodes on the network).

Let's look at what might be contained in a typical block. As this varies from network to network, we'll take a generic, simplified view.
The block header will contain:

- The identity of the previous block in the chain.

The block header might contain:

- Hashes of the data contained in the block's transactions
- A timestamp (that the block was validated)
- Cryptography parameters
- Gas parameters.

Each transaction (and there can be hundreds or a few thousand transactions per block, depending on the parameters set out by the network) might contain:

- A sender's wallet address
- A recipient's wallet address
- The amount of native coin being transferred
- Smart contract parameters and data
- Cryptography parameters
- Gas parameters.

The inclusion of the previous block's identifier in the current header creates a permanent link between the two blocks. The identifier is generated through hashing the data within the block. This hashing and linking process can be re-validated at any time by nodes to ensure that the identifiers are properly linked and that the identifier of each block can only be derived from the original data that was validated when the block was added.

It is this second criterion that makes hashing so critical to the security of the distributed ledger.

3.3.3 Hashing

In the blockchain, data is shared between all participants. Each participant must have a means to know that the data can be trusted. What's to stop a dishonest participant going into one of the old blocks of data and amending the details of a transaction in their favour? As we've seen, this mutual trust is the fundamental bedrock of the distributed ledger and it is achieved through cryptographic hashing.

Hashing is the process of converting data (of any initial size) into a string of numbers and letters. This process has three absolutely critical aspects:

- It is a one-way process; it's impossible to rebuild the original data from the hashed data alone
- It always produces a string of the same length, regardless of the size of the original data
- No two datasets will generate the same result.

The result of the hashing process is therefore a unique fixed-length key that can be entirely trusted to have been derived from the underlying data. As every node in the network has access to the hashing algorithm, this relationship can be tested again and again across the network. Should our dishonest participant edit an old block, the data in the block will no longer produce the identical key.

This is a key point, so it's worth considering an example.

Let's imagine a block (B) that contains the following data:

- The hashed key of the previous block (A)
- Transaction 1 delivering 10 units of tokenised asset to Party Alpha
- Transaction 2 delivering 25 units of tokenised asset to Party Beta
- Transaction 3 delivering 5 units of tokenised asset to Party Gamma.

This data is all hashed together to produce the key to Block B (for simplicity, let's say that the result is abcd1234).

This hashed key is included in the data for Block C. Note that it's not usually stored in Block B as it can be derived at any time from the data within Block B.

Should the dishonest party (Party Delta) attempt to amend all three transactions so that they are the recipient, the hashed key will be recalculated to be (say) efgh5678. The other nodes in the network will detect that this differs from the key stored in Block C and will reject the new block proposed by the dishonest party.

To make the process of hashing more efficient and to reduce the amount of data needed, most blockchain networks use hierarchical structures of transactions rather than hash the entire data set. Such a hierarchy is called a binary hash tree, or a Merkle tree.

Merkle trees and similar constructions are critical to distributed ledger technology. "Merkle trees allow efficient and secure verification of the contents of large data structures. A Merkle root commits to all transactions in a block.[1]"

Think of a tennis draw for a major tournament. All the players are listed on the left-hand side and as each match is played, the winner's name goes into the next round. A Merkle tree works in much the same way, except that instead of the winner, what goes into the next round is the hash of the two transactions. Each round, the two resulting hashes from the previous round are combined until there is only one "winner" – called the Merkle root.

This root is like a fingerprint of all the transactions combined. if even one of the transactions changes, the resulting root will be different. This allows computers to quickly verify whether a transaction is part of a block without downloading all data from the block, making data verification more efficient.

Not all blockchains use Merkle trees, although many use something similar.

Ethereum, for example, uses something called a Merkle Patricia Trie[2]. This is a combination of a Merkle tree and something called a trie (pronounced "try" and derived from the word "retrieve") which is a way of storing data as a key and related data ("key-value pairs"). As Ethereum incorporates smart contracts, the root must not only cater for the transactional data but the impact that transaction had on the smart contract's data.

Accounting Mechanism

There are broadly two ways that networks account for balances: UTXO (Unspent Transaction Output) or account-based.

Why are there two models? Distributed ledger technology was originally designed specifically to support peer to peer cash transactions in cryptocurrencies. The simple accounting methodology adopted by the early networks such as Bitcoin[3] (UTXO) supported that use case but was not particularly flexible. With the subsequent rise of the Ethereum network and the adoption of smart contracts, a more sophisticated accounting mechanism was needed (although even some later networks use a variant of UTXO).

In the UTXO model there is no direct record of a coin balance: the balance in any given wallet address can be found by totalling all of the transactions impacting that wallet, both credits and debits.

Let's imagine Wallet A has received coin in the following shapes:

- Transaction #1 which outputs a credit of 1 coin
- Transaction #2 which outputs a credit of 3 coins
- Transaction #3 which outputs a credit of 4 coins.

These can be summed to give a balance of 8 units.

The transactions are recorded on the blockchain. As the transactions are considered "unspent" they also form part of the UTXO set (which for Bitcoin is recorded separately).

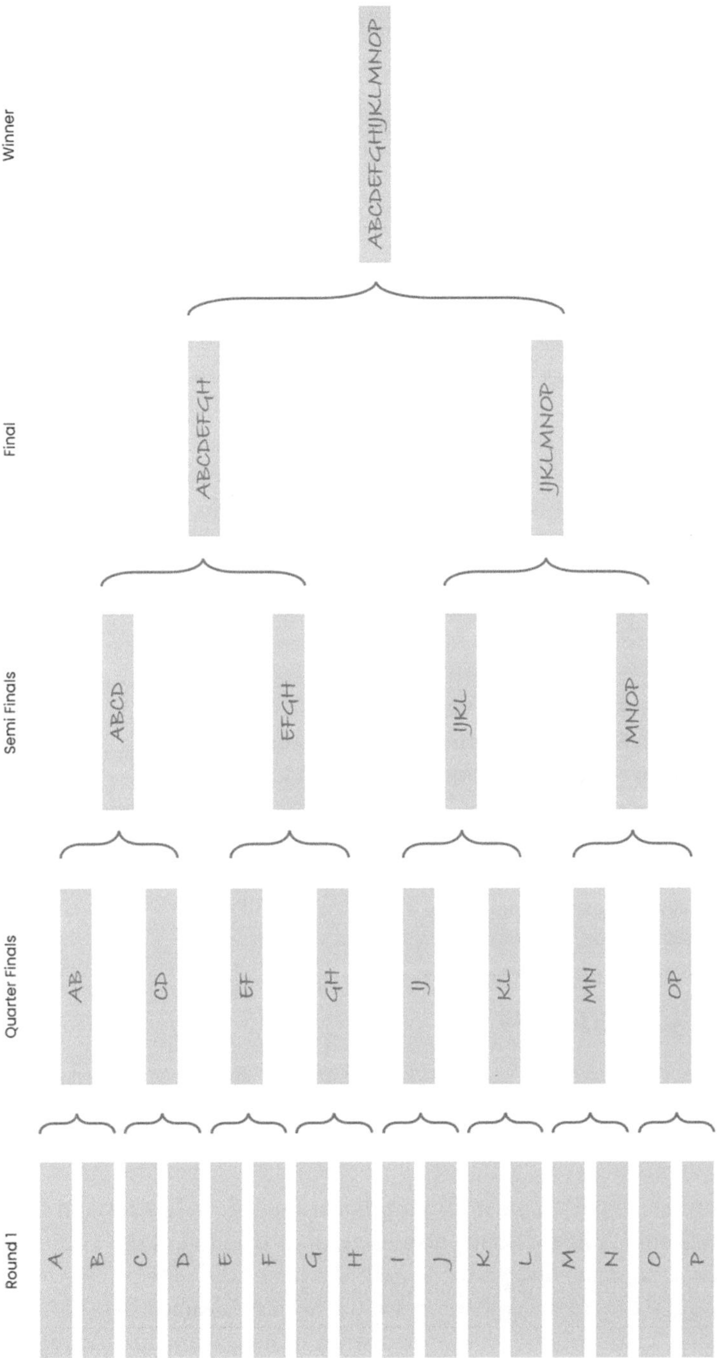

Figure 3.2 Illustration of Merkle Tree Concept.

The owner of Wallet A then wants to sell 2 coins (to Wallet B). The algorithm will look for a transaction in the UTXO set to supply the coins. As there is no single transaction that credited 2 coins to Wallet A, the algorithm will need to get its "unspent transactions" in some other way. Selecting Transaction #2, it will create a new transaction as follows:

- Transaction #4 which takes an input of the 3 coins received in Transaction #2 and has the following outputs:
  - 2 coins to Wallet B
  - 1 coin back to Wallet A as "change"
  - In reality, the change returned to Wallet A will be fractionally lower than 1 coin to pay gas for the transaction.

Although Transaction #2 remains forever on the blockchain (for a full, unarchived node), it is deemed to be "spent" and can be removed from the UTXO set.

The account-based model adopted by later networks maintains an explicit total of coins and tokens in each account as well as other data managed by smart contracts.

For an account-based network, the same sequence of transactions would be accounted for as follows:

- Transaction #1 which outputs a credit of 1 coin
- Transaction #2 which outputs a credit of 3 coins
- Transaction #3 which outputs a credit of 4 coins
- Transaction #4 which takes 2 coins from the balance and outputs them to Wallet B.

Because of the overhead of managing the account balances, the database is larger than for UTXO.

3.4.4 Physical Storage

You might be wondering where this data is actually sitting; which file on a disc drive can you point to and say "there is block number 137".

The answer varies, depending on the blockchain network (as always) but also on the type of node you are running.

Running the Bitcoin Core node program will create a directory on the node called "chainstate." A new data file (extension .dat) is added to the directory each time a block is validated and passed around the network.

Running the Ethereum node program (Geth) also creates a data directory, in this case called "chaindata." Files are stored with the extension .ldb indicating they

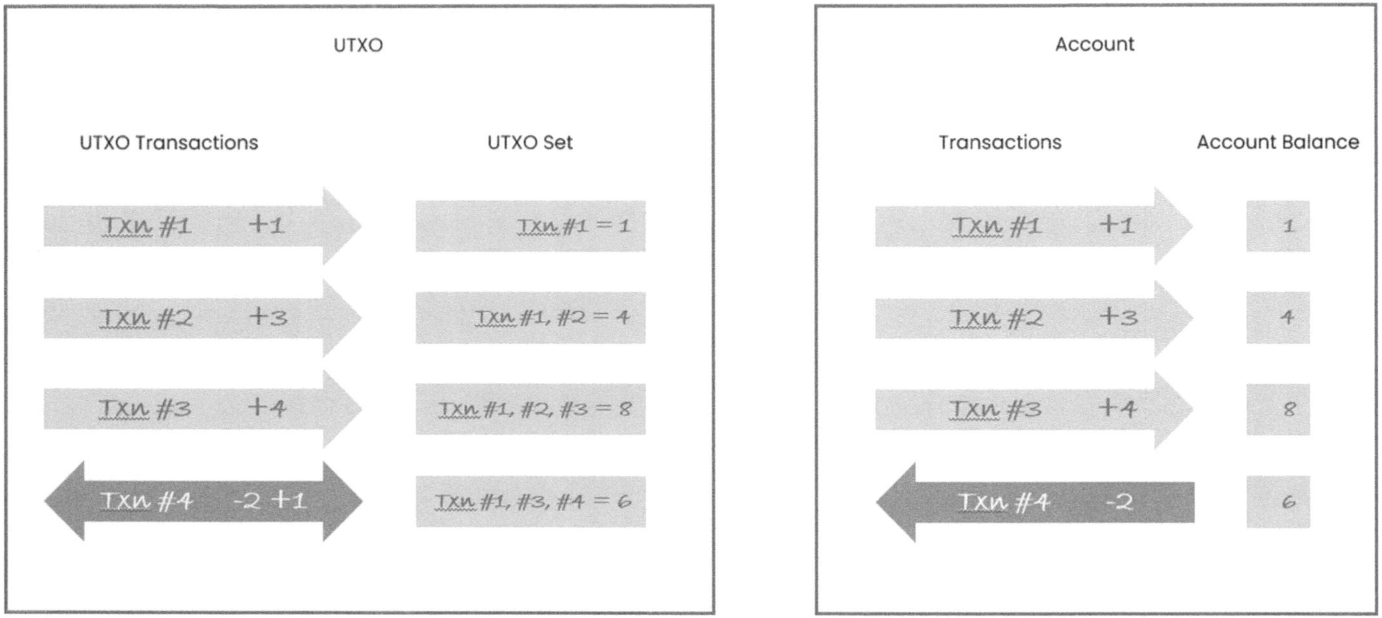

Figure 3.3 Accounting differences between UTXO and Account Mechanisms.

are used by a database called LevelDB which specialises in storing and retrieving data in simple key-value pairs for speed and efficiency.

Bitcoin also uses LevelDB for tracking balances of unspent coins.

For a light node, the data held is significantly lower, as only block headers are retained (with many block headers per file) and there is no database for tracking balances. If a light node needs more data, it will need to contact other (full) nodes in the network to retrieve the data it needs.

The exact details vary depending on the network, but the key common ingredient is that every full node keeps a copy of the full database on its local drive(s).

3.4.5 Data Growth

We are used to thinking about databases as huge sprawling things, even our own personal ones. Think about the different media files – videos, photos and music – taking up vast amounts of space on your phone or your laptop.

Blockchain databases are far more concise. Bulky data is rarely stored within the network itself ("on-chain"). And there are no video or music clips stored in this way. That's the essence of tokenisation: if you buy an NFT representing a piece of digital art, the artwork itself is stored away from the network ("off-chain") – what's on-chain is just a token representing the artwork.

Even so, the databases for these networks are quite large. The Bitcoin database, after 800,000 transactions or so, has reached 400 gigabytes. For Ethereum (with more data to record), the figure is over 1 terabyte. If you tried to run a full Ethereum node on a standard desktop, you'd run out of data storage space pretty quickly. Light nodes don't have the same requirements, typically needing only a few hundred megabytes.

What's to stop these databases growing indefinitely?

The networks take steps to "prune" old data so that the database can stay as small as possible (even for a full node). Bitcoin nodes can prune old transactions and hold just the latest balances (reducing the size of the database significantly). Ethereum takes the same approach, allowing the "state" components to be pruned. An unarchived Ethereum node requires over 12 terabytes of storage. Solana also uses the node's RAM (Random Access Memory) to maintain frequently-used data and reduce storage needs. Multi-chain networks such as Polkadot also reduce the memory demands for the main network by storing only a summary of parachain activity.

Added to these techniques are the financial disincentives to execute operations and hold data on-chain. The more data is needed by a smart contract (and the more operations it needs to perform) the higher will be the gas cost to execute it.

3.4.6 Off-Chain Data

Another way to reduce the amount of data held on-chain is to hold the data off-chain, away from the blockchain network and database.

This has the advantages (especially for very large files) of reducing the overall size of the blockchain database, but has disadvantages in that once it's off-chain, the node program can no longer rely on the data in quite the same way.

Remember the Blockchain Book Club from Chapter 2? Let's imagine that the club have agreed to reserve a table at a tea shop for their next meeting. They want to see if there is enough money in the kitty to cover the cost of the table reservation. The foundation of blockchain is that any one member of the club could perform the calculation and achieve the same result. But what if the data isn't freely and transparently available to all the members? Alexis might get one price from the Tea Shop's website, while Kai might call and get a different price over the phone. Rene knows the owner well, so if they make the call to book the table, the club will get an even better deal. The data is no longer decentralised: there is no longer a single source of the truth on which the members can rely.

Off-chain data can be held in a centralised or decentralised way.

If centralised, a single curator holds the data and manages access to it.

With a decentralised model (such as using the IPFS, the Interplanetary File System), the data is stored in such a way that it is available to anyone with the right key, which is stored on-chain. With IPFS, for example, the data is broken into chunks and stored across the IPFS network, each item tagged with the same hashed identifier (called a "content identifier" or CID). The owner (or other party) can request the data using the CID. The local node requests chunks of data from nearby nodes and reassembles the original file content. Crucially, as the CID is cryptographically derived from the data content, the assembling node can identify if any of the underlying data has been tampered with. Although IPFS itself is free, stored data cannot be guaranteed to be retained permanently unless it is pinned through a (paid for) service provider.

Off-chain data must be introduced carefully to the blockchain world in a way that makes it reliable and transparent.

3.4.7 Getting Off-Chain Data On-Chain

Due their distributed nature, blockchain networks can only rely on calculations that produce the same result no matter which node in the network performs the operation. For this to happen, all nodes must have access to the same data. As we've just seen, off-chain data does not meet that guarantee. Any off-chain data intended for use in an on-chain calculation must be brought onto the chain and be made available to all nodes in the network. Only then can it be guaranteed to be immutable and reliable.

Oracles solve this problem by taking information from off-chain sources and storing it on the blockchain for smart contracts to consume. Once stored, this information is unalterable and publicly available, so nodes can safely use it to compute state changes without breaking consensus. Or put another way, "oracles serve as bridges between blockchain smart contracts and off-chain data sources, enabling real-world data to trigger on-chain execution.[4]"

An oracle is made up of an on-chain smart contract and one or more off-chain nodes.

The oracle smart contract is the on-chain component for the oracle service. It listens for data requests from other smart contracts, relays data queries to oracle nodes, and broadcasts returned data to client contracts. This smart contract may also perform some computation on the returned data points, such as to produce an aggregate value to send to the requesting contract.

Upon receiving a new query, the oracle contract will emit a log event with details of the data request. This notifies off-chain nodes subscribed to the log, who proceed to retrieve data defined in the log event.

The oracle node is the off-chain component of the oracle service. It extracts information from external sources, such as APIs hosted on third-party servers, and puts it on-chain for consumption by smart contracts. Oracle nodes listen for events from the on-chain oracle contract and proceed to complete the task described in the log.

There are many ways to implement an oracle, depending on the specific needs for data:

- Instant access oracles obtain off-chain data ahead of time and store it on-chain. They provide the data instantly to any on-chain smart contract that requests it
- Streaming oracles receive regular updates from off-chain and publish the data on-chain to any subscribing smart contracts
- On-demand oracles wait for a request from a smart contract before retrieving the data from off-chain and supplying it by response to the smart contract
- Computational oracles perform an off-chain calculation as well as simply retrieving data – this is helpful if the computation is complex (and would therefore be expensive on-chain)
- Cross-chain oracles behave in exactly the same way as off-chain oracles but they pass data between different networks.

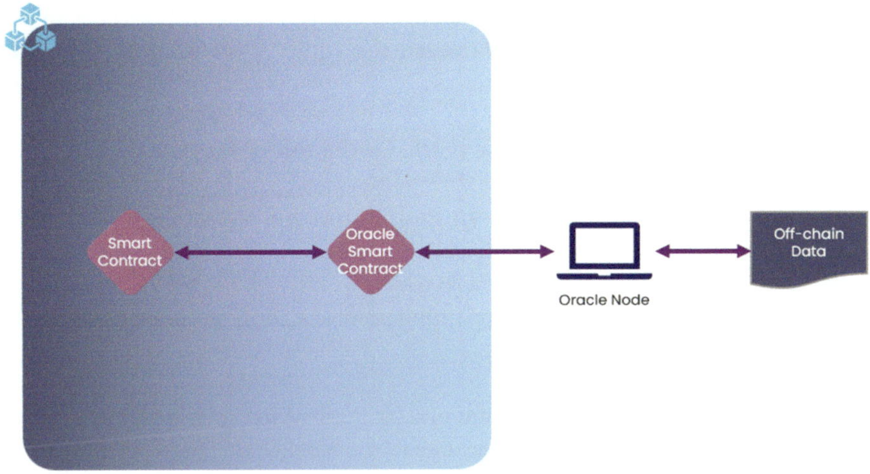

Figure 3.4 How an Oracle brings Data On-chain.

Oracles can also be centralised or decentralised.

Centralised oracles are controlled by a single entity with a single (off-chain) source of truth. These are useful where there is a trusted source of the data. However, this creates a single point of failure (the trusted entity) with no incentive for correctness.

Decentralised oracles are designed to overcome the limitations of centralised oracles by eliminating single points of failure. A decentralised oracle service comprises multiple participants in a peer-to-peer network that form consensus on off-chain data before sending it to a smart contract.

Decentralised oracles attempt to achieve correctness of data using different approaches. This includes using proofs attesting to the authenticity and integrity of the returned information and requiring multiple entities to collectively agree on the validity of off-chain data.

Authenticity proofs are cryptographic mechanisms that enable independent verification of information retrieved from external sources.

Decentralised oracles deal with discrepancies in information retrieved from multiple off-chain sources by either allowing users to vote on the accuracy of the data or by using a mechanism such as a Schelling-point mechanism, where responses are aggregated into a single mean or median value after which nodes are rewarded or punished according to the extent to which their responses align with or deviate from the aggregate value.

Let's consider the need for data such as an equity price that fluctuates in real time. If a smart contract on-chain needed the equity price it could choose to invoke one of the following:

- An instant access or streaming oracle (at the risk of the data being slightly out of date)
- An on-demand oracle (for an up-to-date price but with a short delay while the oracle retrieves the data)
- A decentralised on-demand oracle which would average the values returned and reward the more accurate suppliers (for a more accurate price at the cost of time and rewards).

Not all oracles are software: hardware oracles (embedded in a device such as an Internet of Things sensor) can provide data to the blockchain based on the device's status or location.

For the Blockchain Book Club, an oracle might serve the purpose of checking the club's bank account to ensure the on-chain total balance in the kitty (as represented by the various spreadsheet entries) matches what is actually held at the bank. Jo volunteers to check the bank account on a regular basis. This is yet another kind of oracle (a human oracle), in this case centralised and on-demand.

3.4.8 Getting On-Chain Data Off-Chain

Just as sometimes off-chain data is needed on-chain, data from the blockchain is frequently needed in the real world. An example might be to see the balance in your crypto wallet on your phone.

Blockchain scanners (also known as explorers) allow off-chain actors to access data that is held on-chain. Scanners use oracles to make on-chain data available to the outside world. In the financial industry, blockchain scanners will have many applications such as verifying consumer identities or authorities, or to inspect transactions or balances relating to tokenized financial assets.

Blockchain scanners typically run a full node (or connect to a third-party full node) for the selected blockchain. Each full node contains a complete copy of the blockchain ledger which includes every smart contract, token and transaction on that particular blockchain network.

This raw data copied from the blockchain may be enhanced by some scanners which offer the use of indexes to allow faster retrieval of linked data.

The scanner may link to third parties using APIs. This obviates the need for the third party to build their own connectivity to the blockchain.

Listeners are another way to get data off-chain. These applications respond to events emitted by smart contracts.

Indexers regularly take large chunks of data from a blockchain network and store it in an off-chain cache. The data is indexed for fast retrieval.

3.5 Distributed Data Applied

The subject of data both on-chain and off-chain has many facets and many practical considerations for the would-be user of the distributed ledger. What questions should such a user be asking in respect of their data?
We suggest the following:

- What kind of node to run?
- What data should be on-chain?
- How to get data on-chain/off-chain?

3.5.1 What Kind of Node to Run?

Let's assume for a moment that you are running a business that involves interacting with the distributed ledger in some way. How do you connect to your chosen network? Do you implement a full node with the hardware overheads that implies or go with a light node only, accepting that the reduced hardware spend is worth the potential for slight delays to access (in cases where the light node needs to get more data from a nearby full node). You may, of course, decide that you don't need a node at all and can rely on a third party provider for your access.

If your need for access to data will be frequent, with regular reference to on-chain data, then you are probably better off with a full node. For less frequent access (and if there is little need for historical data) then a light node may do the trick. You should only consider a remote provider if your blockchain access will be infrequent.

If you will be deploying smart contracts or running an oracle, this may predicate the running of a full node by the network itself.

3.5.2 What Data Should be On-Chain?

There won't always be a choice of whether to keep data on-chain or off-chain. For cryptocurrency transactions and simpler tokenised operations, all data will be on-chain. But as smart contracts become more sophisticated, executing complex calculations or interacting with real-world data, a choice will need to be made between keeping data on-chain (immediately accessible but at great cost) or off-chain. In these cases, as always, the design will need to take account of the conflicting needs of accessibility against cost.

We must also always consider our three tests for tokenisation: equitable access, transparency, and trust. If the data needs to be instantly available to multiple parties, then it should be on the blockchain.

Consider a business that wants to tokenise a real-world asset (such as a mutual fund in the world of finance or an Old Master painting in the art world). For a mutual fund, the dataset will include ownership of the fund (which wallets have units and how many), the price of the fund, the nature and allocation of underlying financial instruments, the fund issuer and so on. For a piece of art, the data will include detailed provenance of the ownership to establish its credence. The fund issuer might decide that only the distribution of units should be on-chain, although it may also want to make the price available through an oracle service. The art tokeniser may want to hold the detailed provenance off-chain, linked to an on-chain identifier.

3.5.3 How to Get Data On-Chain/Off-Chain

Most real-world business processes will need to use a combination of on-chain and off-chain data. Imagine that you have deployed a smart contract that has a function to re-evaluate a portfolio of assets against a defined model. The function will need asset balances (on-chain) and asset valuations (which may be off-chain).

Depending on the business need, an organisation may want to deploy (or utilise) a range of oracles, scanners and other tools to effectively move data between the on-chain and off-chain worlds (or even between chains).

Rather than set out specific use cases (which will in any case vary from industry to industry), we have tried to summarise below some different types of interaction and the related configurations:

- **On-chain trigger, off-chain activity**: such as where the minting of a token on-chain is confirmed to the owner (or other interested and authorised party such as a regulator) by email or other messaging capability, or where the purchase of an NFT grants access to the related real-world asset for the buyer
- **Off-chain trigger, on-chain activity**: such as where a real-world payment into a bank account triggers the minting of a stablecoin in? the payer's wallet, or where the receipt at the door of a package triggers the payment in stablecoin by the buyer
- **On-chain trigger, off-chain verification, on-chain activity**: such as where a purchase of a tokenised asset can only take place if certain off-chain permissions have been granted

- **On-chain data, off-chain analytics**: such as where data providers scrape data from the network and make it available in aggregated or enhanced form
- **Off-chain verification, on-chain record**: such as where the blockchain's immutability is used to effectively timestamp an event or record.

Notes

1 Narayanan, A. et al. (2016). *Bitcoin and Cryptocurrency Technologies.* Princeton University Press.

2 Wood, Gavin (2014). *Ethereum: A Secure Decentralised Generalised Transaction Ledger* (Yellow Paper).

3 Antonopoulos, Andreas M. (2017). *Mastering Bitcoin: Unlocking Digital Cryptocurrencies* (2nd ed.). O'Reilly Media.

4 Chainlink Labs (2021). *Chainlink Documentation.* https://docs.chain.link/

Chapter 4

Decentralised Applications

4.1 Introduction

It's now time to look at the "keeping" aspects of ledger-keeping on the distributed ledger: the processes that amend the data in the ledger.

While blockchain technology was introduced initially through the Bitcoin network, it was the advent of Ethereum and the Ethereum Virtual Machine (EVM) that turned blockchain into a truly transformative proposition.

In this chapter we'll look at how smart contracts in virtual machines like the EVM create a decentralised application that can be used by any blockchain participant with reliable results.

4.2 Decentralised Applications: An Overview

Decentralised Applications (also known as dApps) are executable code running on a *virtual machine*, a computer operating across a blockchain network through the execution of smart contracts.

Depending on the blockchain network, a developer will use a specific *programming language* encoded into the network's node program to write *smart contract code*. This code is then compiled and deployed on the network. It contains

DOI: 10.4324/9781003571421-5

functions that can be invoked and data that can be amended or viewed, which are often defined in a relevant *standard*.

As well as a blockchain component, many *decentralised applications* have an off-chain component as well as a front end with which the user interacts directly or through an interface. These components are deployed on servers or other devices (Figure 4.1).

4.3 Decentralised Applications: The Components

4.3.1 Virtual Machines

First, let's look at what is meant by a virtual machine.

In a non-blockchain context, a virtual machine is the name given to a computer that has been emulated through software rather than built physically. Although it ultimately needs a physical server somewhere on which to execute, the characteristics and behaviours of the virtual machine are primarily controlled by software rather than the hardware environment. Many such virtual machines could run alongside each other on the same piece of hardware, each behaving differently according to its specific configuration.

In a blockchain context, a virtual machine might be considered to be exactly the opposite: a single virtual environment that is operated across countless blockchain nodes.

In reality, each node runs its own copy of the software that collectively creates the virtual machine. Critically, due to a concept referred to as *deterministic execution*, each copy can be fully relied upon to produce the same result as all of the others, regardless of the location or hardware configuration of the individual nodes.

The concept of such a blockchain-enabled virtual machine was introduced with the Ethereum network and was referred to as the Ethereum Virtual Machine or EVM. It was through the EVM that nodes were able to execute smart contracts in a consistently reliable way, paving the way to tokenisation. As each node receives and processes a transaction, it executes the functions (or methods) within the related smart contracts. Each calculation is performed entirely in isolation, using data only contained within the transaction itself (or stored in the smart contract's memory from previous transactions). As such, the outcome of the calculation is guaranteed to be the same no matter which node is performing it. This is called deterministic execution: each node can perform the calculation and store the result, knowing that every other node will (by design) reach the identical result.

Following the model established by Ethereum, other blockchain networks (including Solana, Polkadot and Cardano) have also implemented their own interpretations of the virtual machine. However, these different virtual machine

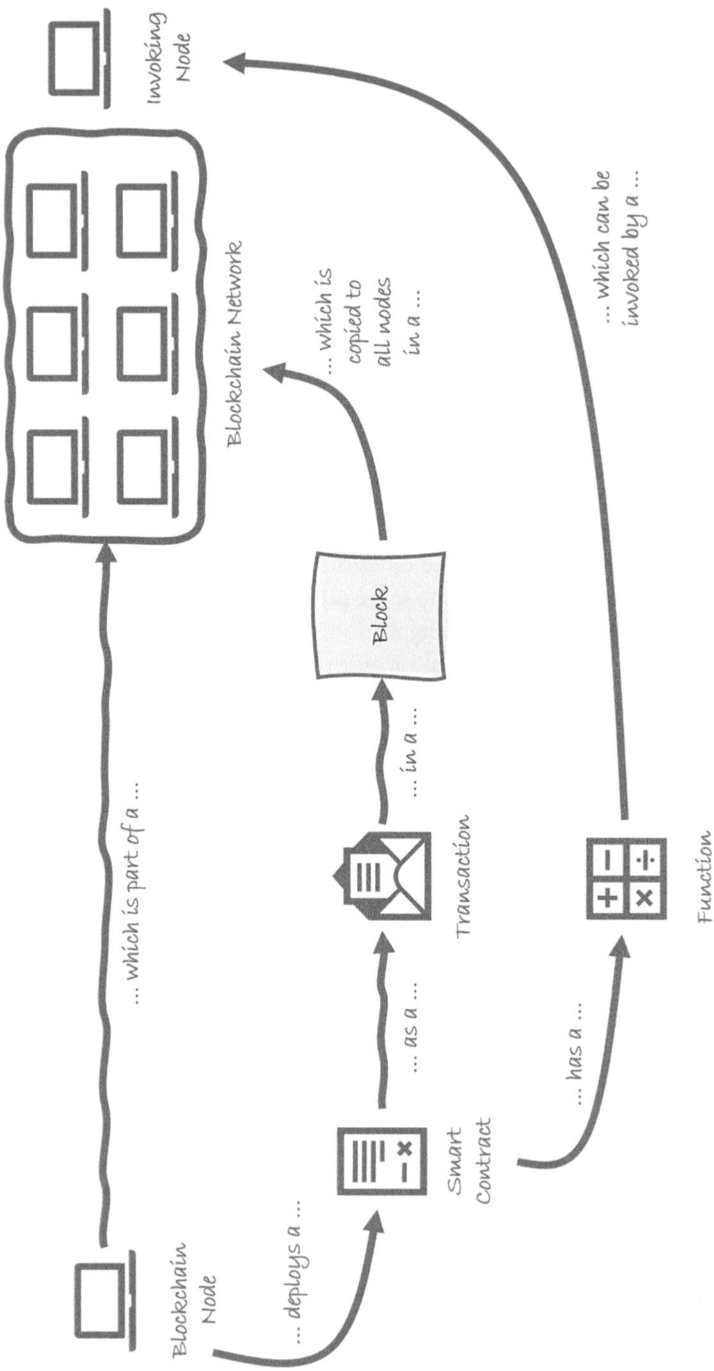

Figure 4.1 Distributed Applications.

environments share a number of common characteristics. While most networks have implemented the EVM or something very similar, there are exceptions as always. Polkadot and Cosmos have repurposed an existing format originally designed for web browsers called WebAssembly or WASM.
By network, then:

- **Bitcoin**: Bitcoin Script (a simple non-Turing complete virtual machine that supports Bitcoin transactions)
- **Ethereum**: EVM
- **Cardano**: Plutus Core (a UTXO-based virtual machine)
- **Polkadot**: WASM
- **Solana**: Solana BPF (Berkley Packet Filter)
- **Cosmos**: WASM (CosmWasm)
- **Tezos**: Michelson VM (virtual machine designed specifically for verification and security)
- **Avalanche**: EVM
- **Algorand**: AVM (Algorand Virtual Machine, designed for high-speed execution and scalability).

The main function of the virtual machine is to execute smart contracts that have been written and compiled into a low-level code (called *bytecode*). Each copy of the virtual machine must process the commands in the same way, to produce a reliable and repeatable outcome (for a given set of input data). This includes the order in which instructions will be accepted, and the ability to run each instruction in a stateless and isolated way (not impacted by other instructions). Many virtual machines process instructions sequentially (although this creates performance issues at large volume) and are adept at dealing with cryptographic operations. Gas plays an important part in the blockchain economy, and virtual machines are able to assess the resource requirements of smart contracts and ensure the right gas is allocated while also limiting the impact of overly complex instructions.

4.3.3 Smart Contract Programming Languages

Before a smart contract can be deployed onto a network, it must be written and tested by an individual or an organisation. The source code is written in a defined language that is specific to the target blockchain network. Once written, the smart contract can be compiled into bytecode that can be interpreted by the virtual machine.

The blockchain node program contains all of the necessary logic to execute these compiled programs. Each of the major networks has its own specific smart contract programming language: Solidity and Vyper (both Ethereum) were the first, followed by Rust (Solana and Polkadot), Michelson (Tezos) and Plutus (Cardano).

The characteristics of each language vary, but most share a set of common features.

For a start, the languages must all support deterministic execution so that given the same input data and instructions, two copies of the code will produce exactly the same output. To do this, the language will have an "event-driven" architecture favouring stateless function calls and will be modular in nature. The executable code must be "Turing complete", meaning that any conceivable calculation must be (theoretically) possible. Once deployed to the network, a smart contract's logic cannot be changed, so most languages have ways to ensure that the code is as accurate as possible, such as robust error-handling and exception processing, safety checks and clear data definitions.

4.3.4 Smart Contract Code

Many explanations about smart contracts (especially explanations to a non-technical audience) focus heavily on the word "contract" and how the smart contract will execute conditionally when certain specified criteria are met.

But the easiest way to think of a smart contract is that it is simply software. Even the least technically oriented person is likely to be familiar with the broad concept of software and how it works. It takes in a number of variables in the form of data, evaluates them and produces an output. Think of your email software: it receives data (an email message), applies some logic (such as detecting spam or allocating the mail to the right inbox) and takes an action (displaying the mail on your screen). A smart contract is no different. It's just a program, written by a developer to carry out specific functions.

A decentralised application may invoke one or many smart contracts, in just the same way that an application running on a desktop or server will invoke multiple programs and functions.

A smart contract will have one or more of the following components.

- *Variables* store essential information used by the smart contract
- *Functions* can be invoked by those with permission to effect a desired outcome
- *Events* are special functions that log transaction activities, helping external applications and interfaces react to smart contract activities
- *Constructor* is a special function that runs once only when the contract is first created.

Variables are the bricks and mortar of a smart contract and come in many flavours depending on where they are stored and who can view or update them.

Data that needs to be kept once the smart contract has finished executing is held in *state variables*. These variables are persistent and define the state of the smart contract. This might be the identity or name of a token, or the total number of such tokens in circulation. Data that is used by the smart contract during execution but can then be discarded is held in *local variables*. It costs more gas to view and update state variables than local variables. There are also global variables managed by the blockchain environment itself which are available to be read by the smart contract as it executes (such as a transaction identifier).

As well as the persistence of the data, each variable has a characteristic that defines its visibility. A *private variable* can be accessed only by the smart contract that defines it. An important concept when writing smart contracts is that of inheritance: one contract can be derived from another and can inherit the characteristics of the parent. This reduces the need for duplication of code in the child contract. An internal variable can be used within both the parent smart contract and any derived smart contracts. Finally, a public variable is visible to any smart contract on the blockchain network.

Functions are the engines of smart contracts. Designed by whoever conceives and deploys the smart contract, they are built into its executable code and are available to be used by anyone who has the right credentials and provides the right data. Like variables, functions come in a number of flavours which define who can use them (*visibility*) and how they interact with the smart contract's variables (*state mutability*).

Functions that are *public* or *external* are available to everyone who has access to the smart contract. Typically, there is a gas fee to be paid as part of the transaction that invokes the function. Public functions may also be called from within the smart contract, whereas external functions must be called from outside the contract. Some functions (*private* or *internal*) are only available within the smart contract itself, performing any required internal calculations. Private functions can only be invoked from within the same contract, while internal functions can also be invoked by derived functions (reducing the complexity of those derived contracts).

Functions are also classed by their impact on the state of the smart contract (the data stored in its state variables). *Pure* functions are just calculators: they neither need access to state data nor do they store it afterwards. *View* functions are able to read (but not update) state variables. Other functions (*payable*) require gas and can update data within the blockchain.

In the same way that software running on your laptop or your phone has an output, so does a smart contract. Output is in the form of changes to data in state variables or in the form of an event. Events are said to be emitted by a smart contract, which actually logs the event as data within the blockchain. This logged event is then available to other applications (either on- or off-chain).

The constructor function is a special function that is invoked once upon the smart contract's initial deployment. This can perform initial calculations or set up state variables (such as a token's name or identity or how many tokens exist).

Below is a simplified version of a standard smart contract written in Solidity, the programming language used for Ethereum smart contracts. This code outlines the basic functionality required to comply with the ERC-20 standard.

One thing to note is just how simple the contract can be. The example below contains all that is needed to launch a tokenised asset (albeit a rudimentary one). That's four variables, three functions and two events, plus a constructor function that runs once as the smart contract is deployed.

We've added some colour-coding to help with the explanation that follows.

Variables are picked out in red.

Functions are picked out in blue.

Events are picked out in amber.

The constructor function is picked out in green.

```
contract ERC20Token {
    string public name;
    string public symbol;
    uint8 public decimals = 18; // 18 is the most common number of
    decimal places
    uint public totalSupply;

    mapping(address => uint) public balanceOf;
    mapping(address => mapping(address => uint)) public allowance;

    event Transfer(address indexed from, address indexed to, uint value);
    event Approval(address indexed owner, address indexed spender, uint
    value);

    constructor(string memory _name, string memory _symbol, uint _
    totalSupply) {
        name = _name;
        symbol = _symbol;
        totalSupply = _totalSupply * 10 ** uint(decimals);
        balanceOf[msg.sender] = totalSupply;
    }
```

```
    function transfer(address _to, uint _value) public returns (bool success) {
        require(balanceOf[msg.sender] >= _value, "Insufficient balance");
        balanceOf[msg.sender] -= _value;
        balanceOf[_to] += _value;
        emit Transfer(msg.sender, _to, _value);
        return true;
    }

    function approve(address _spender, uint _value) public returns (bool
    success) {
        allowance[msg.sender][_spender] = _value;
        emit Approval(msg.sender, _spender, _value);
        return true;
    }

    function transferFrom(address _from, address _to, uint _value) public
    returns (bool success) {
        require(_value <= balanceOf[_from], "Insufficient balance");
        require(_value <= allowance[_from][msg.sender], "Allowance
        exceeded");
        balanceOf[_from] -= _value;
        balanceOf[_to] += _value;
        allowance[_from][msg.sender] -= _value;
        emit Transfer(_from, _to, _value);
        return true;
    }
}
```

Variables store essential information about the token.

- name records the token's name
- symbol records its symbol
- totalSupply records the total amount of tokens created
- balanceOf tracks how many tokens each address owns
- allowance records how much one address is allowed to spend from another's account.

Functions can be invoked by those with permission to effect a desired outcome.

- transfer allows a token holder to send a specified amount of their tokens to another address. It checks if the sender has enough tokens and updates the balances accordingly

- approve gives permission to another address (a spender) to transfer up to a certain number of tokens on behalf of the token holder. This is useful for allowing smart contracts to spend tokens in your account, with your permission
- transferFrom is used by a spender (previously approved with "approve") to transfer tokens from one account to another. It checks both the sender's balance and the allowance set by the token owner.

Events are special functions that log transaction activities. Events help external applications and interfaces react to contract activities.

- Transfer records every time tokens move from one account to another
- Approval logs when a token owner approves a spender to use their tokens.

The constructor is a special function that runs once when the contract is first created. It sets up the token's basic details and assigns the initial total supply of tokens to the creator's address.

In simple terms, the ERC-20 standard defines a common list of rules and functions that a token contract must implement to work seamlessly within the Ethereum ecosystem. This includes keeping track of how many tokens everyone has, enabling token transfers between accounts, and allowing others to spend tokens on your behalf, all while ensuring transactions are secure and recorded.

Functions (including the constructor function) are invoked by deploying subsequent transactions, stating the values of the function arguments. So, to invoke the constructor function to create a smart contract for a token called "ABC Token", with a symbol "ABC" and a total supply of 1,000 units, the deploying transaction would specify the arguments (ABC Token, ABC, 1000).

Similarly, to transfer ten units from the sender (let's call them AddressA) to AddressB, the sender would add a transaction to the blockchain that invoked transfer (AddressB, 10). This would emit the Transfer event with variables (AddressA, AddressB, 10).

4.3.5 Lifecycle of a Smart Contract

Let's look (briefly) at the lifecycle of a smart contract, its functions and its data.

First, the code for the smart contract is written and tested (in a separate test version of the blockchain network called a testnet) by the issuer or their appointed technology team. This is shown in Figure 4.2.

The smart contract is deployed using a transaction on the main network, as shown in Figure 4.3. At this stage, its data (shown in simplified form) is in the initial state: no tokens have been issued.

Users invoke the smart contract's functions (by initiating transactions) to mint tokens. We can think of these tokens as existing independently and being

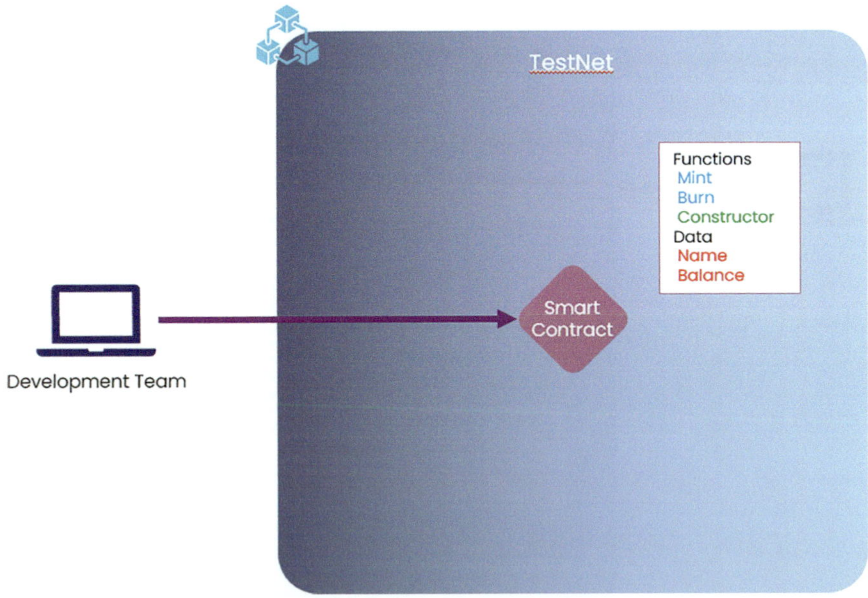

Figure 4.2 Smart Contract Components.

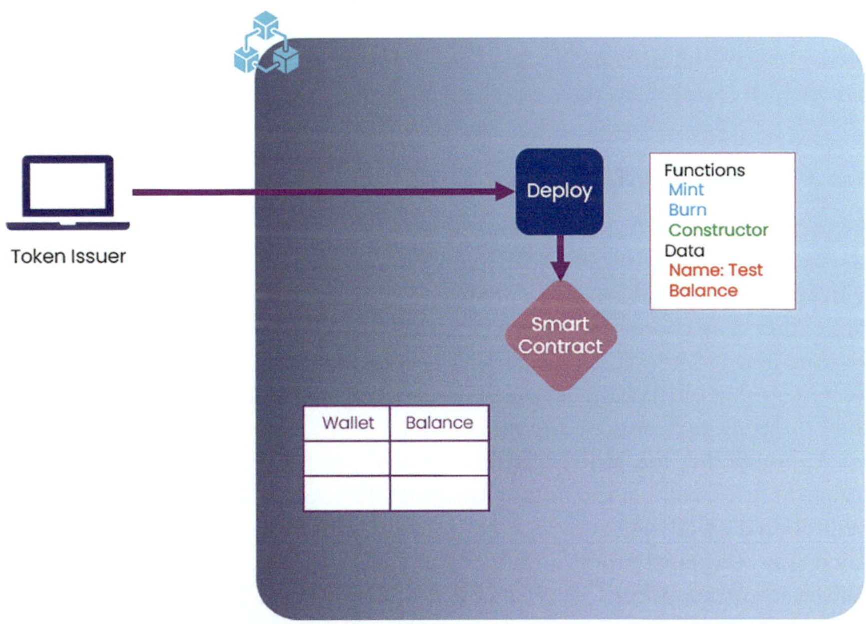

Figure 4.3 Deployed Smart Contract.

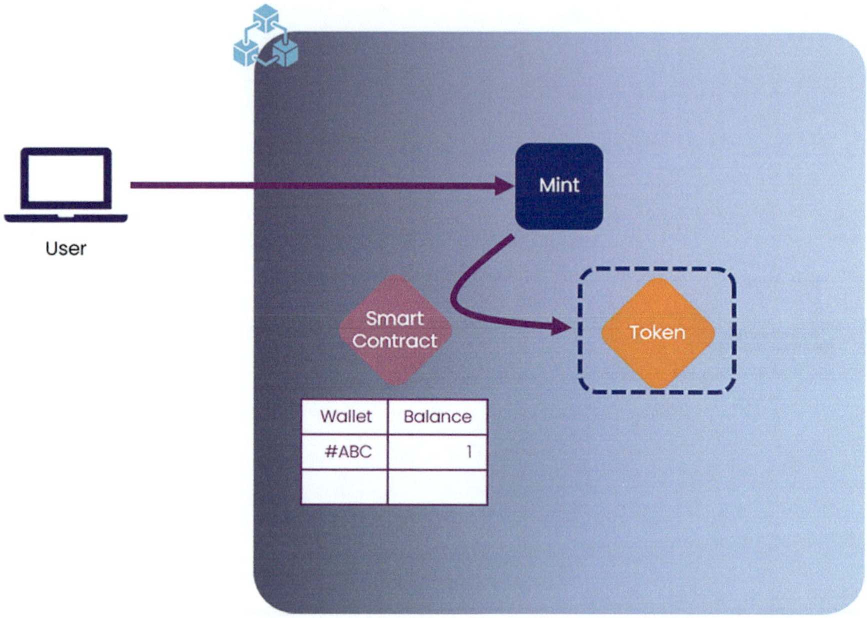

Figure 4.4 Minted Token as Smart Contract Data.

placed in wallets, but in reality they exist only as data in the smart contract's database (which is stored on the blockchain as shown in Figure 4.4).

4.3.6 Smart Contract Standards

As with any software, the developer can write a smart contract however they choose. However, if the developer wants the smart contract to be adopted by the wider community, behaving in a predictable way and providing a predictable outcome, they may choose to follow a particular template, usually called a standard.

An ERC (which stands for Ethereum Request for Comments) is a technical document that blockchain developers use to propose standard smart contracts for the Ethereum platform (among other things).

Although they are, strictly speaking, meant just for the Ethereum network, in reality, an ERC will tend to be adopted for all Ethereum-like networks. ERCs can be proposed by anyone and are then reviewed and discussed by the community. There is no formal approval process for an ERC – acceptance is demonstrated by consensus and adoption. Compliance is also largely self-policed by the community.

In many cases, an ERC is not so much a standard as a *template* for future smart contracts, with a number of pre-defined functions and data components. It is worth remembering that a smart contract is essentially a set of software commands encoded into a transaction that is deployed on the blockchain network.

Some of the more impactful standards include ERC-20 (which was the blueprint for all future tokenisation), ERC-721 (which introduced the concept of non-fungible tokens), and ERC-777 (which enhanced ERC-20 with more functionality).

Below are some of the more impactful ERCs.

4.3.6.1 ERC-20 (Fungible Tokens)[1]

These are the granddaddy of them all, from the tokeniser's viewpoint. ERC-20 sets out the source code for a smart contract to generate and manage fungible tokens – the sort of tokens used for asset tokenisation.

The ERC-20 code (once deployed) implements a number of pre-defined functions, such as:

- **totalSupply**: returns the total supply of the asset tokens available
- **transferFrom**: transfers a number of tokens to a specified address from a specified address
- **allowance**: an amount the spender is allowed to withdraw from the owner.

These functions and the events they spawn are universally adopted, allowing any ERC-20 compliant token to be held in all wallets and to interoperate with other smart contracts.

4.3.6.2 ERC-721 (Non-Fungible Tokens)[2]

This ERC introduced the concept of NFTs on the Ethereum blockchain, where each token is unique and can represent ownership of a specific asset, whether digital or physical. The standard is widely used for digital art, collectibles, and other unique items.

The functions for an ERC-721 compatible token are similar to those for an ERC-20 token, but the transfer function, for example, can be used only to transfer a specified token (indicated by a token ID) rather than a value of fungible tokens as permitted by ERC-20.

4.3.6.3 ERC-777 (Advanced Fungible Tokens)[3]

This is an improvement on ERC-20, introducing several new features aimed at increasing functionality, security, and usability, while remaining backward compatible with ERC-20.

Additional functions include the ability to authorise (and de-authorise) a third-party operator and the ability to mint (create) and burn (destroy) tokens as well as to transfer them.

A significant new concept introduced with ERC-777 is that of hooks, which react to tokens being either received (allowing the receiving contract to perform additional validation or processing) or sent (allowing pre-transfer checks at the sending contract).

Hooks facilitate more seamless interaction between different contracts and Decentralised Applications (dApps) by allowing for automatic notifications and actions upon token transfers.

4.3.6.4 ERC-1155 (Multi-Token Standard)[4]

This supports multiple tokens, including a mix of fungible and non-fungible.

4.3.6.5 ERC-1400 (Security Token Standard)[5]

This is a comprehensive standard designed for security tokens, which represents ownership of real-world assets (like funds, stocks, or bonds) and is subject to regulatory compliance. ERC-1400 builds on the foundations laid by existing standards (like ERC-20) to address the unique needs and legal requirements of security tokens, aiming to standardise their issuance, transfer, and management on the blockchain.

ERC-1400 introduces the concept of partitioning, which allows tokens to be grouped into partitions within a single contract, representing different classes of shares (such as voting rights). It also allows for the integration of compliance checks (for example, KYC/AML) directly into the token's transfer function, ensuring that tokens can only be transferred between addresses that have passed the necessary verifications. It supports conditional transfers, incorporating a system of checks that must be passed for a transfer to be executed. These can include time-based restrictions (for example, lock-up periods), jurisdictional restrictions, and investor eligibility. Where an asset has requirements for legal documentation, the standard enables these to be attached to the token contract, ensuring that token holders have access to all necessary legal information.

Finally, ERC-1400 allows for the creation of mechanisms to recover tokens in case of accidental loss or transfer to an incorrect address, which is a significant concern for valuable security tokens.

4.3.6.6 ERC-3643 (On-Chain Permissioned Tokens)[6]

These represent an automated, on-chain exchange protocol for regulated financial markets based on four pillars:

- A blockchain based identity management system, ONCHAINID
- A set of validation certificates linked to the identity
- An on-chain Eligibility Verification System (EVS)
- A set of compliance rules for each tokenised offering.

Other ERC standards exist, and more are being added all the time as use cases develop and innovators make improvements to distributed ledger capabilities.

These standards (or templates) are all based on the EVM, but the concept is replicated for the other virtual machines. For example, *SPL-Token*[7] ("Solana Program Library") is Solana's equivalent of ERC-20 and ERC-721, while for Tezos *FA1.2*[8] ("Financial application 1.2") is the equivalent of ERC-20 and *FA2* is the multi-token equivalent of ERC-1155.

You may ask, if these ERC templates (and variants for other virtual machines) are not standards, what benefit do they bring? First, knowing that a given smart contract is based on a particular template gives the user confidence in the outcome of an operation, which also encourages interoperability (and therefore adoption). Secondly, it is worth remembering that a smart contract, once deployed, is immutable and cannot be changed (although another, corrected, smart contract could be deployed). If there is a bug in the smart contract's coded logic, that bug will remain forever. One way to reduce the incidence of such bugs is through testing, but another is to use an established template such as ERC-20 as a starting point, adding any specific logic as needed.

4.3.7 Standardisation

Standards are important in any industry, but they are vital in the world of technology and finance, where they ensure that processes can be relied upon to deliver consistent results. If two organisations operate different software applications that need to perform specific functions (whether to validate or to process data), it is critical that each application can rely on the data input to or output by the other.

Standards in the financial world have evolved over decades, and adoption levels are very high. Messaging standards such as ISO 20022 enable organisations' applications to talk to each other reliably, while information security standards such as ISO 27001 ensure that each organisation manages its (and its clients') data responsibly.

The same is very much true of blockchain technology.

However, it is worth noting that standards and innovation are often not comfortable bedfellows. If the technology evolves beyond the scope of the standard, a lot of effort and collaboration can boil down to nothing much.

The video cassette "format war" of the late 1970s and 1980s is a classic case in point. Betamax had first-mover advantage and by some measures could be considered the superior standard, but VHS provided a longer recording length and achieved wider adoption by targeting manufacturers more successfully. Ultimately, however, their rivalry proved to be merely a blip on the technological roadmap, as video cassettes were swiftly supplanted by DVDs and eventually by streaming and downloading.

For blockchain, it may be some years yet before the final panoply of internationally adopted standards is mature, complete, and representative of best practice.

ISO[9] (the International Organisation for Standardisation) is based in Geneva, and operates through a series of technical committees, which typically draw on global industry expertise provided on a pro bono basis by industry players. The technical committee for "blockchain and distributed ledger technologies" is TC307 and it runs various working groups focusing on topics such as digital currencies, security, interoperability and non-fungible tokens.

The technical committee has published a number of documents, only some of which are official standards (the rest are technically "reports" or "specifications" in ISO terminology). More standards are in the process of being defined.

Published standards include ISO 22739 (vocabulary) and ISO 23257 (reference architecture). Technical reports include ISO/TR 6039 (identifiers), ISO/TR 23244 (privacy and personally identifiable information) and ISO/TR 23576 (security management of digital asset custodians). Published technical specifications include ISO/TS 23258 (taxonomy and ontology).

Other industry initiatives may yet become standard. Many are simply proposals at this stage (quite often theoretical in nature), whereas some initiatives are in direct competition with each other, and only time (and adoption) will determine the victor.

4.3.8 Decentralised Applications on your Server, Desktop or Mobile Device

So far, we've talked a lot about smart contracts. But the smart contract is only part of the story. It's possible to create a decentralised application through just the deployment of smart contracts, but this would be potentially inefficient (as there are some activities unsuitable for execution on the blockchain) and certainly wouldn't be very user-friendly.

Most users would expect to use a User Interface (UI) to capture their input and to display any results. This UI capability could be deployed on a laptop as a web page or as a native executable application or on a smartphone or tablet. Once the UI application has been developed and tested, it can be deployed to users through standard channels such as app stores or as a web page.

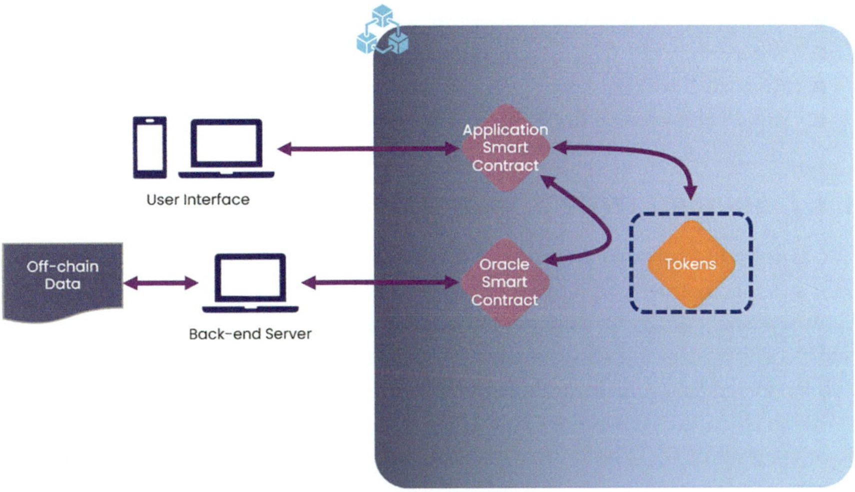

Figure 4.5 Distributed Application Components.

Most applications will also feature calculations or data off-chain, especially where the calculations are complex or the data requirements are sizeable. These off-chain aspects will need standard servers (typically in the cloud) and storage capabilities (such as IPFS or a data vault) and will need to be linked to the on-chain components through oracles and explorers (Figure 4.5).

In cases where a decentralised application is being used in a Business-to-Business (B2B) interaction, it's possible that there is no UI, and the application will gather data and instructions directly from corporate applications running on servers in the organisations' data centres or in the cloud. Although there is no UI in this case, the principle is the same – the interaction with the distributed smart contract is managed from the off-chain applications.

The critical link between the off-chain applications (on mobiles, tablets, laptops, desktops and servers) and the on-chain smart contract is managed through the user's wallet and publicly available libraries which act as a messenger and translator for the different networks (such as ethers.js, web3.js for Ethereum, Polkadot.js for Polkadot and Solana Web3.js for Solana).

4.4 Decentralised Applications Applied

Now that we've learned a great deal more about virtual machines, smart contracts and decentralised applications, it's time to answer some practical questions you may have, whether you're a user or a deployer of smart contracts:

- Should I write a smart contract or a dApp?
- Where should I deploy my smart contract?
- How do I raise an ERC?
- What's the process for writing and deploying a dApp

4.4.1 Should I Write a Smart Contract or DApp?

Just as tokenisation isn't necessarily the solution to every multi-participant process, a dApp isn't necessarily the answer to a distributed process.

It is worth taking the time to analyse whether such an interaction between off-chain components and the distributed ledger is warranted. Many problems could well be solved by more automation and existing architecture.

Even if the analysis points at a dApp, how do you know if you need to write it, or even all of it? Where can you look to find existing components that could be re-used?

And if you're going to write a smart contract, how can you find out if a suitable ERC already exists for you to use or whether you'll need to define your own standard?

Fortunately, the blockchain community comes to your aid.

At each stage, there are multiple resources and libraries to help you.

To look for similar dApps, you can try DappRadar, State of the Dapps, Dapp.com, DeFi Llama or Awesome dApps.

You can search for existing smart contracts in Etherscan Verified Contracts, OpenZeppelin, Smart Contract Sanctuary, Awesome Solidity or Solidity Scan.

And you can look for ERC standards in the Ethereum repository, on the Ethereum Magicians forum or in the EIP GitHub Repository.

4.4.2 Where Should I Deploy My Smart Contract?

Before choosing where to develop and deploy your smart contract, you'll need to consider how the chosen virtual machine will execute the code as well as any other constraints or factors such as gas usage.

Factors to consider include:

- The programming languages available for that virtual machine and their capabilities
- How data is stored and accessed in the virtual machine (in the EVM, storage is persistent but expensive and every operation costs gas; WASM allows for greater efficiency; Solana BPF uses accounts as storage units, meaning contract logic must handle multiple accounts)
- How upgradable you want your smart contract to be (EVM contracts are immutable while WASM and Solana BPF do allow limited upgrades)

- How is finality achieved and how quickly (it's not always instant)
- Cross-chain interoperability (see Chapter 6)
- Parallelism (EVM is single-threaded whereas WASM and Solana BPF both support limited parallel execution).

Each virtual machine carries its own risks which need to be considered and avoided where possible.

EVM, for example, due to its account-based nature and the ability for smart contracts to invoke other smart contracts, can be susceptible to re-entrancy errors (or attacks) where multiple calls are made to a contract before the resultant updates are effected (essentially allowing the withdrawal of the same resource multiple times). Think of this as a cash machine that only updates your balance a few minutes after you withdraw your cash. You could visit the cash machine multiple times, taking out more money than was in your account to start with. By the time all the updates are made, you are overdrawn.

Due to the immutability of deployed contracts, some contracts on EVM virtual machines include a "self-destruct" function (literally "selfdestruct()"). If discovered, this risky command could be invoked by malicious actors to remove the contract (and pocket any spare resources it might have). You're advised to think carefully before including this function.

WASM was not originally designed as a virtual machine and some implementations use local environment variables in calculations, meaning that results are not deterministic (the same inputs may get different results depending on local parameters). Smart contract code should be written to avoid the use of these parameters.

Solana BPF has a strict limit to computations. If a calculation takes too long (or has too many steps), the virtual machine will simply cancel it.

4.4.3 How do I Raise an ERC?

An ERC (Ethereum Request for Comments) is a technical proposal for a new Ethereum standard, such as token types (ERC-20, ERC-721) or smart contract improvements. The process follows Ethereum's Ethereum Improvement Proposal (EIP) framework.

A template exists for ERCs which provides a standard format, including:

- **Preamble**: EIP Number, author, status and type of proposal
- **Abstract**: one-paragraph summary of the proposal
- **Motivation**: why this standard is needed
- **Specification**: detailed technical explanation (including functions and interfaces)

- **Rationale**: design choices and trade-offs
- **Backwards compatibility**: how this ERC interacts with existing standards
- **Implementation**: how the ERC will be implemented
- **Security considerations**: potential risks and mitigations.

Once you've drafted your ERC, making sure it is clear about the problem it solves and any technical details, you can post it in a dedicated repository in GitHub. Once there, it is discussed and eventually approved by the Ethereum community. You may need to amend your proposal during this process.

Following a "last call", the ERC becomes officially approved.

Even then, you will need to ensure adoption through lobbying of the community and by including it in implementations and projects.

4.4.4 What's the Process for Writing and Deploying a Dapp…?

Let's imagine that the Blockchain Book Club have embraced distributed ledger technology and have taken the significant step of converting their laptops-and-messaging virtual blockchain network into a real decentralised application on the Ethereum network.

Starting small, they want to create a token to represent the rewards ledger (members are rewarded for validating transactions and also for making real-world kitty contributions on time). They also want to introduce the capability to use these tokens to vote on club governance matters.

The dApp will have capabilities as follows:

- Buy, sell, and hold tokens, which represent voting power
- Vote on proposals, where voting strength is determined by the number of tokens held
- View results in real-time through a user-friendly mobile interface.

Here's the recipe that they might follow.

The recipe is divided into:

- **Ingredients**: the people, tools, and technologies needed
- **Method**: a step-by-step breakdown of the process, from design to deployment, along with some "Cook's Tips" at each stage, setting out some likely pitfalls and solutions
- **Serving Suggestion**: how the club members will interact with the dApp.

4.4.4.1 Ingredients

- People and skills required:
  - **Blockchain developer**: responsible for writing and deploying the smart contract (should be skilled in Solidity, Ethereum, and gas optimisation)
  - **Backend developer**: designs the APIs and handles blockchain interactions using Node.js and Web3.js
  - **Mobile developer**: builds the mobile application using React Native and integrates Web3 libraries for wallet interaction
  - **Security expert**: conducts smart contract audits and backend security checks
  - **UI/UX designer**: creates an intuitive user interface
- For smart contract development:
  - **Language**: Solidity (Ethereum smart contract language)
  - **Development environment**: Hardhat (for contract development, testing, and deployment)
  - **Libraries**: OpenZeppelin (secure pre-built smart contract modules)
  - **Blockchain network**: Ethereum Testnet (Goerli or Sepolia) for testing, Ethereum Mainnet for production
- Backend Development Ingredients
  - **Languages and frameworks**: Node.js with Express.js for server-side logic
  - **Blockchain interaction**: Web3.js or Ethers.js for calling smart contract functions
  - **Hosting services**: AWS Lambda, Heroku, or DigitalOcean for backend deployment
  - **Database (optional)**: MongoDB or Firebase for off-chain storage
- Mobile Application Ingredients
  - **Development framework**: React Native for cross-platform mobile development
  - **Blockchain interaction**: Web3.js or Ethers.js for Ethereum integration
  - **Wallet integration**: MetaMask SDK or WalletConnect for user authentication and transaction signing.

4.4.4.2 Method

- Step 1: Design the architecture

  The first step involves defining the architecture of the dApp, ensuring it is decentralised and secure. The key components are:

- **Smart contracts**: a set of Ethereum-based contracts to handle token transactions and voting
- **Backend server**: a lightweight server that interacts with the blockchain and serves data to the mobile app
- **Mobile front end**: a user-friendly interface that allows users to buy tokens, vote, and track results.

Each component must be designed to ensure security, gas efficiency, and scalability.

- Step 2: Develop the smart contract

Build a smart contract to perform the core logic of the dApp. It should handle token transactions using an ERC-20 token (OpenZeppelin's ERC-20 contract can be used as a base to ensure security). For the voting mechanism, the smart contract will store proposals and allow users to vote using their tokens (with the number of tokens held determining the weight of the vote). The smart contract logic will need to prevent duplicate votes and allow only eligible participants to vote.

Key considerations:

- The ERC-20 standard ensures compatibility with wallets and exchanges
- Users must approve the contract to spend tokens before voting
- The contract must emit events when a vote is cast to enable real-time updates in the app.

Cook's tips for smart contract development:

- **Gas optimisation**: minimise storage costs by using mappings instead of arrays
- **Security audits**: perform thorough testing to prevent exploits, such as reentrancy attacks
- **Testnet deployment**: deploy contracts to a test network (Goerli or Sepolia) before going live.

Step 3: Build the backend

Build a backend process to provide API endpoints for retrieving proposal data and checking user balances, interacting with the smart contract using Web3.js or Ethers.js and handling transactions such as voting or token awards.
The backend should be:

- **Lightweight**: minimise reliance on off-chain storage to maintain decentralisation
- **Real-time**: implement WebSocket connections to update the mobile app with live voting results
- **Secure**: never store private keys on the server. All transactions should be signed by the user's wallet.

Cook's Tips for backend development:

- **Avoid storing private keys**: always require users to sign transactions in their wallet rather than exposing private keys
- **Error handling**: ensure the backend gracefully handles failed transactions due to network congestion or gas issues
- **Real-Time updates**: use blockchain event listeners to notify the front end of new votes.

Step 4: Develop the mobile application

Build an intuitive mobile app to allow users to connect and sign in to their wallet (MetaMask or WalletConnect), award VOTE tokens and view balances, share and view governance proposals (using a real-time feed from the backend), vote on proposals by staking tokens, and to track voting results in real time.

To ensure usability:

- The app must handle transaction failures gracefully
- Gas fees should be estimated before transactions to inform users of costs
- The UI should provide clear feedback when votes are submitted.

Cook's Tips for mobile development:

- Optimise for slow networks: use local caching to improve performance
- User-friendly wallet integration: ensure MetaMask or WalletConnect is seamless
- Provide gas fee estimates: inform users of transaction costs before execution.

Step 5: Test

Test the components of the application individually and together to ensure the dApp functions correctly. Test the smart contract using Hardhat and Mocha to simulate contract interactions and ensure proper token transfers and voting behaviour. Test the backend by verifying API endpoints and contract calls. Test

the mobile app (with real users where possible), conducting UI/UX testing, including edge cases such as failed transactions and network issues.
Testing Checklist:

- Ensure that reward tokens can be awarded to members
- Ensure only token holders can vote
- Prevent duplicate voting
- Confirm smart contract events are emitted and captured correctly
- Test on multiple devices and network conditions.

Cook's Tips for testing and debugging

- **Use a testnet first**: always deploy contracts on a test network before mainnet
- **Simulate high load**: test how the system handles multiple concurrent votes
- **Check for gas efficiency**: ensure transactions are optimised to minimise costs.

Step 6: Deploy

Once the testing stage is complete to your satisfaction, it's time to deploy your dApp. Start with the smart contracts by deploying as a transaction on the Ethereum network. Launch the backend by hosting on AWS Lambda, Heroku, or DigitalOcean. Then publish the mobile app on Google Play and the Apple App Store.

Ensure a smooth launch by monitoring smart contract activity using Etherscan, track errors on the backend and mobile applications and by ensuring the new users are ready for the application.

4.4.4.3 Serving Suggestion

When presented to the members of the Blockchain Book Club, the dApp will allow them to:

- Connect their wallet and load their balance
- Accumulate VOTE tokens to gain voting power
- Browse active proposals and select one to vote on
- Cast a vote, signing the transaction securely
- Monitor results in real-time through the app.

Notes

1 https://ethereum.org/en/developers/docs/standards/tokens/erc-20/
2 https://ethereum.org/en/developers/docs/standards/tokens/erc-721/
3 https://ethereum.org/en/developers/docs/standards/tokens/erc-777/
4 https://ethereum.org/en/developers/docs/standards/tokens/erc-1155/
5 www.polymath.network/erc-1400
6 www.erc3643.org/
7 https://solana.com/docs/tokens
8 https://octez.tezos.com/docs/user/fa12.html
9 www.iso.org/home.html

Chapter 5

Identity

The foundations of blockchain are data ownership and transparency.

Data is owned by individuals (not captured by corporates) and is visible to all. Ownership brings with it the requirement to establish the identity of the owner while transparency comes with its own downside in that data on a blockchain network is visible to anyone who knows where to look.

The challenge is to be able to establish irrefutably the credentials of the viewer and their rights of access to data, granting access to those who have permission and denying it to those who do not.

Identity is key to the successful protection of sensitive data.

We each have an identity. For thousands of years, identity was largely a matter of physical recognition. When you walk past a friend in the street, you recognise them from their physical characteristics: their height, weight, face, body shape, even the way they walk. As the world became more connected and a person's individual influence stretched further afield, new ways were needed of confirming their identity: that they were who they purported to be.

Documents came into play: initially letters of introduction penned by local dignitaries, safe-conducts signed by military leaders, letters patent, letters of credence and ultimately the government-issued passports we all know today. But such documents were no absolute guarantee of identity: they could be lost, purloined or forged. Famously in the 1820s, a British soldier named Gregor MacGregor

DOI: 10.4324/9781003571421-6

forged a series of documents that established him as the fictional ruler of the equally fictional Central American country Poyais. Using his fake credentials, MacGregor persuaded hundreds of British investors to buy land and even to build a settlement in the region he claimed to rule (with largely fatal consequences). Even today's modern passport – with all its watermarks, colourful inks, holograms and biometric chips – is not secure against the counterfeiters.

In the conventional digital world, the most common way we identify ourselves is with a logon credential: a username (or email address) and a password. But this falls well short of identifying a person – passwords can be guessed or stolen (especially when written down). A username and password combination is less a way of identifying a person and more a means to allow whoever presents them to access the data they protect.

More recently, usernames and passwords have been supplemented (and in some cases supplanted) by less transferrable (or guessable) credentials. In fact, we've come full circle it seems. Our phones recognise our faces or our fingerprints (and even the way we walk), while many financial and other sensitive websites require multi-factor authentication so that online credentials are backed by something physically accessible by the user such as a code sent to a phone or an authenticator application that can only be opened following a biometric check.

Blockchain enables us to take access security a step further by introducing new ways to manage identity that differ greatly from traditional centralised systems.

In this chapter we'll look at how the blockchain community and technologies combine to ensure that identities are managed better and that data is kept private.

5.1 Identity: An Overview

Establishing a user's identity is a key component of blockchain operation and security. The distributed ledger enables new approaches to identity, while presenting its own challenges.

A *Self-Sovereign Identity* (SSI) is an identity uniquely linked to a user and managed by them with no reliance on a central authority. On the blockchain, an SSI might be implemented as a *Decentralised IDentifier* (DID), a document (the *DID Document*) stored on the network that defines a person's digital identity such as their public keys. Crucial to self-sovereign identities is a means to validate that the identity is genuine, with reference to *verifiable credentials* such as a government-issued passport.

On a public database such as a blockchain network, it is important to keep personal details separate from identifiers. This is called *pseudonymisation*. The identifiers present on-chain (such as wallet addresses and public keys) have no direct link to a real-world person or entity. Although an outside observer can see transactions and positions relating to a given wallet or key, they can't easily infer real-world information from it (unless the link is disclosed).

While the identifiers are present *on-chain*, sensitive or revealing data is typically stored *off-chain*, or even *off-line* in a data vault. This latter approach is known as *cold storage* – data is separated from the public internet and is only made available by the data curator through defined interfaces. This approach is even more effective when combined with *Zero-Knowledge Proofs* (ZKP), where data can be verified without revealing the data itself.

These different concepts are layered and combined to create a robust security for users, even in a distributed environment.

5.2 Identity: The Components

5.2.1 Self-Sovereign Identity and Digital Identity

How many different online user identifiers, passwords and so on do you have? Do you even know?

The average modern internet user could have between 70 and 200 different identifiers that they use to log into email, social media, financial and gaming applications as well as the apps they use for work. And this number is likely to grow in the short term with the proliferation of online services leading to further fragmentation.

Proliferation in itself is an issue, but the main problem with credentials curated by organisations is the fact that it is the organisation that owns and manages – "captures" – the associated data and your access to it. The individual is entirely dependent on the organisation for continued access. It is the organisation that stores and manages the individual's data and it is the organisation's application that grants the individual access to it. If the organisation decides, for whatever reason, to revoke that access, the individual user (you, the data subject) can no longer view or manage their own data.

In the world of blockchain, this all changes.

There is no central organisation between the user and the data. No central application that can be discontinued or taken down, no central authority to revoke access.

While this is a fundamental tenet of distributed ledger technology, it does present certain logistical issues: without a central authority to confirm a user's identity and to authorise user access, how can a user's identity be established unequivocally?

The answer might be the Self-Sovereign Identity, or SSI. An SSI is an identity that each individual may assign to themselves. There is no central authority

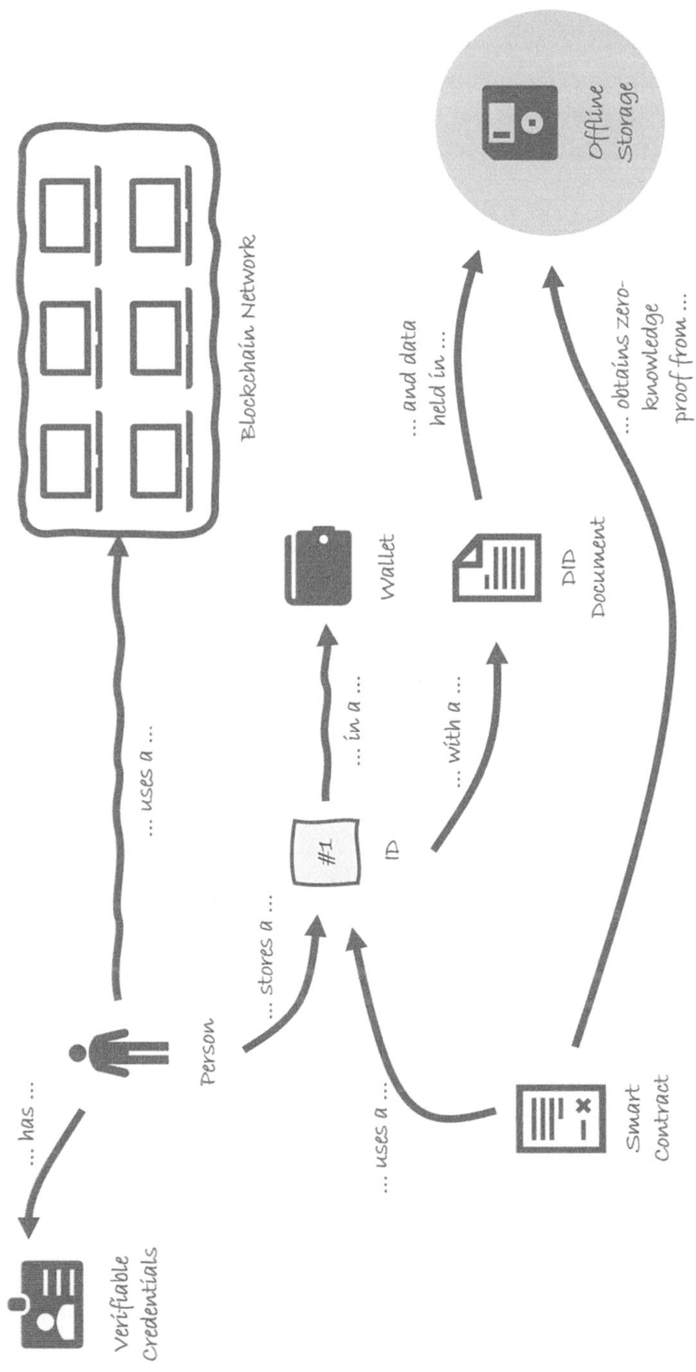

Figure 5.1 Identity.

to confirm or police it. As such it can never be revoked or limited. One example is the fingerprint. Our fingerprints are unique to every one of us and (certain macabre possibilities aside) can never be revoked or removed from us. Fingerprints or other biometric credentials can be used to absolutely and uniquely identify us. But, of course, we need to be present to provide this proof of identity – through a fingerprint or face scan.

Online, something else is needed – a *digital* fingerprint.

The Decentralised IDentifier (DID) is perhaps that.

"A Decentralized IDentifier (DID) is a new type of identifier that enables verifiable, self-sovereign digital identities.[1]" A decentralised identifier is not necessarily the same as a self-sovereign identity. An SSI might still be held centrally, while a DID might be curated by a central authority. However, a DID that is also an SSI creates the possibility of users assigning their own identifier and that identifier being used across one or more distributed networks without the need for a central authority.

So, rather than just using their fingerprint, the user constructs a numeric code that represents them. This code is then supplemented with additional data about the consumer, which may include the means by which they verified their identity: that they are who they say they are (which may be a document issued by a central authority such as a passport).

The data is then stored in a DID document on a blockchain network, secured by a private key. It contains personal data that can provide validation through zero-knowledge proof (without ever revealing the data itself) as well as other data such as public keys and contact information.

SSIs empower individuals to own and control their identities without reliance on centralised authorities. DIDs enhance security by leveraging cryptographic techniques to offer a more secure method for authentication, significantly reducing the risk of identity theft, data breaches, and fraud. They promote interoperability, spanning multiple platforms and use cases, and they enable selective disclosure and zero-knowledge proofs, allowing users to share only the necessary information for the job at hand.

At the core of the DID is a DID document.

This is a document stored on-chain which defines the DID, who it belongs to and how it was verified, along with key cryptographic information. The exact contents of the document vary depending on which network rules are followed (called the "DID Method"), but the World Wide Web Consortium (W3C) has proposed some standard fields including:

- The ID itself (a string of characters)
- Verification method (a list of one or more public keys specified by the DID owner)

- Authentication (which of these keys can be used by the DID owner to prove their identity)
- Key agreement (which of these keys can be used by others to communicate securely with the DID owner)
- Service (defines where and how others can interact with this DID).

Alongside the DID document are the DID method and the Verifiable Credentials (VC).

The DID method defines how the DID was generated and stored. These rules differ depending on the network used to store the DID (such as Ethereum, Hyperledger Indy or ION). This can affect how the ID itself is generated (locally or off-line), where the document is stored (on or off-chain) and how it can be accessed or even revoked.

Being able to create and own an identifier is one step – but can it be trusted by others? This where the concept of verifiable credentials comes in. These are a means for a party ("the verifier") to check the authenticity of a set of credentials issued (by "the issuer") about a subject ("the holder"). For example, as part of a job application, the company may wish to verify the status of a degree issued to the applicant by their university. The university (in this case the issuer) may offer a service whereby the proof of the applicant's degree is stored on-chain (secured cryptographically against tampering). The applicant (the holder) can provide the hiring company (the verifier) with the location of the credential. The hirer can compare the university's public key to verify that the submitted credentials are valid and can be trusted.

Other aspects of a DID include who can control the data (the DID Controller) and where the blockchain aspects of it are stored (Verifiable Data Registry or VDR).

Although W3C has begun to assert some standardisation in this field, the practical implementations of DIDs vary across different networks, meaning that there is currently little scope for interoperability and a degree of uncertainty which has a negative effect on adoption.

Nevertheless, the practical applications of DID are impressive, in theory. Imagine a world where I can define my own ID and store it on the blockchain network of my choice (whether native to the blockchain or stored off-line with a blockchain anchor). I can use it to store public keys for my own use and for other parties to use to contact me securely, as well as adding credentials from multiple authorities, each protected cryptographically. If any third party wants to verify my identity or some aspect of my life such as my degree or my date of birth, the data is readily available.

National governments can issue digital passports for travel or for financial verification. Universities can issue diplomas and degrees, which potential employers can check before offering a job. Financial organisations will be able to store credit scores and KYC data to be used during financial transactions. Health organisations can store vaccination records. With a standardised, interoperable DID, all of these credentials could be checked and verified, usually without revealing the data itself.

Sadly, we aren't there yet. The proliferation of methods as well as security concerns are just two of the barriers to adoption of the DID, especially while simpler alternatives exist. Rather than refer to an encrypted database to verify a user's age, many websites simply ask the user for manual confirmation. This is neither secure nor reliable, but it works (for now).

5.2.2 Pseudonymisation

Take a look at your passport and its unique passport number (in the UK it's a 9-character string). Now imagine that there's a public database of every passport number and a list of the countries where that passport has visited and been checked by border control. Anyone could look up a given passport number and find out where it (and its owner) had been.

A scary prospect?

Not really.

Because the passport number on its own doesn't mean anything (to most of us). Only when it is coupled with a (more secure) database showing which passport number belongs to which person does this information become of interest.

This is known as pseudonymisation. Data visible to the general public is only linked to an identifier, with no direct onward link to a real-world person.

A blockchain is a distributed database, visible to any network participant. Data that represents wallets, tokens and portfolios is available to anyone who has access to the network. However, just like a passport number, a wallet address is simply an identifier: it doesn't give any clue to the real-world owner of the wallet and its contents. Typically, that information is withheld from the blockchain and is known only to the data's controller(s).

By keeping real-world identities separate from the on-chain addresses, blockchain systems mitigate some privacy risks. Even if a competitor or unauthorised person were to scan the blockchain, they could see transactions flowing between addresses and balances held at each address, but they wouldn't easily be able to identify the real-world entity behind each address.

During blockchain's infancy, the only use case and transactions were simple cryptocurrency transactions. Satisfaction of the use case (trustless peer-to-peer financial transactions) required only an identifier (the wallet address). The real-world recipient of the transacted coins remained a secret, known only to the parties involved in the transaction (often just the recipient).

Even in such simple scenarios, however, pseudonymisation is only partially effective. There are many ways in which a wallet address might become privately or publicly identified with a real-world person:

- A trusted third party may have access to the link, such as a crypto exchange that requires customer details before it will allow trading to take place
- Transaction counterparties may deliberately or inadvertently reveal the link between an on-chain transaction participant and the real-world entity with whom they transacted
- The owner themselves may have publicly revealed their wallet address (again, this may have been deliberate or by mistake)
- A determined researcher, armed with blockchain data and corroborating real-world data such as social media posts and pictures, may be able to identify a wallet's owner from behavioural or financial patterns (such as a large corporate transaction or large holding).

Not all of these are obvious, such as simply telling other people what your wallet address is. Some exposure of your real-world self is inevitable if you use any intermediaries to help navigate the blockchain. You may have documented your credentials online, such as in a DID Document; once you've given another actor (for legitimate reasons) your keys or identifiers, they can use link those credentials to your real-world identity. Or you've perhaps completed KYC ("Know Your Customer") for a financial firm who can likewise identify you from their own records.

These are acceptable risks; you are still better off than today as although these parties can identify you, they still have no control of your data or your assets.

Other ways to reveal yourself are less understandable, such as publicly revealing your wallet address on social media (unless it's to receive a large number of payments).

Then there's data analysis. Firms such as Chainalysis (who claim to have mapped over 1 billion addresses to real-world entities[2]) analyse blockchain data to identify clusters of activity both on and off-chain to draw conclusions about who owns which addresses. For example, even if a user maintains multiple addresses, they may input two or more of the addresses for the same transaction. Then KYC data from another exchange can be used to identify that user as a real person. Alternatively, firms can use data added to social media, unshielded IP addresses, or even on the dark web to make these links.

Users who really want to stay pseudonymous while they transact might want to think about using blending services to merge their transactions with others, deal in "privacy coins" that hide addresses, or use exchanges that don't require KYC.

It's worth noting that many tokenisation scenarios will create close links between on-chain data and off-chain identity. Health records will need to be pseudonymous on-chain while maintaining a very strong link to the actual patient (who does not want to arrive at a new hospital only to discover that their health records can't be obtained because there is no link from their real-world credentials to their on-chain data). Real-world financial assets often require more stringent KYC and AML than one might currently expect for crypto holdings, and the same applies to more exotic assets such as works of art. The DID Document described above creates a link between the real-world person and their on-chain credentials.

For those wishing to remain anonymous, it will be critical to manage these different use cases carefully, to ensure that publicly available information about a wallet address can't be linked to use cases where discretion is required.

In practice, pseudonymisation is really only effective if combined with other privacy measures. These include practical steps taken by the data owner such as using multiple addresses (so activity is spread out and harder to link) or using additional cryptographic tools (like mixers or privacy layers on certain blockchains). For businesses developing tokenised products, it would be wise not to place any clear personal data on-chain, but instead to use references and pseudonymous identifiers. If personal information is only ever held in a secure off-chain system, even if the blockchain data is publicly inspected, it is less likely to expose an individual's identity without access to the separate off-chain data.

Pseudonymisation thus serves as a first line of defence: it obscures direct identity links in a transparent system, buying privacy and a degree of security through obscurity, while still allowing the system to function and be auditable. It's a balance between transparency (everything is visible) and privacy (true names are hidden), which is a recurring theme in blockchain identity management.

5.2.2.1 Cold Storage and Off-Chain Data

One way to make data more secure is to keep it away from the blockchain database. Data can be held separately off-chain, or even isolated from the internet completely, in cold storage.
Note the difference:

- On-chain data is data held on a blockchain network, present and visible in every node on the network
- Off-chain data is not held on the blockchain but may still be freely available depending on how it is stored; it might be on a publicly visible global network, or behind the firewalls of a curating organisation

- Cold storage (or off-line) data is not accessible to the public internet, held on servers that can only be accessed using specific data requests or following specific hardware operations (such as plugging in a hardware module or USB stick).

Providers will manage the data and store it safely, allowing access only through their proprietary software using a defined identifier. This makes the data more secure against attack as even if a malicious party obtains the identifier, they may not have authorisation to use the organisation's interface to obtain the underlying data.

The initial application of off-line storage was to ensure the protection of private keys, but as tokenisation increases in both volume and scope, more and more data (particularly personal data such as names and addresses) will be used by smart contracts and decentralised applications. Data complexity and sensitivity will evolve away from simple wallet addresses and token quantities to include health, wealth and other data that falls under regulation such as GDPR. This presents a double risk, as the data may be prone to attack and may also be in itself an indicator of the identity of the data subject.

For example, data needed for a cryptocurrency transaction includes only a wallet address, a balance, a transaction quantity and a recipient address. It's hard from this data to identify the real-world individual executing the transaction. Once the community of tokenised applications includes activities such as know your customer (KYC) with complex data such as name, address, tax details, wealth and health and other indicators, it will be possible to use this data to trace the real-word individual.

This risk can be reduced if sensitive data is held off-line – all that's left on the blockchain is a pseudonymous identifier (with no real indication of where and how to use that identifier to unlock the sensitive personal data held in cold storage). This is further complicated by the immutable nature of the blockchain – once data has been written to a block it cannot be removed. If personal data ever gets recorded (and is later discovered to be sensitive data), it's too late to remove it.

Individuals will have different reasons for wanting to keep their data off-chain (and off-line). Cold storage solutions exist to meet each of these different scenarios.

The first (and in many ways simplest) means of cold storage is applicable for cryptographic keys: off-line storage for your private key. This could even be low-tech such as writing it down on a piece of paper and storing it in a safe or a box file. If you're worried about wear and tear or fire damage, there's even the option to etch your wallet's seed phrase onto metal plates. There are also plenty of providers of electronic key storage solutions. Usually, these incorporate a chip that holds the wallet information and then a means of communicating locally with a PC (such as through Bluetooth or via a USB cable). A final option for the eager crypto trader is an off-line computer that is never connected to the internet ("air gapped").

For more complex data, IPFS (Interplanetary File System) or a similar service may be the right answer. Data is held in globally-accessible files but is fixed to an on-chain key known only to the data owner.

For more industrial uses, however, it is best to use the services of an off-line data vault. Sensitive data is stored in an off-line database that can be accessed only through a defined protocol using the correct code. Solutions vary in sophistication (and cost). Providers typically maintain a centralised storage which is heavily protected both physically and digitally, using robust datacentres and network airgaps to limit unauthorised access to the data.

As use cases become more sophisticated, data managers will use more complex models to protect their data. Techniques will be mixed and matched as needed – with less protected keys available for mundane operations and highly secure keys protected in off-line vaults called on only for high-value transactions. Both decentralised and centralised data storage options can be incorporated into applications to interact with off-chain data in real time.

The case for tokenisation also becomes more complex. When deciding whether a tokenised approach is relevant for a use case, an organisation or group of organisations will need to consider not just whether there needs to be equitable access to trusted data, but how that data needs to be protected and stored. In most scenarios, only data that directly relates to identity and permission will be tokenised, while more verbose and sensitive data will remain untokenised and held securely off-chain, or off-line.

5.2.3 Zero Knowledge

Linked to the concept of cold storage is that of "zero-knowledge proof". This allows applications to test the validity of data without learning anything about the data itself. This adds yet another layer of security: at no stage does the sensitive data leave the haven of its off-line vault.

Imagine that an individual has recorded their personal data in an off-line vault and has placed a token on the blockchain as a pointer to that vault. If the individual needs to interact with an application that wants to confirm some aspect of their data (let's say they must be older than 18) they can supply their identifier to the application which can query the off-line store through an API. The storage facility can provide a true/false response to the application. At no stage does the individual's actual age (the sensitive data) leave the confines of the vault. Only the identifier and the response are ever sent.

The concept of zero knowledge proof is that one party (the "prover") has secret knowledge and can prove this to another party (the "verifier") without revealing the knowledge itself. The proof must be complete (so that the verifier is able to believe the prover) and it must not be possible for the prover to provide false proof to the verifier.

A commonly-used thought experiment to illustrate this concept is Ali Baba's cave. The cave is essentially two long tunnels that meet far inside the mountain (out of sight), joined by a magical door. The prover knows the secret password that opens the door and wishes to prove this to the verifier. Once the prover has entered the cave (regardless of the entrance used) the verifier calls out a tunnel entrance ("left" or "right"): if the prover can exit via the required tunnel repeatedly, the verifier must accept that the prover knows the secret password to open the door between the tunnels (as without the knowledge of the password, the prover would only be able to guess the right exit 50% of the time).

As with most analogies, this is helpful but doesn't give the full picture. To be useful in a business application, any proof must be obtained quickly, ideally in a single pass, rather than through repeated proofs to rule out random chance (known as an interactive zero-knowledge proof model).

Similarly, any proof mechanism for use in a blockchain scenario would need to be trustless – the proof should be entirely self-contained, not relying on the good intentions of the proof provider. This one-shot trustless proof mechanism is known as non-interactive zero-knowledge proof.

Two common mechanisms are the zk-SNARK and zk-STARK.

The zk-SNARK (Zero-knowledge Succinct Non-interactive Argument of Knowledge) "allow[s] a prover to convince a verifier of a statement's validity with minimal communication.[3]" The mechanism is fast and requires very little data to be exchanged. Although the act of verification itself is trustless, the mechanism does require a trusted party to initially set up cryptographic parameters called the Common Reference String (CRS) which is used by provers to cryptographically hash their proof.

The zk-STARK (Zero-knowledge Scalable Transparent Argument of Knowledge) mechanism instead uses publicly known (and reliable) hash functions. zk-STARKs are capable of larger computations as they break down more complex proofs into a series of smaller proofs.

These proofs are fundamental to scaling blockchain operations as they support the use of Layer 2 networks, providing a large number of proofs in a single transaction without the need to transmit the associated data (the Layer 1 network doesn't need the knowledge, just the proof).

This is how a ZKP (Zero-Knowledge Proof) might work in the scenario where a user wants to prove to an online supplier that they are over 18 without revealing their actual birthdate. Let's assume that the user's passport (issued by the national government) has been stored off-line in a secure database and digitally signed. The user runs a local algorithm that combines the data from the passport and the current date to verify that the user is over 18 and creates a cryptographically signed proof using the government's public key. The user sends this proof to the supplier who can decrypt it using the government's public key, proving beyond doubt that the user meets their age thresholds but learning nothing more.

In essence, a ZKP allows compliance and verification checks to be performed in a decentralised system without exposing user data. This provides trust without sacrificing privacy – a key trade-off in more complex tokenised applications. It also aligns with one of the fundamental tenets of data management: share only what is necessary.

5.3 Identity Applied

Collectively, Self-Sovereign Identities (SSIs), pseudonymisation, cold storage and off-line storage combined with Zero Knowledge Proofs (ZKP) provide a layered approach to data and identity security in a tokenisation context.

For an organisation (or group of organisations undertaking a collective endeavour) looking to build a tokenised application, what are the questions that need to be asked about identity?

- What data should be on-chain?
- How will users and other participants be identified?
- How are private keys and credentials secured?
- How do we strike a balance between trust and privacy?

5.3.1 What Data Should be On-Chain?

One of the first considerations is deciding what information actually needs to be stored on the blockchain versus what should stay off-chain.

As a rule of thumb, sensitive personal data (names, addresses, medical information, financial details) should not be published in clear text on a public database. The best data architecture will use the blockchain for what it's good at (integrity, timestamps, tokens, references) and keep confidential data elsewhere in secure storage. For example, if you're building a tokenised health records platform, you might design it so that the blockchain is only used for the management of identifiers and access permissions while personal and health data (such as name and address, date of birth, and detailed medical history) reside in an encrypted database controlled by the health provider or the patient.

The organisation should also consider compliance with data protection laws such as GDPR, which require that only necessary personal data is recorded, in as secure a manner as possible. The prudent use of off-chain and off-line data storage goes some way towards satisfying this requirement.

The key question for the data architects to ask is: "Do we really need to put this piece of data on the blockchain?" If the answer is "No," then don't do it. And if it's a "Yes," ensure the data is pseudonymised or encrypted in such a way that it's meaningless to anyone without the proper keys or context.

5.3.2 How Will Users and Other Participants be Identified?

In a conventional application, user and other data is typically curated by a centralised organisation. In such a linear scenario, it is relatively easy to define rules for the identification of users and other participants.

For a distributed application, this is less obvious. When there are multiple organisations involved, who is responsible for onboarding participants? Who curates and manages the critical link between on-chain identifiers and real-world entities? Who can be trusted to ensure the data remains valid and secure? In such a case, self-sovereign identifiers might be the way to go. New participants can bring and use their own existing Decentralised IDentifier (DID) along with the related verifiable credentials.

An alternative is for one of the organisations to act as a gateway, verifying and onboarding new participants. But rather than set up a record within the organisation's own database, the outcome is a decentralised identifier similar to a DID that all organisations on the network can access.

An alternative is to integrate with existing providers of identifiers or federated identity systems ("identity as a service"). Users can log in using an identifier and credentials that have already been verified externally by this trusted partner, saving time on KYC and other validation.

If you do decide to maintain your own separate identity database, then this may limit future interoperability and may be a barrier to entry for additional participants who will need to integrate to your local systems to access the identity database and be sure that the participant is and remains valid.

5.3.3 How are Private Keys and Credentials Secured?

We've seen that in any blockchain-based system, private keys are the linchpin of security. They control access to wallets, allow signing of transactions, and prove ownership of an identity such as a DID.

For an organisation planning a tokenised product, deciding how private keys are managed – and secured – is critical.

There are broadly two options: user-managed keys or custodial keys.

With user-managed keys, each user is responsible for their own keys. They might use a mobile wallet application or a hardware module. While this embraces the spirit of decentralisation and self-sovereignty, it comes with its own risks and challenges: what if the user loses their key? What if it is stolen? What guarantees does the organisation or collective have that every user will keep their keys secure and how will the organisation detect (and indeed react) if an identity is stolen and used maliciously?

A custodial arrangement is more akin to the operation of traditional credentials:

- The organisation or a service provider holds the keys on the user's behalf
- Users typically log into the application with a username and password and the organisation controls direct access to the wallet
- Users can ask the company to recover the identity if they forget details.

Users may not even realise that blockchain keys are involved. They just use the service with normal login credentials, and behind the scenes the system signs transactions or performs other blockchain operations using their private key as needed. If choosing this approach, the organisation will need to invest heavily in security infrastructure such as hardware security modules, use of cold storage, and multi-signature approvals.

Organisations may also adopt a hybrid approach such as using multiple keys (one for the user and one for the organisation) or where the user is responsible for their own security but the organisation provides a recovery service.

For complex tokenisation solutions, an additional consideration is the deployment of any smart contracts. Certain functions within the smart contract can only be performed by the entity that deployed the contract, identified by their private key. If this private key is lost or misappropriated, the entire decentralised application and any tokens associated with it are at risk.

For any given configuration, it's critical to clearly identify the required strategy and back it up with fault-tolerant approach to security so that users and other participants can be confident that their underlying data is protected.

5.3.4 How do we Strike a Balance between Trust and Privacy?

Although the initial use cases for blockchain were unregulated (by definition), real-world tokenisation use cases will often be for domains that are subject to regulation. Health, real estate and financial applications, even decentralised applications, will need to meet regulatory requirements for data protection and consumer safety.

The challenge is to meet these needs without simply reverting to a centralised system (which would defeat much of the purpose of using blockchain). To address this, organisations should embrace mechanisms such as verifiable credentials and zero-knowledge proofs as core parts of their solution. Essentially, how can personalised data be stored safely and be made available to applications as needed without exposing it to public scrutiny?

Does the decentralised application even need to know the data? Can a user's credentials or identity be validated using a third party to supply cryptographically secured proof without the application ever being exposed to the underlying data? For example, for an application conducting financial transactions, rather than fully onboard a client and record their details on a KYC database, the organisation could use an external third party to perform KYC checks, storing a "KYC valid" token for the relevant identifier.

As is often the case, there is no single right answer. The nature of the business itself will often define the approach to be taken. But wherever possible, organisations should consider taking data out of their own product and using zero-knowledge proofs to verify identity and permissions.

Notes

1 www.w3.org/TR/did-core/

2 www.chainalysis.com/

3 Ben-Sasson, E., Chiesa, A., Genkin, D., Tromer, E., & Virza, M. (2013). SNARKs for C: Verifying Program Executions Succinctly and in Zero Knowledge. In R. Canetti & J. A. Garay (Eds.), *Advances in Cryptology – CRYPTO 2013*, Part II (Lecture Notes in Computer Science, Vol. 8043, pp. 90–108). Springer. doi:10.1007/978-3-642-40084-1_6

Chapter 6

Interoperability

What is blockchain interoperability and why does it matter?

One definition is that "blockchain interoperability is the ability of blockchain networks to communicate with each other, sending and receiving messages, data, and tokens."[1] It is how activity in one network can become aware of activity in another network and, where necessary, act upon that. Remember that due to the deterministic nature of blockchain operations, the network cannot ordinarily rely on data outside the network.

Interoperability matters because as blockchain networks proliferate and diversify and as tokenised applications become more complex with greater ambition, it will become increasingly likely that tokens on one network will need to interact with tokens on a different network with different governance structures and rules. To quote IBM: "True interoperability enables seamless communication across permissioned and public blockchain networks.[2]"

Let's take a look at some examples to illustrate why interoperability grows in importance as complexity increases.

Consider first a simple cryptocurrency transaction involving the native coin of a blockchain network. Party A (the sender) instructs a transaction to move a quantity of coin from their own wallet to that of Party B (the recipient). The entire transaction is conducted on a single network, and the characteristics of the

DOI: 10.4324/9781003571421-7

transaction (speed, finality and so on) are the same for both parties. Once the transaction is final, both parties can safely agree on the outcome.

Now consider a more complex case involving smart contracts and tokenised real-world assets. As before, Party A wants to send a quantity to Party B, the recipient. But in this case, Party A is also the issuer of the asset (let's call it Fund #1) and is selling it to Party B in exchange for a tokenised currency such as a government-issued stablecoin, a Central Bank Digital Currency (let's call it CBDC #1). These tokenised assets are issued through the deployment of smart contracts. For various very sound business and operational reasons, the two issuers have decided to deploy their smart contracts on different blockchain networks. In order to ensure that Party A and Party B exchange Fund #1 and CBDC #1 at exactly the same time (to avoid the risk that one party owns both assets while the other owns neither), the two smart contracts will need to orchestrate synchronous transactions on their own local networks and perform what is known as an atomic swap (or "delivery versus payment" in old language). This would be compounded if the rules for finality differ dramatically between the two networks, as each transaction must retain the ability to be reserved locally until finality on the other network could be guaranteed.

We could make it even more complex if we imagine that Party A requires Party B to pass a KYC check before being able to purchase Fund #1 and that this is achieved through a KYC token stored on a third blockchain. In one transaction, therefore, three smart contracts would need to coordinate a KYC check, a movement of Fund #1 in one direction and a movement of CBDC #1 in the other. Without interoperability, this transaction will never take place.

There now exist hundreds of blockchain networks, each behaving differently in terms of how transactions are initiated and processed, how smart contracts are supported and executed, how data is stored and accessed, and how participants get access or contribute to the community of users.

In this chapter we'll look at why interoperability matters and how it can be achieved with a range of approaches and protocols.

6.1 Interoperability: An Overview

Blockchain interoperability involves enabling communication and data exchange between smart contracts operating on multiple, different blockchain networks.

Networks can differ in terms of their consensus mechanisms, smart contract languages, governance, and transaction characteristics. These differences create challenges in areas such as communication, transaction finality, reconciliation, and token availability.

Cross-chain interoperability can be approached through transformation methods like "*lock-and-mint*" or "*burn-and-mint*," where tokens are recreated on target networks, but these require trusted intermediaries and carry inherent risks.

Alternatively, cross-chain messaging techniques, including *notary schemes*, *light clients*, and proposed *standardised protocols* like ERC-7786 and ERC-7802, allow data to move between chains without transferring tokens. Notary schemes rely on oracles, while light clients verify blockchain data directly. Standardised protocols help unify messaging and token interfaces across blockchains.

Another approach is for an issuer to issue tokens natively on multiple networks. While this increases accessibility, it fragments liquidity.

Cross-chain processes must manage *asynchronism*, where off-chain operations may lag behind real-time changes. In contrast, smart contracts within the same network benefit from synchronous execution and shared state, simplifying interoperability (Figure 6.1).

6.2 Interoperability: The Components

6.2.1 Network Operational Differences

As we noted in Chapter 2, not all blockchains are created equal. While networks such as Ethereum, Cardano, Polkadot, Solana, Avalanche, and Cosmos strive for similar outcomes, they often achieve these in very different ways. They vary in terms of consensus mechanisms (PoW, PoH, PoA and the many variants of PoS), smart contract languages, transaction speed and throughput, finality, and even governance processes.

Not all of these differences impact how interoperability can be achieved between one network and another, but many do.

As an example, let's return once more to the Blockchain Book Club. A second club (The Blockchain Coffee Club) has set up their own virtual blockchain network, also using laptops and spreadsheets to record members' credit balances, the overall kitty and a tokenised inventory of coffee. The Blockchain Coffee Club has bought some rare coffee beans which the members of the Blockchain Book Club want to buy for their next meeting.

On the face of it, the transaction seems simple: the Blockchain Book Club will debit cash from the kitty ledger and the Blockchain Coffee Club will credit cash to their own ledger and debit the coffee inventory. But there's an issue: the Blockchain Coffee Club is run by ex-treasurer Sam, who cannot be trusted. Furthermore, the club operates a designated proof of stake consensus mechanism whereby as soon as Sam verifies a transaction, it is considered to be final by all the

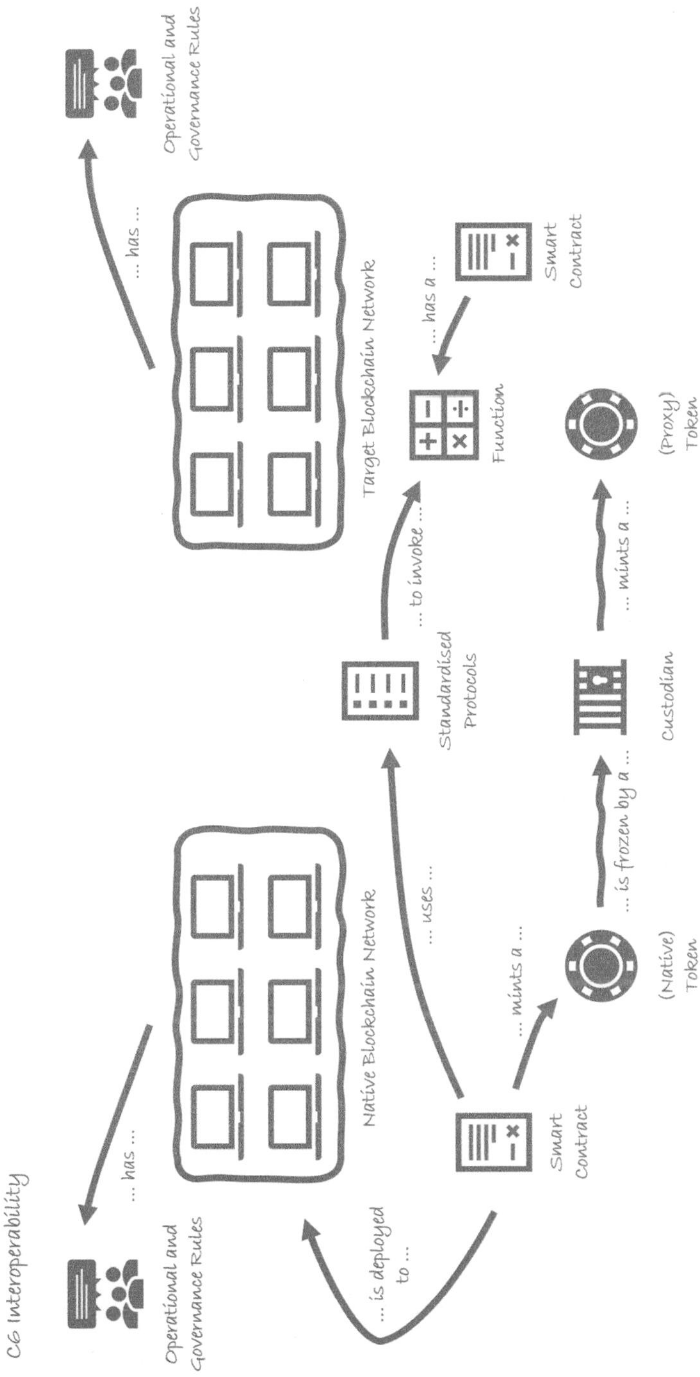

Figure 6.1 Interoperability.

other members. To make matters worse, Sam is currently away on business and has only intermittent access to the virtual network.

Even this simple scenario presents a number of interoperability issues.

The first (and perhaps most obvious) is that of *communication* between the networks. Each club operates a communications network between its members, but there's no agreed protocol for communication outside the network. How will this work? Will a member of the Blockchain Book Club send a message to Sam? Can these communications be delivered reliably? Can Sam still be trusted? Will Sam be available to process the message? How will the response be sent?

The second issue is that of *finality* and is related to the third issue, that of *transaction speed*. In the Blockchain Book Club network, finality of the transaction is achieved on confirmation from the verifier (whoever is first to check the transaction) whereas the Blockchain Coffee Club rely solely on Sam to verify and provide finality. Due to Sam's unavailability, these two activities will almost certainly not coincide, so how are they to be synchronised and what is the process for backing out the transaction in one network if it is not finalised in the other?

A further issue is that of *reconciliation*. One of the key advantages of a distributed ledger is the reduction (or even avoidance) of the amount of reconciliation required: there are no separate databases to reconcile. As soon as two different networks need to agree a value or a quantity (whether transaction or as a balance), reconciliation is back on the table – each network needs to be sure that it has received (and processed) the right information.

Related to the issue of reconciliation is that of token *transformation*. The Blockchain Coffee Club have tokenised their coffee inventory. If the Blockchain Book Club want to do the same for the coffee they have just bought, they will need to build their own tokenised inventory on their own network, while the Blockchain Coffee Club will need to record the change in ownership on their ledger. The native tokens on the Blockchain Coffee Club's network will be effectively transformed into tokens native to the Blockchain Book Club's network. These two pools of coffee tokens need to be carefully managed (and reconciled) to ensure they remain in step.

These issues may seem simple and easily fixed in our virtual manual network, but for complex automated interaction across the entire community of blockchain users they will all need to be fixed reliably and at scale.

And real-world blockchains face additional challenges such as differences in governance, privacy levels, gas costs and technology (such as the smart contract programming languages used on different networks). It may seem obvious, but it's worth noting that you can't simply port a smart contract from one network to a new one and expect it to function.

6.2.2 Network Organisation Differences

As well as technical and operational differences, blockchain networks differ in how they are governed. This may impact access to the network and its data or it may impact how operational changes are effected.

Permissioned networks may not allow interaction with public networks: data within these networks may be hidden or unavailable.

Each network has its own unique governance structure. Participants may or may not be involved in decisions to introduce operational changes. As such, changes may be introduced unilaterally which could impact (or even stop) cross-chain operations.

Gas costs may also become a factor. Just because a multi-chain process makes economic sense when it is developed does not mean that it will always do so: gas price fluctuations on the target or native chain may impact costs in an unpredictable fashion. For networks where gas prices are flexible based on transaction volumes, economic factors may vary from moment to moment.

6.2.3 Interoperability Through Transformation

As we've just seen, tokens can't simply be passed from one blockchain to another: the token is just data stored within a smart contract and the smart contract (or its data) can't be moved from network to network.

So how can a real-world asset that's been tokenised on one blockchain network be made available to a participant on a different network?

One solution is transformation or bridging, where a new token is created on the target network.

There are broadly two approaches to transformation, known respectively as "*lock-and-mint*" and "*burn-and-mint*" transformations.

In the "lock-and-mint," approach, the native token on the original network is frozen and a proxy token is created on the target network. This is sometimes called a wrapped token or a pegged token (these mechanisms differ subtly but the overall concept is similar). With the "burn-and-mint" approach, the native token is destroyed ("burnt") and a new token created ("minted") on the target network.

There is complexity and risk in either approach[3].

A trusted party is required to control the transformation, either by isolating or destroying the native tokens and then issuing proxies on the target network. This may be the original issuer of the token or a third party. This introduces risk in that the third party might (whether maliciously or by accident) break the link between the native token and the proxy, rendering the latter worthless. This risk can be mitigated by using oracles (operated by yet more trusted parties) or even humans to validate that the link remains in place and ensuring any transaction that tries to break the link has been properly authorised.

All of this introduces complexity and cost into the process of transferring and owning these mirrored tokens.

Transformation is common in the crypto world – wrapped Bitcoin tokens (WBTC) are available on many networks. This is driven by the communities on the target networks wanting a mechanism to exchange Bitcoin. In the world of tokenisation (as opposed to native coins) it's less clear who would be prepared to bear the cost and risk of enabling such transformation. If an issuer has launched a token on one network, they might reasonably expect users and owners to interact with them directly on that network rather than transform the tokens away to a different network. If there isn't the demand for the tokens elsewhere, organisations are unlikely to pay for the development and operation of a transformation mechanism.

Figure 6.2 shows the differences between "lock-and-mint" and "burn-and-mint" transformations.

6.2.4 Interoperability Through Cross-Chain Messaging

An alternative to transforming the native asset is to leave it in place on the original blockchain network and use cross-chain messaging to make the link to the target network.

We'll look at three ways this can be done:

- Notary schemes
- Light clients
- Standardised protocols.

Notary schemes involve the use of oracles to attest that an event has taken place on the native network, allowing certain dependent activity to be initiated on the target network. As for the transformation option, this approach relies on the operation of third parties and involves a level of trust that the third party will execute its function competently and honestly.

A *light client* is where one blockchain participates as a node in another blockchain and is able to empirically verify that events have taken place on that network by checking block headers. This is an inherently trustless approach but adds complexity and may not even be possible if the two networks do not operate in a coherent fashion.

In an effort to avoid bespoke solutions to the interoperability issue, the blockchain community has made a move towards more *standardised protocols*. Organisations such as Chainlink and Axelar seek to provide generic solutions that can be used in a range of scenarios, rather than a one-off solution for each combination of token and network. These solutions do not remove the need for

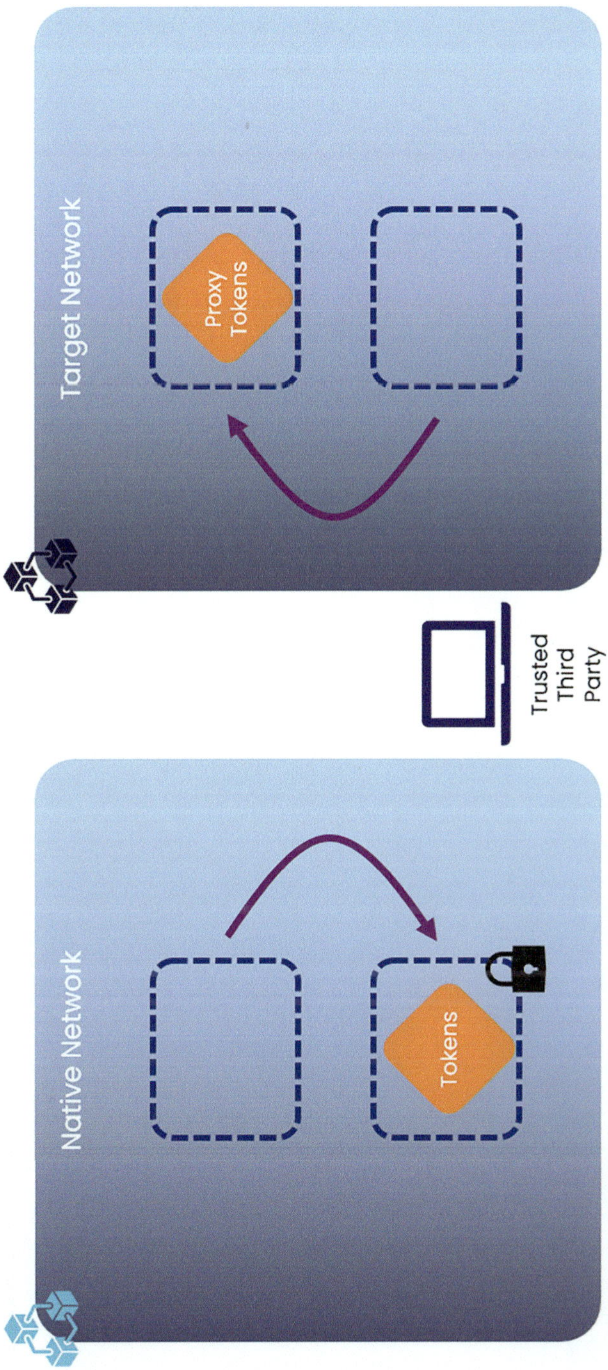

Figure 6.2 (a and b) Transformation through "Lock and Mint" and "Burn and Mint".

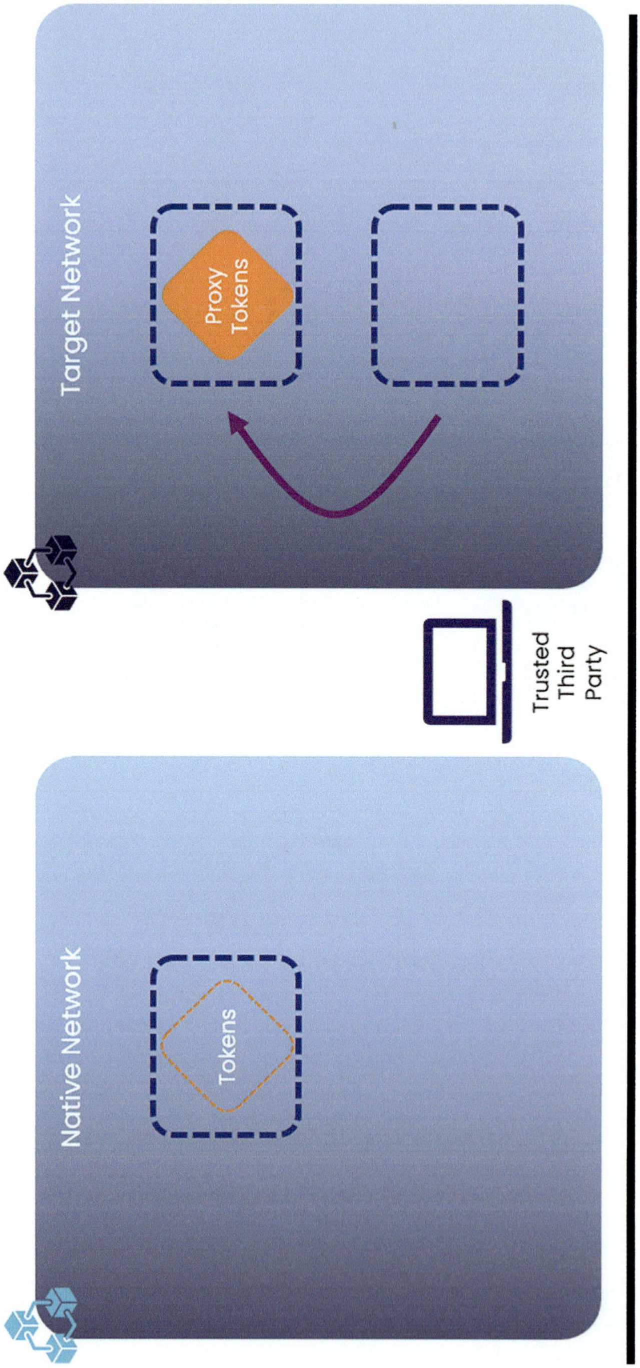

Figure 6.2 (Continued)

a trusted party – indeed, they combine many of the techniques above such as oracles and light clients to pass data between networks.

These standardised protocols take broadly one of two forms: one uses messages passed by oracles between networks while the other provides the capability to directly invoke smart contract functions on another network.

In addition, a number of standard templates have been developed.

ERC-7786 (Cross-Chain Messaging Gateway)[4] is a proposed standard that defines a universal interface for smart contracts to send and receive messages across different blockchains. It is a blockchain-agnostic protocol and allows a wide range of payloads. Data in the call includes the identity of the receiver (or sender), a number of attributes (as defined key-value pairs) and an unstructured payload.

ERC-7802 (Crosschain Token Interface)[5] is a proposed standard that seeks to provide a standardised interface for the cross-chain transformation of tokens, providing a standard "burn" and "mint" function for both export and repatriation of the native token.

Figure 6.3 shows how a smart contract on one network can invoke a function on the native network.

6.2.5 "Interoperability" Through Multiple Native Tokens

An alternative approach to managing interoperability and the issues it raises is to avoid it completely. Depending on the tokenisation use case, it may be appropriate for the token issuer to simply mint tokens on multiple networks, allowing potential owners or users to select the network of their choice before each transaction.

This approach would involve more work for the token issuer, as they would need to deploy smart contracts to multiple blockchain networks. Another downside would be that the token population would become fragmented, with pools present on each network.

This approach does have merit, though, where the fragmentation would not be an issue.

In the financial markets, for example, where there is a secondary market for issued shares, the approach would create smaller liquidity pools. If Investor #A owns tokenised shares in a wallet on one blockchain network, they would not be able to sell those shares directly to Investor #B. In the mutual funds market, however, there is no secondary market. All purchases and sales are bilateral and involve the fund manager, who in this case is the token issuer. The fund could be tokenised on multiple networks, and the investor would be able to choose which network to use to complete their purchase or sale.

Franklin Templeton, one of the largest fund managers in the world, has taken exactly this approach for their money market fund (Franklin OnChain U.S.

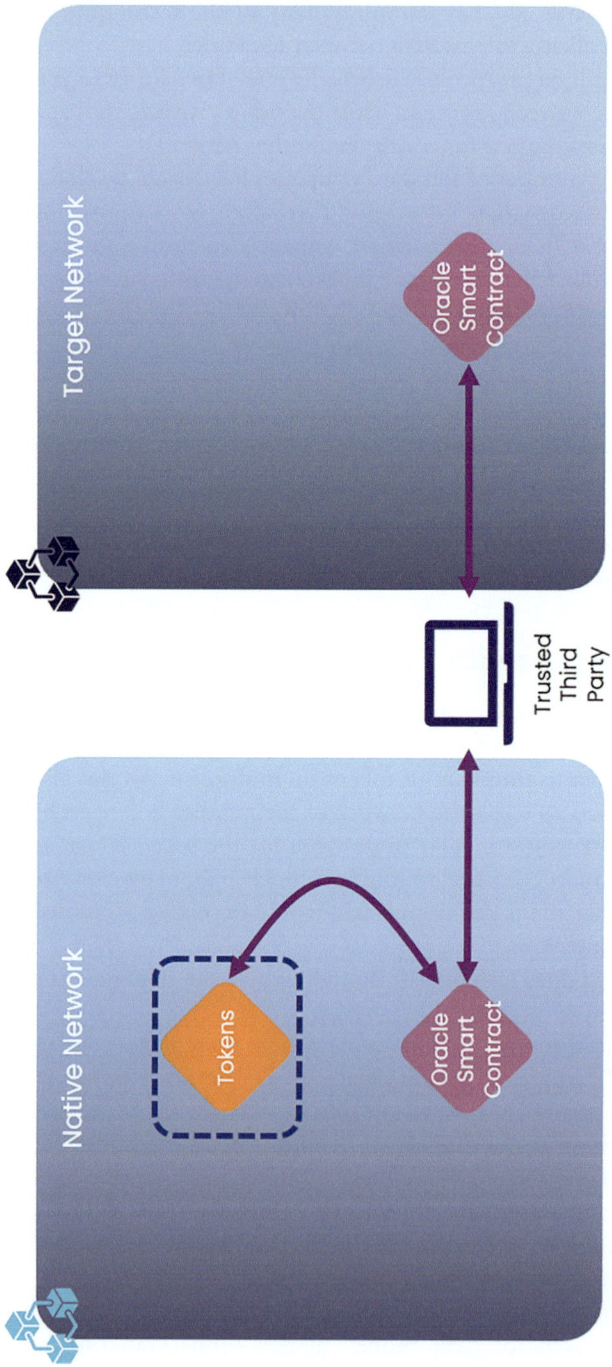

Figure 6.3 Interoperability through Messaging.

Government Money Fund), tokenised as the BENJI. It is available through a range of networks including Stellar, Polygon, Arbitrum, Avalanche and other EVMs.

6.2.6 Asynchronism

One of the key issues faced by cross-chain processes is that of asynchronism. While the process is off-chain gathering data, the native data may be in a state of flux (or vice versa). Keeping everything in the same network avoids this problem.

Asynchronism introduces risks that reference data becomes out of date or that resources are spent twice. This requires careful management by the controlling process to ensure that nothing is committed until all processes have completed (at the risk of tying up resources while waiting for everything else to catch up).

Let's look at a simple example where a tokenised real-world asset is being distributed to a new owner, who must meet certain eligibility criteria (such as their nationality or age). This personal data is held on a different blockchain network to the tokenised asset. The sale process must allocate the asset to the new owner but must then pause while it checks the eligibility off-chain. If the asset was not properly earmarked during this pause, there's a risk that another transaction will come in and distribute the asset to someone else, meaning that the whole transaction needs to be restarted. If the reference data is transient (such as a permission or authorisation), then there's a risk that as soon as it's been checked on the other network it changes to an invalid state. The transaction will still go ahead, potentially timestamped after the change of permission.

The potential risks of asynchronous processing will differ for every use case, so this complexity needs to be built into the cross-chain communication and management processes.

6.2.7 Interoperability Between Smart Contracts

So far, we've talked about interoperability between networks. There is another kind of interoperability: between smart contracts on the same network.

Many (if not most) smart contracts have this interoperability built in. If they follow the basic standards for tokenisation (such as ERC-20 and ERC-721), they will be able to communicate with each other. This is possible because the network has defined rules on how to execute the code in these templates and the data can be shared between the contracts as it is all on the same network. You can see how this becomes more complicated as soon as you try to achieve the same result for a cross-chain process.

An advantage of on-chain interoperability is that the data is in the same state for the whole network, avoiding asynchronous issues.

6.3 Interoperability Applied

Given the different approaches to interoperability, what are the factors that a token issuer (or other multi-chain participant) must consider when designing their processes?

These questions should be answered:

- Who is involved in the process?
- What are the tokens or data to be moved between chains?
- What is the best mechanism to move data between chains?
- What are the operational and governance differences between the networks?
- What are the legal and regulatory issues?
- Self-build or standard?

6.3.1 Who is Involved in the Process?

This is a key question. Interoperability is less likely to result from a private process belonging to a single organisation. Typically, multiple organisations are involved. There may be data providers, service providers, validators, buyers/sellers and issuers to name but a few.

With such a mix, it's unlikely that all parties will share the same legal structure – some might be consortia or government bodies, while others might be private individuals.

Not everyone needs to be involved in the design stage, of course. But where data or services are being provided by other parties, the process design will need to include appropriate permissions and authorisations.

It's worth remembering that the operators of the blockchain networks are also involved in the process and should be included in the design.

6.3.2 What are the Tokens or Data to be Moved Between Chains?

Before deciding which blockchain networks to use and how to deploy smart contracts, the potential issuer must first consider what cross-chain interoperability is actually needed by the process. Does the process require the movement of tokens from one network to another? Can this be avoided by multi-network issuance? Is there data native to one chain that needs to be read (or even amended) by a process on another chain? Can that data be obtained elsewhere?

It's important to understand the full data flow, and (it may go without saying) to minimise cross-chain activity where at all possible. Any data that can be managed on-chain in a synchronous fashion will save on cost and, more importantly, risk.

6.3.3 What's the Best Mechanism to Move Data Between Chains?

The answer to this question will really depend on what data is being moved.

Data that needs to be simply interrogated can be brought on-chain through oracles or even queried directly on its native chain through cross-chain messaging, possibly using standard protocols. When updating data, it is more likely that the right solution is to use cross-chain messaging, so that the data is updated in its native network. The main issue in these use cases is to ensure that the data is protected from unauthorised access and can be relied on to be both current and valid.

For asset tokens such as mutual funds, the choice of whether to lock-and-mint or burn-and-mint depends on whether a suitable custodian can be found to freeze the asset while its proxy is in operation on the target network. The risk with any such bridge (especially as the value of the tokens increases) is that malicious agents may be able to break out the frozen assets or mint assets that haven't been locked, essentially creating false value from nothing. Risks can be reduced by choosing well-known bridge providers, minimising the amount of trust required (perhaps by engaging third-party auditors or using independent validators), and building in rollback protocols in case a malicious operation is discovered.

6.3.4 What are the Operational and Governance Differences Between the Networks?

We've already seen that networks have different operational procedures, such as how consensus is reached, the frequency and speed with which transactions are processed, and the rate at which finality is achieved. Any cross-chain process will need to take all of these differences into account, such as by delaying finality on a chain that typically has simple finality rules, building in the capability to roll back transactions and so on.

But connecting two or more blockchain platforms isn't just a technical endeavour. It is also a governance challenge. As well as having operational differences, each network will have its own governance structure, stakeholders, and decision-making processes. By linking networks with an interoperable process, you are also creating an enduring dependency on these governance functions.

How will software upgrades (which may affect the operational rules) be managed on each network? Is the organisation sufficiently plugged into the governance structure to ensure that interoperability with other networks is considered before any rule changes are implemented? Can the timing be influenced to minimise risk and impact?

Another potential hazard is a blockchain fork. What happens if one of the networks is compromised to the extent that a fork is required? Which fork does the cross-chain process follow? Or does it follow both, creating an increased management overhead with yet another set of governance rules in play?

There are other considerations such as economic (gas) factors that are within the remit of the governance body for each blockchain in the cross-chain process.

Each of these considerations must be catered for in every combination of networks. What might work for Chain #A and Chain #B may not work for Chain #A and Chain #C. A critical part of the design process for a cross-chain process is to identify, resolve and define these considerations across all possible configurations.

6.3.5 What are the Legal and Regulatory Issues?

Blockchain networks may be (generally) global and borderless, but their users are not. The issuers of tokens will usually be operating within a defined jurisdiction. For example, if a token for a mutual fund asset is issued on a global blockchain, the asset will be regulated by a regulator, perhaps the SEC or the FCA. If that asset is transformed into a proxy token on another network, do the same rules apply to the proxy token? What if it is bought on the target network by a sanctioned participant who would be ineligible under the regulations for the native token? Who monitors and applies those rules?

The same issues arise from data associated with tokenised processes. Suppose Chain #A operates in the EU and thus under GDPR rules, and it shares some personal data to Chain #B (which may be a public chain). Once that data is on Chain #B, how does the data controller in Chain #A ensure that it is protected, only used for appropriate operational reasons and is deleted in due course? Of course, this is another good argument as to why sensitive or personal data should be held securely off-chain so that the only things transmitted are pointers, but even then there are access and authorisation considerations to bear in mind – even a pointer must be managed appropriately.

Errors (and hacks) happen. In cases where data is compromised, it must be clear which jurisdiction applies. If a user buys a proxy asset on Chain #B but it does not arrive (having been "lost" somewhere between Chain #A and Chain #B), to which body does the user go for recompense? In the absence of clear regulation, this may be something that needs to be clearly defined by all the participants involved in the cross-chain process, including the governance bodies of the involved chains.

6.3.6 Self-build or Standard?

Finally, there is the question of whether to go it alone and build a fit-for-purpose bespoke interface or to use an existing interoperability platform.

Each approach has its own merits. Much will depend on the details of the particular use case.

Building your own interface means that the solution will fit to your exact requirements. You will have full control over the design, security and functionality and can adapt the solution to meet the particulars of even the most extreme use case. As the owning organisation, you will have full control of the software and its future operation.

It is, however, expensive and time-consuming, requiring very specific skills and expertise in the technology space. Furthermore, you'll be locking yourself into a solution. Blockchain technology and usage is evolving fast, and you may find that your solution is outpaced by other similar operations and security features, leaving your processes exposed to malicious operators. As new networks are added to the blockchain world, it will be your responsibility to evaluate whether your interoperable solution should be extended along with the resulting build.

Adopting an existing interface (or following a standardised protocol) will be faster and (initially) less expensive. It will also bring with it a range of security features (such as a network of oracles and validators) and will be adapted as new networks and security capabilities become available.

The downside to using an existing solution is that it might not be a perfect fit for your exact use case. It's also likely that operational costs will be higher than a solution that you run on your own behalf.

It is also possible to take an existing solution and customise it. Many such solutions are open source, making the software available to be adapted to specific needs.

Notes

1 www.chain.link
2 IBM. (2020). *Blockchain Interoperability White Paper*. https://www.ibm.com/
3 Chainalysis. (2022). Cross-Chain Bridge Hacks Report. Chainalysis. https://www.chainalysis.com/blog/cross-chain-bridge-hacks-2022/
4 https://www.erc7786.org/
5 https://eips.ethereum.org/EIPS/eip-7802

Chapter 7

Risks

All change comes with risk.

Risk that the new model is underdeveloped, misunderstood, more exploitable or just not as operationally robust as the old.

We've already looked at some of the risks associated with blockchain and tokenisation: security and governance risks on public blockchains, cryptography risks from unimaginably fast quantum computers, identity risks, and even finality risks in cross-chain interoperability.

In this chapter we will consider a number of types of risk, the potential impact and any mitigation that might be put in place.

7.1 Risks: An Overview

Legal and *regulatory* uncertainty remains a major barrier to adoption, with differing global frameworks often leading to friction, particularly in cross-border applications. Even if the legal status of a token has been clearly defined, interpretation by national regulators may vary, complicating interoperability.

Blockchain networks, themselves, present numerous risks, particularly in public environments. These include governance disputes during forks or upgrades,

DOI: 10.4324/9781003571421-8

consensus vulnerabilities like 51% attacks, and privacy threats arising from public identity exposure. The security of private keys and the resilience of cryptographic methods are critical concerns, especially as quantum computing progresses. Smart contracts also pose significant threats, from unauthorised access and flawed logic to the risks of immutability, making correction of errors challenging.

Operationally, issues emerge from the permanent nature of transactions and reliance on third-party code and data sources. *Poisoned oracles*, defective contract logic, and reliance on outdated or inefficient contracts all add complexity. The *fragmentation of token liquidity* across chains, often due to bridging mechanisms, introduces challenges in maintaining market depth and transactional fluidity. Additionally, fluctuating gas costs and the inability of some blockchains to scale efficiently with business demand present further limitations.

Collectively, these risks highlight the importance of comprehensive design, robust governance, and due diligence in any tokenisation initiative that seeks to avoid significant *reputational* damage for its operators.

7.2 Risks: The Components

7.2.1 Legality and Regulatory Risks

There remain a number of legal risks and regulatory barriers that may hinder global token adoption.

First and foremost, establishing the legal framework for tokens is key, as the case study from our legal experts later in this chapter clearly shows. Even then, there will be conflicts and friction between the legal framework of the marketplace for the tokenised operation and the legal framework for the blockchain network (or networks) employed to execute the operation.

For regulated markets (such as in the financial industry), once the legal status of a token is clear, regulators will need to opine on the status of the tokens within their market. Again, different regulators may take a different view so cross-border operations will become increasingly complex until a harmonised world view becomes established.

7.2.2 Blockchain Network Risks

As we've already seen, there are a number of risks associated with the use of one network or another. Typically, these risks relate to the use of public networks, although the risk is potentially offset by the benefit of greater accessibility.

In brief, the risks are:

- **Governance risk**: interactions with the network's governance may cause issues when presented with major decisions such as network forks or functional upgrades
- **Consensus risk (the 51% attack threat)**: the risk that a malicious agent overwhelms or subverts the consensus protocol to create and verify erroneous transactions
- **Identity risk**: the risk that users are no longer anonymous due to the public nature of the blockchain
- **Private key and cryptography risk**: the risk that a user's private key is irretrievably lost or stolen and used to remove value from the user's holdings, or that advances in quantum computing invalidate existing cryptographic security measures
- **Smart contract usurpation risk**: the risk that unauthorised users gain access to a smart contract and are able to execute its functions
- **Finality risk**: the risk that finality is not immediate on some networks, meaning that dependent ("real world") activities may need to be coordinated or delayed
- **Interoperability risk**: the risk that having adopted an interoperability solution that involves a third party, that third party is no longer able (or willing) to support the solution, potentially leaving orphaned or valueless assets in the target network.

7.2.3 Operational Risks

There are some purely operational risks associated with the use of blockchain technology.

The first risk (let's call it "immutability risk") stems from the fact that transactions on a blockchain are immutable. In many automated systems, there are ways to recover from erroneous transactions, such as backing out the input or directly editing the database through the intervention of operators. In a blockchain environment, this becomes – whilst not impossible – more difficult as the underlying erroneous transaction has become immutable and cannot be erased. This leaves reversal as the only option available to the correcting organisation.

Smart contracts are programs and as with any program there can be defects. Any organisation (or person) invoking a smart contract function runs the risk that the function does not work correctly. Traditionally, an organisation running software takes responsibility for testing it before deployment into a live environment – with a smart contract, the executing organisation may need to rely on the deploying organisation to have thoroughly tested the smart contract's capabilities. All users will need to take care to ensure they only invoke smart contracts that have been tested and are bug-free (and that the functions themselves do what they are supposed to, whether by accident or malicious design).

A smart contract, once deployed, is also immutable, meaning that its coded functions cannot change (although data-driven parameterised functions may behave differently from time to time). The risk here is that processing becomes tied to the smart contract, even though later smart contracts may be more effective. Management and version control of third-party-deployed smart contracts will become critical to effective and accurate operation in a tokenised environment.

Similarly, organisations may be at risk from erroneous or misleading data brought into the blockchain by a third-party node, a so-called "poisoned oracle". As with all data provision, it's a case of "caveat emptor": the data user must take sufficient steps to ensure that the data comes from a verifiable and trusted source.

Where native tokens are bridged to non-native chains (whether through lock-and-mint or burn-and-mint), there is a risk of reduced liquidity as discrete token pools are created on each new network. The organisation responsible for the market or safe operation of the tokenised solution will need to ensure that liquidity pools are balanced, using a process of repatriation as required.

Finally, there are cost and scale risks:

- **Cost risk**: the risk that gas costs for a public network increase or are algorithmically increased at particular times of the day (and without notice)
- **Scale risk**: the risk that operations on the network are unable to keep pace with business volumes.

7.2.4 Reputational Risk

As always, with a new endeavour, there are reputational risks to consider. Building and publicly launching a tokenised solution may be a huge success, but encounters with any of the legal, network or operational risks we've already covered may cause undue damage to an organisation's reputation. This risk may be exacerbated if the failure is a direct consequence of blockchain network vulnerabilities, building on the already toxic impact of numerous cryptocurrency failures.

7.3 Case Study: The Legal Framework in England and Wales

In their Joint Report "Tokenisation in the context of money and other assets: concepts and implications for central banks", the Bank for International

Settlements (BIS) and the Committee on Payments and Market Infrastructures (CPMI) defined tokenisation as:

> The process of generating and recording a digital representation of traditional assets on a programmable platform. This definition… reflects that the issuance, recording and transfer of tokens relies on the execution of applications that exist on programmable platforms.

- Digital tokens are entries in a database that are recorded digitally and that can contain information and functionality within the token themselves. Digital tokens can represent financial or real assets.
- Programmable platforms are the technologies that allow eligible participants to develop and execute applications that update a common ledger. In the context of money and other assets, one of the technologies that has gained prominence is Distributed Ledger Technology (DLT).[1]

Tokenisation is in its ascendancy. In terms of commercial transactions, it offers much in the way of increased efficiency, greater transparency and reduced friction between systems; mostly because it allows the aggregation of assets and interests into tokenised forms onto a single system that can be accessed by multiple parties. In many ways, therefore, it might be difficult to see why adoption of tokenisation has not occurred both more quickly and more extensively than is currently the case. One of the main reasons has been, and continues to some extent still to be, legal risk, as the BIS-CPMI Report indicates:

> Legal risk arises from the unexpected or uncertain application of a law. With respect to token arrangements, it could arise in cases where the application of existing laws to the concept of tokens is not clear or certain… the legal and regulatory status of a tokenised asset may differ across jurisdictions, particularly as some jurisdictions may adopt token-specific legal frameworks while others apply existing legal frameworks. For example, questions may arise as to whether certain tokenised assets reflect a legal claim or property right; and whether this legal status is consistent with the status of these assets when not in tokenised form. Such issues of legal treatment will be especially relevant in cases of default or insolvency.[2]

The legal problem in relation to digital assets such as tokens is that they do not fit into the categories with which the law has been familiar for hundreds of years. One of the most pressing problems with this is, as alluded to in the excerpt from the Report above, the question of property rights: that is, will the law recognise the holders of tokens as having property rights in them? Such uncertainty might well come as a surprise to many who might have invested in, or purchased, such tokens without asking the question. Most non-lawyers who pay money in exchange for something would probably presume that such payment gives them property in the thing for which they paid, and consequently the protection of the law when that thing is damaged, taken from them or destroyed. As a matter of the law of England and Wales (and many other jurisdictions across the world), there was however until very recently no such certainty and several questions remain unanswered today.

For example, English common law had historically divided personal property rights (that is, rights to property other than land) into two categories: things in possession and things in action.

Things in possession are all of those physically tangible things that can be held, touched, passed from hand to hand, and physically modified and destroyed: everything from bags of gold to horses, to cruise ships and to laptops.

Things in action on the other hand are all those things that could not be perceived, identified or dealt with in the physical world but can instead only be recognised and managed through legal action; the most obvious examples being, say, debts and contractual rights.

The factual differences between the things in each category are important not least because they determine, for instance, the remedies that are available when things go wrong. Most notably, for instance, the legal remedies available when the rights to each type of thing are infringed and are different. And it is this difference that shows most clearly why digital assets present such a problem to these established legal lines.

The crucial distinction lies in the alienation of the thing in question.

Things in possession could, in a factual sense, be taken from their holder without consent. I can, for instance, take another person's watch from them, wear it myself and thereby deny them the ability to do the same. (That is not to say that they would not have a legal claim against me but the factual state of affairs is what is important for present purposes because it explains why things in possession and things in action are treated differently by the law.) Things in action, on the other hand, cannot as a matter of fact be taken from their holders without their consent. A person who is owed a debt by another cannot have that right removed without a legal process. Consequently, holders of things in possession require certain legal protections that those holding things in action do not, such as the means to sue someone who has taken factual possession of an asset belonging to them.

This distinction is relevant to the digital assets problem because digital assets are susceptible to involuntary alienation. It is possible, as a matter of fact, to take another's digital asset without their consent (by, for example, hacking their wallet and transferring that asset to another location). This makes them look like things in possession. The problem for the law, however, was that it regarded digital things as being intangible and there was very strong authority to the effect that intangible things could not be possessed. As a genuinely novel legal phenomenon, digital assets do not sit comfortably into either category – they can be involuntarily alienated but they are also not obviously tangible in the traditional sense because they cannot be perceived with the unaided senses, or passed from hand to hand in a physical way.

The Law Commission of England and Wales was tasked with finding a solution to this problem; a problem that threatened to stifle the productive use of digital assets, such as tokenisation, in the economy. In 2023, it published its Final Report on Digital Assets, containing recommendations to Government and guidance to the courts on how the law should develop in order to accommodate digital assets and thereby ensure that they could be a positive force for growth and commercial progress. In essence, it recommended the development of a third category of personal property into which digital assets that exhibited certain characteristics could be put. This would ensure that, where appropriate, digital assets could attract the legal protection of property rights, despite the fact they might in some ways behave in unfamiliar ways. For instance, whilst things in possession can be transferred from hand to hand, the transfer of digital assets will often look more like an extinction (of, say, a token in a particular location) and a creation (of a token of corresponding value in another location). Analysing such assets in the clean lines of a third category means there is less likely to be confusion about the way in which the law should respond to their functions. This is now largely a job for the common law (that is, for the courts to decide), although there is also a very short bill currently being considered by the UK parliament that, if enacted, will simply clarify that:

> A thing (including a thing that is digital or electronic in nature) is not prevented from being the object of personal property rights merely because it is neither—
>
> (a) a thing in possession, nor
> (b) a thing in action.

Whether or not this Bill becomes an Act, however, (and if it does, it will be known as the Property (Digital Assets, etc) Act), the increasing propensity of the common law to recognise digital assets as property is very good news for the practice of tokenisation. Without legal recognition of property rights in tokens, holders would have far fewer protections when things go wrong, particularly where they have lost possession of their tokens or where the custodian of their tokens becomes insolvent. This would have obvious chilling effects on the appetite of parties to engage in tokenisation. The recent Law Commission recommendations and common law developments have already done much to dispel such doubts, and travel seems set to continue in the same direction for the foreseeable future.

7.4 Risks Applied

So, how do organisations evaluate these risks and seek to mitigate them? Asking these five questions might help:

- Is the legal and regulatory environment clear?
- Which blockchain network(s) should we use, and how do we assess their associated risks?
- How will we secure and manage smart contracts throughout their lifecycle?
- Are we prepared to manage operational risks?
- How will we maintain liquidity and ensure scalability across multiple networks?

7.4.1 Is the Legal and Regulatory Environment Clear?

Start by assessing the legal classification of the token: is it a utility token, security token, stablecoin, or NFT? Then, determine the applicable regulations in every relevant jurisdiction. This may include understanding licensing requirements, AML/KYC obligations, and securities law implications.

Engage with legal counsel experienced in digital asset regulation early in the process. Build and maintain a regulatory map for each jurisdiction you operate in, outlining the position of relevant regulators.

Participation in industry forums and regulatory sandboxes would also be recommended to understand community thinking and best practice as well as testing the boundaries of compliance before broader deployment.

Finally, it might be advisable to avoid building in hard rules that cannot be flexed, as laws and regulations evolve.

7.4.2 Which Blockchain Network(s) should We use, and How Do ee Assess Their Associated Risks?

Choosing the right blockchain network is critical to the success of any tokenisation initiative. Factors such as public or private networks, consensus mechanisms, governance models, and finality times all have security, operational, and financial implications.

To mitigate network risks, organisations should conduct a thorough evaluation of the network's governance structure, assessing its ability to evolve and manage forks without disrupting operations. Consensus security should be analysed, especially for networks with lower hash power or validator participation. Finality times should be matched to business needs; for example, financial applications may require faster, deterministic finality.

Diversifying across multiple networks or using modular chains with interoperability frameworks can reduce dependency on any single network. Additionally, establishing SLAs with infrastructure providers and monitoring network health continuously will help manage ongoing risks.

7.4.3 How will We Secure and Manage Smart Contracts Throughout their Lifecycle?

Risk mitigation starts with formal development standards. Smart contracts should be developed using well-vetted libraries and undergo extensive unit and integration testing. Organisations should perform internal code reviews and also commission external audits by third-party security specialists. Where possible, upgradability patterns such as proxy contracts should be employed cautiously to allow for post-deployment fixes.

Strong version control is recommended, especially when relying on third-party contracts. Metadata and changelogs should be published to on-chain or off-chain repositories to ensure transparency. Finally, implementing circuit breakers or administrative controls (with careful governance) can provide a failsafe in case of contract exploitation.

7.4.4 Are We Prepared to Manage Operational Risks?

To address immutability risk, organisations must adopt robust pre-validation and simulation practices before any transaction is submitted to the chain. For example, user interfaces should simulate the exact result of smart contract calls before confirmation. Additionally, processes should be in place for issuing compensating transactions if a reversal is needed.

Data integrity from oracles should be managed through careful vetting of data providers, redundancy (using multiple independent providers) and by validating incoming data against historical norms or other datasets. Poisoned oracles can be detected by anomaly detection algorithms and economic disincentives.

For cost volatility, using Layer 2 solutions or alternate chains with lower fees (such as Arbitrum, Optimism, or Avalanche) can provide financial predictability. Organisations can also adopt fee prediction tools and budget buffers. Wherever possible, schedule non-urgent transactions during off-peak hours (keeping a close eye on when "off-peak" really occurs).

7.4.5 How will We Maintain Liquidity and Ensure Scalability Across Multiple Networks?

To manage liquidity, organisations should establish or participate in decentralised liquidity pools across all target chains and employ Automated Market Makers (AMMs) with dynamic rebalancing mechanisms. Cross-chain liquidity protocols or aggregation tools (for example, Thorchain, LiFi) can streamline access to fragmented liquidity. Periodic "repatriation" of tokens to rebalance pools may be required, and this process should be automated where possible.

Liquidity is always likely to be most abundant on the token's native chain, so operating a solution aimed primarily at the native node for each token might be an option. Alternatively, the use of a token aggregator could ensure that all tokens are held on their native network.

Scalability must be addressed by selecting chains that align with expected transaction volumes and performance needs. Where scalability of a chosen network is uncertain, consider a modular architecture using rollups or sidechains. Monitoring tools should track TPS (Transactions Per Second), block times, and pending transaction backlogs to predict congestion trends.

Strategically, organisations should adopt a modular deployment strategy—starting with a single chain and expanding based on demand—to limit exposure while maintaining growth flexibility.

Notes

1 Joint report to the G20 by the Bank for International Settlements (BIS) and Committee on Payments and Market Infrastructures (CPMI), October 2024, p.4.

2 Joint report to the G20 by the Bank for International Settlements (BIS) and Committee on Payments and Market Infrastructures (CPMI), October 2024, p.4.

TOKENISATION USE CASES

II

In Part II of this book, we will take a deeper dive into the "so what?" of tokenisation and set out several industry-specific use cases to demonstrate how tokenisation can be deployed in the real world and the places where work is done. In so doing, we'll highlight the potential impact, positive and negative, that tokenisation could have.

Tokenisation isn't just an elegant redesign of database technology.

When the core, compelling characteristics of data used in distributed ledgers and tokens (equal access, transparency and trust) are made available to consumers, industry, public service and administration and the knowledge economy, the results can be transformative with positive impacts on productivity, operational process and more.

Several of these industry-specific applied use cases were first profiled in our sister book, *Blockchain Applied* (Stephen Ashurst and Stefano Tempesta, Routledge/Taylor and Francis 2022). Building on that, we've circled back round to present the subjects again, updated to cater for the latest developments in tokenisation technology.

DOI: 10.4324/9781003571421-9

Chapter 8

Money

It seems only fitting to start our journey through the practicalities of tokenisation with a chapter on money.

Money, it has been said, is just a shared illusion: a belief that the coin in your hand (or token in your app) will be accepted by others in exchange for goods or services. This belief is rooted in trust. Fiat currencies ask you to trust governments. Stablecoins ask you to trust private issuers. Cryptocurrencies ask you to trust code.

Blockchain's creation was entirely derived from a challenge to traditional forms of money: to replace them with a more democratic alternative. Whether it will ultimately succeed in this goal remains a matter of debate, but it's clear that blockchain – through tokenisation – can provide a range of tools to replicate and enhance the exchange of money, reimagining it for the digital age.

8.1 Money Overview

Once upon a time, people bartered.

Chickens for grain. Shoes for eggs. Give the baker enough flour for thirteen loaves of bread and get only twelve in return. This works fine in local communities for a narrow range of commodities, but begins to break down as trade

DOI: 10.4324/9781003571421-10

expands both geographically and in scope. What happens when the shoemaker doesn't want your eggs? Or when the chicken market is too far away?

What was needed was a medium of exchange. Say hello to money.

The first coins (introduced over 2,500 years ago in the eastern Mediterranean region) were made of a blend of gold and silver, called electrum. They were standardised in weight and stamped with the king's mark for authenticity. Early coins held a worth attributable to the metals used in their construction (their "intrinsic" value). Later, the Romans introduced the first "fiduciary" coins: assigned a value by decree, greater than by their intrinsic value. The first tokens, if you will.

But coins are heavy and easy to steal, especially in transit. A more convenient means to exchange and record value was needed: the ledger.

The first ledgers hailed from the very earliest of civilisations in Mesopotamia and the fertile lands of the Tigris and Euphrates rivers where trade between city states flourished. Use of these ledgers later spread to Egypt and Greece, and throughout the Roman Empire.

Ledgers grew in complexity to meet the demands of commerce. The Tang dynasty introduced double-entry ledgers to manage their complex trading arrangements with multiple cultures along the Silk Road. While Muslim requirements to account for indebtedness and to perform complex calculations for inheritance led to Muhammad ibn Musa al-Khwarizmi's ninth century work *The Compendious Book on Calculation by Completion and Balancing* which introduced the concept of balance and "restoration" (*al-jabr* – from which we get "algebra"), leading to the construct of an equation where the components on the left-hand side are balanced by the components on the right-hand side.

Europe lagged behind due to the use of Roman numerals which made calculations difficult. The adoption of Arabic numbers led to an explosion of arithmetic and the art of double-entry bookkeeping was introduced in the banking families of Italy in the 12th and 13th centuries. Luca Pacioli recorded these practices in his book *Everything about Arithmetic, Geometry and Proportion*. Written in Italian vernacular (rather than Latin or Greek), this influential tome popularised Arabic numerals and spread double-entry accountancy practices throughout Europe.

For hundreds of years, movements of money and goods were recorded in ledgers across the globe. Almost all of these ledger entries were made in relation to one of the following:

- **An item of goods or a commodity**: that had intrinsic value
- **Specie money**: where the value of a coin was derived from its constituent commodities (such as gold, silver and copper)

- **Representative money**: often issued as paper or promissory notes that guaranteed a value of a specific commodity that had been set aside and held in reserve.

The Bank Charter Act of 1844 gave the Band of England the right to issue bank notes that could be redeemed either for gold or equivalent bank credit. From 1931, the Bank no longer redeemed their notes (or bank credits) in gold. The United States followed in 1971 as part of the "Nixon shock" of financial measures taken to address rising inflation, bringing to an end the Bretton Woods system that linked international currencies to the price of gold.

Since then, paper money has been issued globally (typically by central banks) in a form that doesn't necessarily relate to a quantity of any commodity. The intrinsic value of most coins in circulation is a fraction of their face value. Fiat money's value is derived from the perceived creditworthiness of the issuing authority, which requires absolute trust from the recipient of the issuer's good standing and ability to so redeem.

The key entities and actors involved in the circulation and exchange of money can be summarised as follows:

- **Individuals**: buyers and sellers who exchange money for goods or services (the "retail" market)
- **Commercial Organisations**: that exchange money for goods and services (the "wholesale" market)
- **Banks**: who facilitate the flow of money through clearing, deposit-taking and lending
- **Central Banks**: who provide financial and banking services for a country's government and commercial banking system, implementing monetary policy and issuing currency.

8.2 The Role of Blockchain in Money

First and foremost, blockchain and distributed ledger technology was created to generate and distribute *cryptocurrencies*, digital coins linked inextricably to the mechanics of the blockchain network itself.

With tokenisation, it became possible to create tokenised money that could be supported by real-world value. These tokenised forms of money were inherently more stable than cryptocurrencies and became known as *stablecoins*. Stablecoins derive their value either from algorithms or from a collateralised quantity of a real-world currency. Tokenised coins issued by central banks or governments are known as *Central Bank Digital Currencies* (or *CBDCs*).

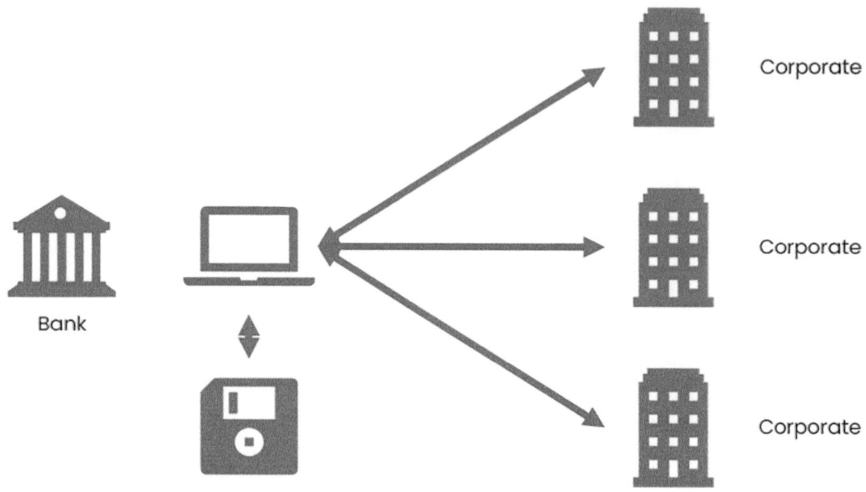

Figure 8.1 Money before Tokenisation.

Other forms of tokenised money exist (or things that might seem to be tokenised money) such as *Non-Fungible Tokens* (*NFT*s) and *Memecoins*.

Figure 8.1 shows how traditional money is controlled by the bank in its role as a "trusted third party," while Figure 8.2 shows the same relationship conducted via the blockchain using a form of tokenised money. Each participant has direct access to their tokenised currency.

8.2.1 Cryptocurrencies

Blockchain and distributed ledger technology supports the exchange of value through a number of related but different mechanisms. The first is through *cryptocurrencies*, the original raison d'être for Blockchain. Cryptocurrencies are a new form of money: they don't have an intrinsic value and there is no promise made to honour their value. Any value they do have derives purely from the willingness of others to exchange them for real-world currencies that have a more robust and demonstrable worth.

Crucially, cryptocurrencies can be issued by anyone, whether individuals, commercial organisations, banks or central banks. This is both a blessing and a curse, democratising the generation of money but opening it up to instability and dramatic fluctuations.

As we are a book on tokenisation (as opposed to merely blockchain and definitely not crypto), we'll leave cryptocurrencies there for now.

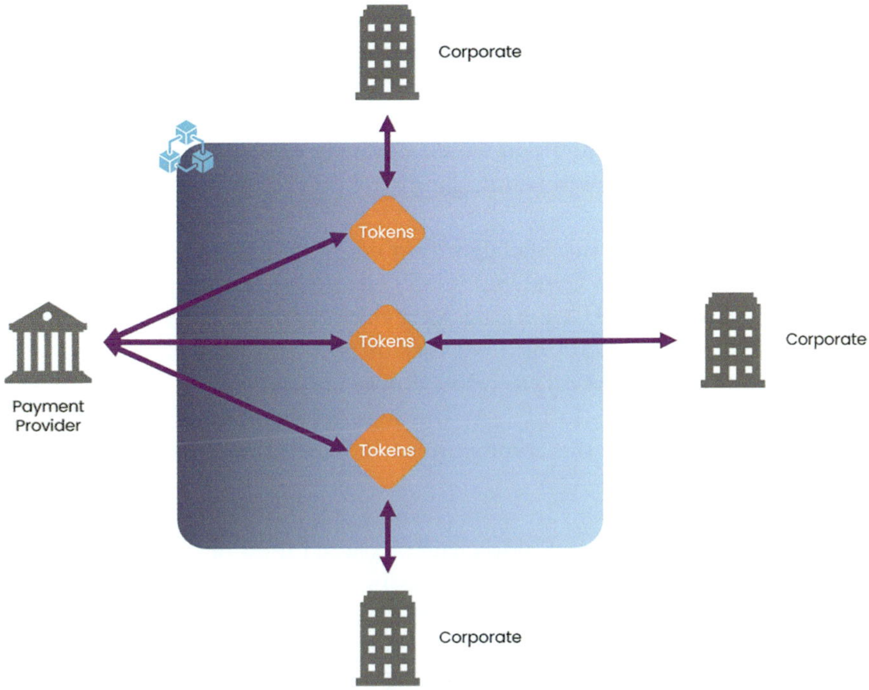

Figure 8.2 Money Tokenised.

8.2.2 *Stablecoins*

With tokenisation, it becomes possible to create tokenised money that can be supported by real-world value.

The most successful of these tokenised currencies are pegged to an existing currency such as the US Dollar and have become known as *stablecoins*. The method of pegging varies but typically falls into one of two camps: algorithmic (where the value of the token is mathematically linked to the value of the dollar) or collateralised, where a quantity of real-world currency is locked up and represented by tokens. In both cases, a merchant might reasonably expect to receive an equivalent amount of value by exchanging the tokens for real cash.

Algorithmic stablecoins generally use incentives to encourage behaviours in the community of owners. If the value of the coin rises above a threshold (typically 1 USD), users are encouraged to mint new tokens, raising the supply and bringing the price down. Conversely, if the price falls, users are encouraged to burn tokens to reduce the supply (raising the price).

This isn't a precise science, and the risk is that the coin fluctuates mildly around the threshold value. This makes algorithmic stablecoins unsuitable for exchange in large numbers. Imagine if you wanted to buy a house with stablecoins. Buying at the wrong time might add 5% to your house purchase – more than any fees or duties you would normally expect to pay and certainly wiping out any value growth you might expect on your property for a number of months if not years.

An additional risk is that the algorithm might fail spectacularly, as was the case in May 2022 for the TerraUSD (UST)[1] stablecoin. Launched on the Terra blockchain network, UST's pegging mechanism allowed either the exchange of UST directly for 1 USD or a conversion to 1 USD value of LUNA (the network's native coin). As crypto prices dipped, holders of UST began to exit, converting their holdings to LUNA. This lowered the price of LUNA further, creating a run that saw the cryptocurrency's value crash from $80 to virtually zero.

Collateralised stablecoins are more reliable but re-introduce the need for trust into the trustless ecosystem of blockchain. A trusted third party must lock away $1 for every dollar's value of issued stablecoin. It is this locked-away value that supports the stablecoin's value in the marketplace.

The two largest such coins are USDT and USDC, supported by Tether and Circle Internet Financial respectively. USDT has a circulating supply valued at $150 Billion at time of writing, mostly collateralised using US Treasury bills (around 80%), Bitcoin (around 5%), gold and other investments held with a major global custodian. USDC has a supply valued at just over $60 Billion and is fully collateralised (mostly in US money market instruments).

In many ways, collateralised stablecoins are the workhorses of the world of commercial tokenisation.

8.2.3 CBDCs

If stablecoins are privately issued digital money, CBDCs are the state's answer. Think of them as digital banknotes minted not by companies, but by governments, backed by the government's ability to pay.

Not all central banking functions are suitable for blockchain. For example, execution of economic policy may not benefit from blockchain implementation. Additionally, central banks may be averse to core blockchain concepts like mining, gas, and anonymity.

Central banks are both attracted to and repelled by digital currency. The technology itself (blockchain) offers efficiency and adoptability compared to current systems. However, the paradigm change raises concerns. Central banks exist to control currency and economy – a purpose that seemingly conflicts with blockchain's decentralisation ethos.

A hybrid option may exist: distributed but not decentralised. Central bank currencies such as GBP, EUR or USD could be issued on a proprietary blockchain maintained by the central banks. The data would be decentralised, but control of money supply and liquidity would remain centralised. As digital tokens were issued, corresponding physical currency would be withdrawn, maintaining the same money supply level.

The scope and application of CBDCs is also hotly debated.

Retail CBDCs (for everyday use by individuals) could streamline day-to-day payments such as shopping on the High Street, as well as reducing banking costs and providing access to money for those without commercial bank accounts. But a retail CBDC raises concerns about surveillance and monetary overreach. Do you want your government to see every latte you buy?

Wholesale CBDCs on the other hand would be for the sole use by banks and financial institutions within the automated monetary systems of the world's financial markets. These could improve settlement speed, reduce counterparty risk, and modernise interbank transfers. Most central banks agree that wholesale CBDCs are less controversial and more immediately useful.

Central banks are at a crossroads with blockchain technology and tokenisation. While the technology offers potential benefits in efficiency, transparency, and security, it also challenges the traditional centralised control model of central banking. The future will likely involve careful integration of blockchain technology while preserving central banks' core functions of economic stability and currency management.

8.2.4 Other Forms of Money

The rapid rise of *Non-Fungible Tokens* (NFTs) as a speculative vehicle, followed by an equally dramatic fall, demonstrated that NFTs are not a viable substitute for money. When the real-world asset that the token represents has value, the token itself does not. At the peak of hysteria, when NFTs for worthless digital sketches were trading for vast sums of money, the token itself was (and still is) valueless in itself.

As with cryptocurrencies (and of course blockchain and the distributed ledger), this lack of value stemmed not from the NFTs themselves but from the nature of the real-world assets they were used to represent. In more trustworthy circumstances, where an NFT is used to represent a piece of artwork or other asset that has genuine value, it is a different story: the NFT can be a viable tool to distribute ownership.

It is true, of course, that the monetary value of something is based entirely on what somebody else will pay you for it. I can buy an old pair of boxing gloves on eBay for about £5. Compare that to an almost identical pair worn by Muhammad Ali during his iconic victory over Sonny Liston in 1964, which fetched a cool $836,500 the last time they were auctioned.

More recently, there has been a degree of interest in "*memecoins*". Initially, memecoins were also cryptocurrencies, but as this required a new blockchain network to be instigated and managed for each new coin launch ("Initial Coin Offerings" or ICOs), a more attainable approach was needed.

Most memecoins are now simply tokens on a network such as Ethereum.

Memecoins are in many ways the lowest common denominator for tokenisation: they are neither native coins for a blockchain network providing operational value through gas payments, nor do they represent a real-world asset that has value in its own right. Any value attached to memecoins derives purely from the community that adopts them: if someone else will buy a memecoin from you, it has the value that they are prepared to give you for it in return. Tokens like Dogecoin or Shiba Inu may be fun and viral, but they are not money in any traditional sense; they are speculative assets wrapped in humour and hype, lacking the substance to serve as serious instruments of value.

This was thrown into the public eye when the $TRUMP memecoin hit the headlines in January 2025. Launched on the Solana network just before Donald Trump's inauguration, 200 million $TRUMP coins were issued into circulation, rising rapidly from a value of a few cents each to over $70 per coin before declining almost as fast. The high-profile launch led to hundreds of copycat coins (many spammed into Trump's own wallet by those hopeful of gaining notoriety and "value" as a result), numerous spam and phishing attacks, and the deployment of malicious dApps seeking to defraud members of the general public.

An exciting (or draconian, depending on your perspective) potential application of tokenisation is the concept of "programmable money". This might be some form of stablecoin where the underlying smart contract can apply conditions or restrictions on how the money can be spent. This could apply to charity donations that can only be spent by the underlying charity, or welfare tokens that can only be spent on essentials such as food and clothing.

8.3 Money Applied Use Case: Splitting the Bill

This section explores how tokenisation could transform the UK's central banking system by introducing a digital pound sterling. Through a comparative narrative, it illustrates both the current state of electronic payments and a potential blockchain-powered future.

8.3.1 Current State: Traditional Banking Settlement

Today, when Martin needs to repay Stuart £30 for their shared work dinner, the process involves several intermediary steps and institutional delays. On a Friday afternoon around 5pm, Stuart shares his bank details via WhatsApp, and Martin initiates the payment through his mobile banking app.

Though Stuart receives a notification about the incoming £30 and confidently withdraws cash from an ATM for his taxi ride home, the actual settlement between banks hasn't occurred yet. Since the Bank of England (BoE) has closed for business at 4pm, Martin's bank merely creates a ledger entry in its internal systems.

UK retail banks compile their daily ledger balances and report them to the BoE. With the weekend approaching, Martin's bank records a £30 liability in its BoE account, while Stuart's bank registers a corresponding credit expectation. The actual reconciliation and settlement between the banks only happens when the BoE reopens on Monday at 9am. Only then do both banks update their internal records to reflect the completed transaction.

This process highlights the time gap between payment initiation and final settlement, requiring banks to maintain sufficient liquidity for all pending transactions over non-working days.

8.3.2 Future State: Blockchain-powered Digital Currency

In the envisioned blockchain future, the BoE still oversees pounds sterling but has introduced a blockchain-powered "stablecoin" version available as tokens that can be transferred between BoE-provided digital wallets, alongside traditional currency forms.

When Martin wants to repay Stuart in this scenario, Stuart shares his GBP token wallet address through Tokenbase, their shared digital wallet application. Martin simply logs into Tokenbase and transfers £30 in tokens directly to Stuart.

The difference becomes immediately apparent: Stuart receives the £30 tokens instantly in his wallet. Without delay, he can order a taxi and transfer the same tokens to the taxi company's wallet upon arrival home. The BoE records all these transactions in a new block on the GBP blockchain, with everything settled in real-time because all participants (Martin, Stuart, Tokenbase, and the taxi firm) are registered BoE token account holders.)

This blockchain implementation eliminates the weekend delay and settlement uncertainty of the traditional system. Payments are processed, verified, and settled immediately, regardless of banking hours or working days.

The narrative illustrates how central banking thrives on reliable, resilient, secure, and immediate settlement systems – all attributes that a well-designed blockchain infrastructure could deliver. The decentralised yet permissioned nature of such a system offers the security benefits of distribution alongside the regulatory controls necessary for a national currency.

For Martin and Stuart, the difference is simple but profound: no more wondering whether a payment will clear over the weekend, no more delays between transaction initiation and completion, and no more reconciliation discrepancies between financial institutions.

For the broader financial system, the impacts extend to more efficient capital utilisation, reduced counterparty risk, greater transparency, and potentially lower costs for end users. Everyone in the central bank ecosystem – from individual consumers to retail banks to the central bank itself – stands to benefit from faster and more accurate gross settlement, decentralised account management, and optimised liquidity requirements.

The blockchain-powered future of central banking isn't just about technological modernisation – it represents a fundamental reimagining of how money moves through an economy, with the potential to make financial transactions as immediate and seamless as sending a text message. While significant regulatory, technical, and transitional challenges remain, the illustrated benefits make a compelling case for central banks to seriously explore blockchain-based digital currency implementations.

8.4 How has Tokenisation been Applied?

Beyond the immediate consumer advantages illustrated in the narrative, implementing blockchain technology at the central bank level offers several systemic benefits:

- **Reduced liquidity requirements**: retail banks would no longer need to maintain large liquidity reserves to cover pending transactions. With instant settlement, banks can optimise their capital utilization more efficiently
- **Lower capital adequacy standards**: financial institutions would require less capital to be held at the central bank, as the risk profile of transactions decreases significantly with real-time gross settlement
- **Enhanced monetary policy implementation**: the central bank gains immediate visibility into money supply movements, enabling more precise and responsive monetary policy adjustments. Every transaction is recorded in real-time, providing unprecedented transparency for economic analysis

- **Improved transaction transparency**: all parties in a transaction chain gain greater visibility into payment statuses, with instant confirmation replacing the uncertainty periods of traditional banking
- **Instantaneous gross settlement**: the elimination of batched settlements and clearing periods means that transactions are individually processed and completed in real-time, reducing systemic risk.

While the technological feasibility of blockchain-based central banking is increasingly evident, several important considerations remain before widespread adoption. The role and future status of traditional financial intermediaries, particularly retail banks, will need careful attention. Their business models would require significant adaptation as certain intermediary functions become automated or redundant. Furthermore, central banks must ensure that blockchain implementations support rather than hinder their ability to execute monetary policy through interest rates, inflation targeting, and other economic tools.

While blockchain can reduce certain risks, new forms of systemic vulnerabilities may emerge that require thorough analysis and mitigation strategies.

8.5 Legal Factors

Here, we analyse the impacts when tokenisation is applied to the ownership of assets, such as art or music, through the issuance of NFTs.

Currently, ownership of an asset such as a work of art or a song would be limited to one legal entity. For example, an artist creates a work of art, and sells it to one legal entity, who becomes the owner with papers to evidence it.

By tokenising the asset, the right to the artwork is converted into a digital token. In current practice, this would usually mean issuing an NFT for a piece of content or the rights associated with it. Each token represents a fraction of the artwork's ownership which can be issued on platforms and split across legal entities as owners of the property. Tokenisation of creative content such as art or music raises questions about the copyright laws. The rights granted by the token will depend on the legal rights that have been defined for the token. The NFT might grant the owner the right to display or resell the digital art, but the artist themselves would retain the copyright.

In 2021, Kings of Leon became the first major group to release an album ("When You See Yourself") as an NFT. They offered three versions of the NFT: a special album package, a golden ticket and an exclusive audiovisual art selection. Each of these variations offered fans a specific reward for purchasing the NFT and it generated over two million dollars in sales. This was an example of how tokenising their music allowed Kings of Leon to innovate the marketing and sales of their album and reach out to their fans in a new, more personalised way.

The benefits of such tokenisation of real-world assets through NFTs include enhanced liquidity and fractional ownership which makes the art more accessible and tradeable as the investor no longer needs enough capital to buy the whole piece outright, increasing the global reach of the art because the art tokens can be traded worldwide, which in turn also reduces costs.

A key difference between tokenised and non-tokenised art is the level of ingrained security and provenance as the blockchain records the transactions rather than the owner requiring physical proof of ownership with a non-tokenised asset.

The use of NFTs for creative content is already a reality, although it remains commercially niche. As the legal and regulatory landscape for digital assets continues to evolve, this use case could continue to develop into a commercial normality.

Note

1 Liu, Jiageng, Igor Makarov, & Antoinette Schoar. (2023, May 22). *Anatomy of a Run: The Terra Luna Crash*. Harvard Law School Forum on Corporate Governance. https://corpgov.law.harvard.edu/2023/05/22/anatomy-of-a-run-the-terra-luna-crash/

Chapter 9

Trade Finance

Trade finance, also known as procure to pay ("P2P"), is the day-to-day activity by which organisations source, order, invoice, purchase, pay for and reconcile the delivery of materials and goods in their supply chain. It may also refer to procurement of services, though professional services are usually delivered via specific service agreements.

Trade finance is vital for business management. When efficiently organised, the benefits of trade finance include reduced project delivery risk, better cash flow forecasting, and more satisfied suppliers.

When poorly executed, trade finance threatens to interrupt key activities. The question is not "Can you afford to have a formalised trade finance system?" but "Could your organisation afford to have a significant trade finance failure?"

9.1 Trade Finance Overview

Simply put, trade finance is buying goods from suppliers using finance or credit. Enterprises procure, daily, billions of dollars' worth of materials from each other and third-party suppliers. In larger organisations, enterprise-level procurement is carried out within structured software systems subject to procurement policies. The trade finance lifecycle might look something like this:

DOI: 10.4324/9781003571421-11

1. **Request**: internal request for materials within the buyer organisation
2. **Request For Quotation (RFQ)**: the buyer organisation processes a request into external-facing standardised format
3. **Quotation**: suppliers respond with quotations
4. **Purchase Order (PO)**: legal instrument setting out procurement details such as quantity, price, and delivery date
5. **Goods Receipt**: delivered goods must be inspected and accepted
6. **Supplier Invoice**: the supplier issues an invoice for payment
7. **Release Payment**: the buying organisation makes payment following validation
8. **Credit Note/Delivery Note Adjustment**: final reconciliation changes.

Trade finance is a journey moving through specific transactions between legal entities, currencies and across borders. It directly correlates with payment and cash transactions. It is typically an enterprise-level operation carried out inside organisations, often confidentially, though it interfaces with external suppliers.

Figure 9.1 shows the complex interactions required for a supply chain under a trade finance agreement.

9.1.1 Trade Finance Software and Policy

Trade finance is usually configured via integrated software systems managed by trained staff or external partners. Trade finance systems may be purchased from third-party vendors or built in-house, hosted on-premises or via the cloud. For smaller organisations, trade finance may be done ad-hoc via spreadsheets, emails and cash ledgers. All of the above are valid and all exist today – and will continue to do so – but all are full of cumbersome friction, latency and cost and none are "distributed" in the ways described in Part 1 of this book.

Every organisation has varying policies over control of trade finance data, security and access. We find examples in industries such as construction, hospitality, automotive, shipping, aerospace, consumer goods and retail. Governments and non-governmental organisations also use trade finance systems to streamline procurement.

Trade finance solutions may span multiple jurisdictions, currency areas, customs boundaries and time zones. Multiple factors increase complexity, alongside risks of errors, fraud, delays, and breaks in the supplier value chain. Most breaks are caused by day-to-day activity of staff and actors, not system failures.

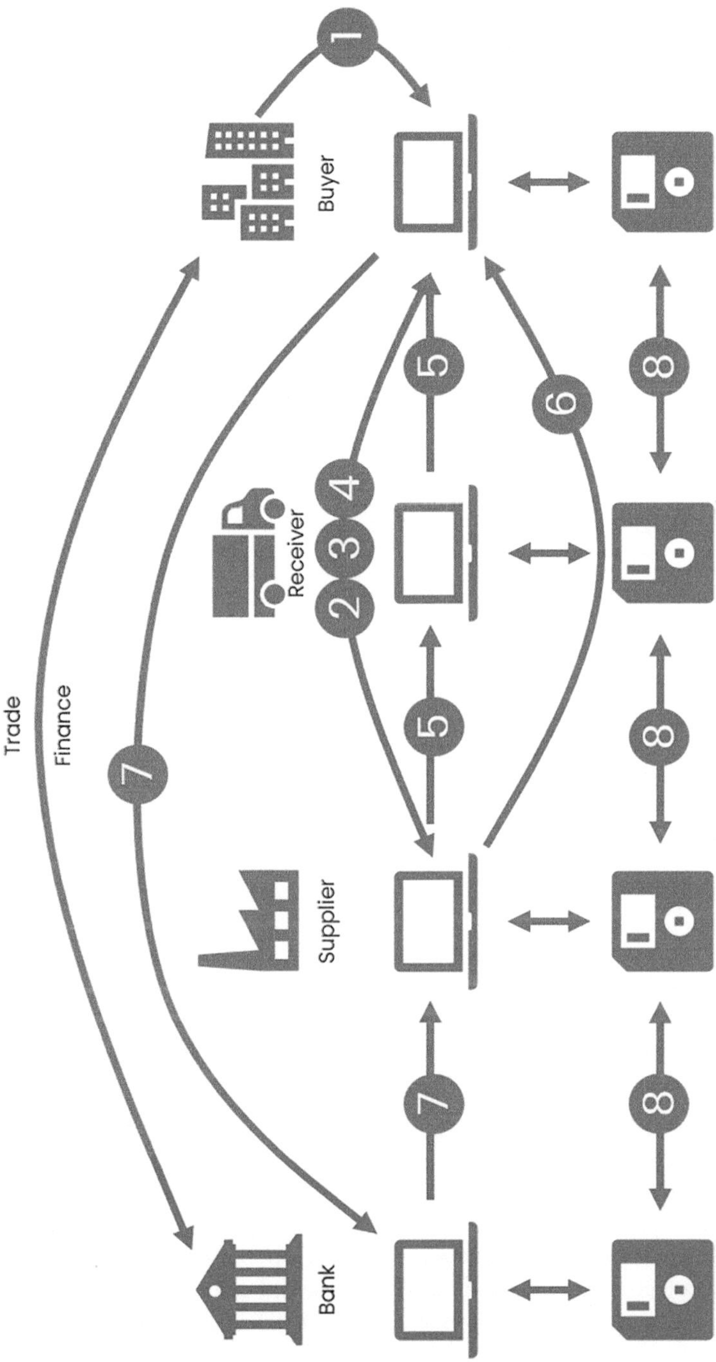

Figure 9.1 Supply Chain before Tokenisation.

9.1.2 Key Entities and Actors

Trade finance has a number of key entities and actors, often where each has a contractual role or a specific function set down and defined in legal agreements, purchase orders and service agreements. The below are some examples of key entities and actors in the trade finance process:
Legal Entities:

- **Buyer**: the organisation with full legal status procuring goods
- **Supplier**: legal entity, often external to the buyer, providing goods
- **Bank/Finance Provider**: operates on behalf of the buyer with interest in ordered goods
- **Receiver**: entity responsible for overseeing movement of goods

Actors:

- **Project Manager**: professional ensuring smooth running of ordering and delivery
- **Auditor**: acts on behalf of buyer/suppliers to ensure standards are maintained
- **Bookkeeper**: keeps an accurate record of all trade finance aspects.

9.1.3 Trade Finance Types and Models

Trade finance operates through established and conventional types and models. Variation is commonplace, and custom trade finance arrangements are as old as trade and commerce itself. Without being an exhaustive list, the below are some examples of trade finance types and models:

- **Payment on delivery**: the buyer settles the invoice immediately following delivery
- **Payment by rolling line of credit**: the bank settles the buyer's liabilities to suppliers
- **Payment on account**: a revolving credit account between the buyer and the supplier
- **Internal trade finance**: the buying organisation manages its own process and system
- **Externally outsourced trade finance**: the organisation delegates procurement
- **Ad-hoc/project-related trade finance**: a project-driven approach
- **End user computing trade finance**: used by smaller organisations.

9.1.4 Challenges in Trade Finance

Trade finance is a useful component in the cashflow and payment aspects of international commerce. Its use speaks to the continuing need for trade finance, and yet there exist significant constraints and headwinds to the wider adoption of trade finance, some of which are set out here:

- **Credit note/delivery note reconciliation**: reconciling the layers of trade finance, and the data necessary, is a burden on all actors in trade finance. Errors, manual processes, reconciliation breaks and poor-quality data all inject friction into the trade finance process in the form of additional cost, effort, risk and complexity
- **Fraud in delivery and payment**: criminals, opportunists, even employees: the fragmented trade finance "stack" provides plenty of opportunities for leakage such as corrupted orders, proofs of delivery or skimming and associated payments
- **Change of supplier/third-party**: lack of supplier information and data governance means there are frictions in trade finance with potentially impersonated suppliers or even, through disorganisation rather than criminal intent, delay and extra costs
- **Cross-currency and cross-border issues**: currency variance and trade movements within the trade finance lifecycle causes expense, along with customs friction and paperwork that must be mostly manually processed
- **Government procurement rules**: government and legislation creates extra layers of complexity and rules
- **Changes of ownership**: when entities become unable to pay liabilities, or when ownership changes, trade finance can be interrupted.

9.2 The Role of Blockchain in Trade Finance

Blockchains and tokens offer a compelling solution to trade finance complexities. As a distributed ledger technology, the blockchain enables multiple entities to represent, share and validate identity, transactions, tasks, delivery and payment data with equal access, transparently and immutably which in turn fosters great trust.

In Chapter 1, we introduced our three standard tests for blockchain and token relevance. For trade finance, these could be interpreted as follows:

- **Transparency**: the ability to match lines of credit to risk
- **Requirement for trust:** the counterparties in the supply chain clearly need to trust each other
- **Equitable access**: all parties can view and verify all stages of the chain.

Tokenisation is reshaping trade finance, offering transparency, immutability, security and equal access to data that can be trusted. Smart contracts will increasingly automate trade finance process stages, incorporating business rules for quality acceptance, payment dates and enforcement criteria.

When comparing current non-tokenised systems with potential blockchain-powered systems, the key difference becomes apparent: with a tokenised architecture, all stages/statuses for all parties are updated automatically, making information equally accessible, transparent, synchronous, immutable and fully reconciled across the entire trade finance cycle.

Figure 9.2 shows how the traditional web of complex interactions has been replaced by a simpler, more direct access for each party to a common, shared, decentralised record on the blockchain.

9.3 Trade Finance Applied Use Case: The Bridge to a Better Future

In civil engineering, massive building projects must contend with complex financial arrangements.

A new road bridge is taking shape in Kent, England. This joint venture between Highways England and Kent County Council isn't just connecting two physical locations: it is showing how traditional trade finance systems and blockchain technology create vastly improved experiences for everyone involved.

9.3.1 The Case of the Missing Concrete

Picture a hot summer's day at a bustling construction site. A massive truck loaded with twenty tonnes of liquid concrete rumbles up to the delivery zone of the bridge project. The driver, wiping sweat from his brow, hands over a file of paperwork with barcodes to the project manager waiting at the site.

Under the traditional system, what follows is the friction of documentation and delays. As workers pour the concrete, the project manager scans barcodes, signs papers, and keeps copies. The driver, after completing delivery, returns to base with his set of papers. Meanwhile, behind the scenes, the buyer and supplier independently enter data into separate software systems and different databases,

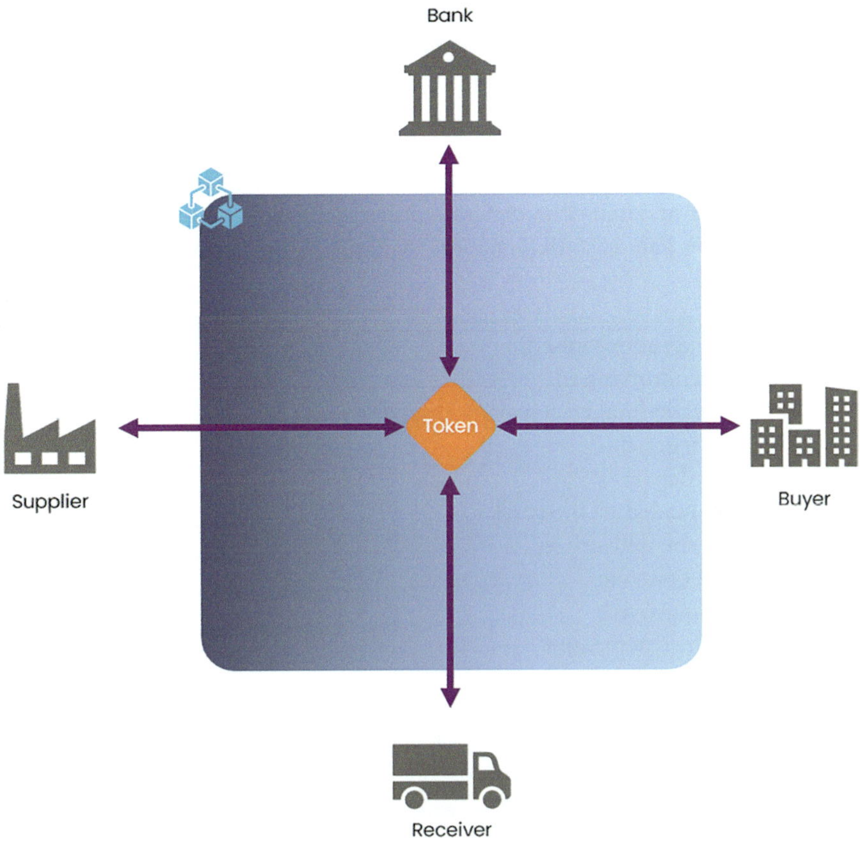

Figure 9.2 Supply Chain Tokenised.

then struggle to reconcile any differences between their records and the physical delivery.

Only after this time-consuming reconciliation between supplier and buyers can the buyer instruct the bank to release payment to the supplier. Days might pass before the supplier receives the consideration due for the concrete that's already setting in the bridge foundation.

Now imagine the same scene, but with distributed ledger technology and tokenisation underpinning the process. At the start of this version of the story, the project manager instructs the concrete company to deliver concrete to the site. The bank or trade finance company is contacted by the supplier and buyer and mints a token for the concrete order, including details such as quantity of the order, cost, delivery date and so on; and the token is now visible to all parties – the buyer, the supplier and the bank or trade finance company.

Back in the "real world", the loaded concrete truck soon arrives at the site with its valuable cargo. The driver presents his phone app that displays the order token to the project manager. As the concrete pours, the project manager confirms the delivery on their app which causes the data on the smart contract of the order token to also be updated. The concrete order token has smart contracts within it, as described in Part 1, so that changes in status of the delivery can be recorded for example:

- Supplier (pseudonymised)
- Buyer (pseudonymised)
- Bank or trade finance company (pseudonymised)
- Order instructed
- Cost of order
- Concrete loaded to the truck
- Arrival at the delivery site
- Unloaded concrete
- Delivery approved
- Payment instructed and
- Payment received.

Using apps to interface with the blockchain, all of these smart contracts can be updated instantly, so that everyone involved (the buyer, supplier, bank, and receiver) sees the updated status of the order, the concrete and the payment. There is very little friction in terms of delays, costs and so on. The difference this time is that the bank can immediately check that the concrete is delivered and release payment to the supplier.

No paper shuffling, no reconciliation meetings, no delays.

The concrete is delivered, payment is made, and the project continues without interruption. All powered by immutable, equally accessible, transparent and trustworthy tokens.

9.3.2 When Credit Meets Construction

For the next phase of the Kent bridge project, financing becomes critical. Under the traditional model, the buyer sends out requests for quotations to trusted suppliers. After selecting the winning bid, the buyer and bank negotiate a line of credit to cover all expected purchase orders, plus a contingency buffer.

The bank must set aside substantial liquidity, waiting for a stream of delivery notes to trigger payments. At project completion, after extensive reconciliation, the buyer repays the entire credit facility. This approach ties up capital, increases costs, and amplifies risk for all parties.

Tokens and distributed ledgers can transform this cumbersome financial choreography. The buyer still sends out requests and selects the winning concrete supplier, but because the bank exists as a node on the "concrete order token" network, it can see each transaction in real time, synchronously; and it can rely on the data as being approved by consensus, not just by one party but all.

This real-time-access, transparent, trustworthy and frictionless method drastically reduces the size of the credit facility that must be maintained, cuts the total cost of credit, releases liquidity in the banking system for other purposes, accelerates supplier payments, and minimises liabilities and risk for the bank. The financial side of the project flows as smoothly as the concrete being poured into the bridge foundations.

9.3.3 The Bridge to Benefits

For banks, blockchain is more than a technological upgrade, it's also a shield against fraud in the trade finance value chain and a catalyst for efficiency.

The immutable and transparent nature of blockchain transactions gives banks and trade finance companies greater confidence in each payment. Cash flow projections become more accurate, credit arrangements more efficient, settlement times dramatically reduced, and identity more easily proven.

Buyers find themselves navigating simpler trade finance. The complexity and friction that once characterised procurement using trade finance and to manage the risks that built up over time using traditional tech stacks gives way, using the distributed ledger, to a much more streamlined process. Delivery risks diminish as trust in orders, delivery and payment becomes transparent and traceable. With access to greater visibility across the entire procurement cycle, buyers gain protection against the type of catastrophic failures that brought down companies involved in the trade finance industry in the past.

For *suppliers*, blockchain addresses persistent pain points. Payment delays, drowning in paperwork, and wrestling with reconciliation issues and arguments – as well as the risk of fraud – fade away. Instead, suppliers enjoy faster payments, better trust between themselves, their buyers, banks and trade financiers, and improved customer relationships. Managing their own supply chains becomes more efficient, allowing them to deliver with greater confidence and precision.

Project managers, those responsible for on-the-ground and complex deliveries, find their burden lightened. The risks that once shadowed every delivery (reconciliation errors, reporting challenges, potential fraud, late and slow payments and disgruntled suppliers, and coordination failures) diminish under blockchain's better and simpler functionality. Accuracy, transparency, immutability, and portability become the project manager's new allies.

9.3.4 The Future Taking Shape

Back at the Kent bridge site, work continues with new efficiency. Where once there were delays waiting for payment authorisations and reconciliation meetings and arguments between buyers, suppliers and banks/trade financiers, now there is smooth, less interrupted progress. The concrete foundations set firmly, steel beams rise, and the bridge takes shape against the English sky.

The blockchain-powered future of trade finance isn't just about faster payments or reduced paperwork – it's about transforming relationships between buyers, suppliers, banks, and project managers. It's about building trust alongside infrastructure. It's about ownership and access to information equally.

As the Kent bridge nears completion, it stands as both a physical structure connecting communities and a symbol of how blockchain/distributed ledger technology bridges the gaps in traditional trade finance. The concrete may be the same, but the way it's delivered, paid for, and recorded represents a fundamental shift in how large-scale projects can be managed and financed.

For the government agencies funding the bridge, for the banks providing the financing, the suppliers delivering materials, and the teams on the ground building it, tokenisation has created a shared reality where information flows as smoothly as traffic will one day flow across the finished bridge – without bottlenecks, without detours, and with unprecedented visibility for all involved.

9.4 How has Tokenisation been Applied?

Trade finance is a vertical industry currently full of duplication of effort, data, process and cost. What this also means on a practical level is that there are multiple places for error, potential criminal activity (or at the very least, incompetence) and poor practice to hide.

Decentralising the stages and steps of trade finance, and deploying, via blockchain, better accuracy, security, speed and access to information means a better overall trade finance system and fewer issues both micro and macro.

It is no accident that trade finance has been seen as an early adopter of distributed ledger technology. Given its obvious challenges, trade finance is sorely in need of the solutions that blockchains can offer.

Tokens, as we have seen in Part I, rely on smart contracts, distributed data, distributed applications, on-chain and off-chain data, trustworthy identity and network interoperability.

Taking each of these headings in turn, the below are some pointers as to how and where the trade finance industry might potentially benefit from using distributed ledgers and a "concrete order token":

- **Smart contract**: the concrete order token enables the automated processing (using smart contracts) of buyer orders; credit decisions and liability management versus events by trade financiers and banks; delivery management by project managers; and payment and risk mitigation for suppliers
- **Distributed data**: there are obvious benefits in all parties having access to the same data at the same time, all the time. This compares with the current "stack" where data about delivery, payment and other key information is asynchronous and full of delays, leading to mistakes and mistrust, as well as the possibility of error and fraud
- **Distributed application**: there are opportunities for dApps that focus on trade finance to develop over time, for example, where communities of buyers, suppliers, project managers and trade financiers/bank enhance their tokens for even-more efficient concrete orders and delivery
- **On-chain and off-chain data**: obviously, details on individual buyers, suppliers, bank/trade financiers should be maintained as private and, therefore, off-chain. But there are interesting possibilities for the extension of some aspects of on-chain data that enhance productivity and creditworthiness; for example, those suppliers with the best quality track record or those buyers who are most active in a market and therefore might qualify for a bulk order discount
- **Trustworthy identity**: as with all financial services, identity is key to trust and a vital component in defeating fraud. The potential for the distributed ledger to enhance the identity element of trade finance is strong and, as we discussed in Chapter 5, a real-world benefit
- **Network interoperability**: there is unlikely to be only one blockchain network option for the trade finance industry. Understanding how "concrete order tokens" might be issued on different networks, how cash and/or stable coins interact with the "top three" trade finance networks, and – crucially – how "delivery versus payment" would work across different networks are important questions.

9.5 Legal Considerations for Trade Finance and Tokenisation

Many of the legal use cases for adopting tokenisation remain in their initial stages. However, one example of a use case that is already being widely implemented is the idea of using tokens to digitise and track ownership of trade documents or goods in a supply chain.

Historically, a paper document was required to evidence the ownership of, or rights to, goods as they were transferred from seller to buyer through a supply chain. There are huge efficiencies that could be created through the adoption of tokenisation for supply chains, as digital tokens can be transferred in minutes, rather than several days. However, for the industry to transition from paper to any form of tokenisation or electronic trade documents, it was essential to have the legal framework that confirmed that the technology would be enforceable.

An electronic Bill of Lading (eBL) is a prime example of how tokenisation is already being implemented into the supply chain, supported by the legal underpinning of the UK's Electronic Trade Documents Act 2023 (ETDA) which grants eBLs, electronic Bills of Exchange and other negotiable trade documents the same legal status as paper originals. The eBL is a digital token that represents the title to goods in transit, and it registers each transfer on the blockchain as the goods move from seller to buyer. In September 2023, Lloyds Bank completed the first transaction under the ETDA when a digital promissory note was issued in which the retailer promised to accept liability when settling a collection for the purchase of clothing from one of its suppliers. This streamlined the transaction as the use of the digital promissory note meant that the key documents arrived two days earlier than they would have done if a paper promissory note had been used.

There are numerous other benefits drawn from the use of electronic trade documents, including the prevention of damage, loss, theft or fraud of the paper documentation that was historically used to evidence the rights to the goods. The Bills of Lading or Bills of Exchange are essential documents for supply chains and the loss or damage of these documents can cause major issues. Through the tokenisation of these trade documents, the process becomes far more secure and reliable. The blockchain retains an immutable record of the transactions and transfers. It cannot be accidently destroyed or amended.

Electronic trade documents are already becoming a practical reality, especially with the defined legal infrastructure in the UK and in other jurisdictions. It will take time for industry wide uptake and implementation as it will require system integration and recognition in the remaining jurisdictions.

Chapter 10

Healthcare

Healthcare is a vital worldwide industry worth trillions of dollars of revenue and expenditure in both the private and public sectors.

On a more human note, leaving aside the economic aspects, healthcare touches the lives of all of us from cradle to grave. Modern healthcare reaches from the wealthiest countries and communities to the less developed parts of the world through vaccine programmes such as the Global Polio Eradication Initiative (GPEI).

Medicines and pharmaceutical research, physical and mental health therapies, diet and exercise, medical equipment and apparatus, dentistry and optometry and all branches of professional medical services are part of the global healthcare industry.

Getting healthcare right is an imperative for all of us. Making healthcare more efficient and personalised is a key measurement for the future of healthcare, so that advances in science and research can be brought to bear on disease, ageing and the other challenges faced by the human race.

This chapter looks at how healthcare software and data works today and how tokenisation could improve it now and in the future.

DOI: 10.4324/9781003571421-12

10.1 Healthcare Overview

Healthcare is primarily a human-to-human service but with technology, software, data and automation embedded throughout. "Healthcare" is an elastic term, which includes personal healthcare, medical machinery, supplies, professional services, research and highly sensitive and personalised medical data. Patient records, clinician data, research information, and treatment information are vital components of healthcare software, which is also impacted by healthcare decisions and policy derived from local, national and international government and financial infrastructure.

In software and data terms, medicine today is practised and consumed predominantly by humans and systems working in unison: from blood tests to operations to pharmaceutical research programmes and vaccine programmes. All medicine makes extensive use of software and data. Medical data is strictly confidential, highly personal, varied, and critical. Getting it right can be – literally – a matter of life and death for patients.

Healthcare software supports the vast global healthcare sector and is, in itself, a multi-billion-dollar industry. Most healthcare software and data are, however, designed by third-party companies and even academic institutions, not by medical practitioners themselves. There is an important difference between the profit drivers of healthcare software providers versus the care and compassion of healers that can, sometimes, cause friction.

This chapter focuses on real-life application of blockchain and tokenisation in healthcare scenarios of today and sets out an applied basis on which the interests and outcomes of actors in the healthcare industry, for example software suppliers, patients and medical professionals, might be better aligned for the benefit of us all.

10.1.1 Healthcare Policy and Challenges

Healthcare software has a complex history.

Even today, paper documents and files play a significant role in healthcare globally. Digital healthcare solutions offer far greater efficiency, access, and analysis benefits over the use of paper, but create new risks like data breaches and concerns over control and exploitation of patient data. More digitalisation of healthcare software can mean greater personalisation of healthcare, with obvious benefits for patient outcomes and efficiency, but would need to be accompanied by greater patient ownership and control to get buy-in at scale from communities of patients and medical practitioners.

Healthcare software policy tends to direct itself towards regulatory and patient-level outcomes, and is often focused on real-world patient or consumer-oriented issues including:

- The impacts of poorly administered patient-level clinical research data
- Rules around the exploitation (for research purposes) and commerciality of patient data
- How to deliver personalisation in healthcare using software and data as a driver for that
- Increasing patient ownership and engagement and thereby scale adoption of healthcare software and data.

10.1.2 Key Entities and Actors

Key actors in the healthcare sector include:

- **Medical practitioners (physicians, nurses and support staff)**: front line users of healthcare software. Understanding their requirements is key to designing the right healthcare software solutions. Medical practitioners are responsible for patient outcomes, and healthcare software must be designed to augment this life-and-death responsibility
- **Patients**: both subjects and objects of healthcare software. They engage as users and recipients of care yet are not typically considered the primary users
- **Hospitals, clinics and surgeries**: healthcare facilities are nodes of care provision. They connect various users, records, and integrations – does the MRI database connect with local surgeries?
- **Pharmaceutical research and testing entities**: pharmaceutical research and testing has a huge role to play in the global healthcare industry but is a background actor in terms of primary care. These entities are long-term actors (medical research can span decades) and are focussed on ensuring healthcare software, data, and patient outcomes are progressed, audited, and accessed correctly.

10.1.3 Healthcare Types and Models

- **Healthcare software components**: healthcare software components have no single standard. The industry is very large globally and historically healthcare software applications, data and operating systems have been deployed on a customised and case-by-case basis. This increases the complexity and friction inherent in healthcare software and diminishes interoperability, making healthcare software integrations more complicated and detracting from efficiency and productivity.
- **Healthcare data requirements**: by definition, healthcare data is personal and incredibly sensitive. Management of this data must ensure:

- **Privacy**: patients want assurance that access to their own data is restricted
- **Trust**: earned by healthcare software providers who demonstrate security and privacy
- **Access**: equitable access to healthcare data is vital for patient and practitioner confidence and engagement
- **Security**: prevention of unauthorised access to healthcare software and data is critical.

- **Healthcare transactions**: every action in healthcare software systems engages with healthcare data "transactions". Examples are:

  - Medical practitioner updates (notes, diagnoses, prescriptions)
  - Prescription processing
  - Patient treatment tracking
  - Patient admission, treatment and discharge records
  - Clinical and pharmaceutical research and development and testing outcomes.

- **Healthcare software specialisations**: healthcare software often clusters around medical specialisations like surgical, paediatrics, and gerontics (elderly care).
- **Potential breaks in the healthcare software model**: an infinitely variable, healthcare software is required to keep pace with a core of activities and not to "break" that model; some obvious examples would be:

  - **Incorrect diagnosis**: caused or made more likely potentially by healthcare software and data not having integrity or becoming corrupted
  - **Lost or changed data**: healthcare data relating to a patient must be immutable; changes would potentially create a serious risk for the patient's treatment and liability for the medical practitioner
  - **Incorrect prescription**: again, healthcare data that is not accurate, accessible or trustworthy in the context of prescriptions might delay treatment or even potentially worsen a patient's experience and outcome.

General challenges:

- **Litigation risks**: healthcare software and data both play a part in medical practitioner litigation risk. Ensuring patient data has the right levels of access, transparency and can be trusted are central to the management of this risk. As we have discussed in other chapters of this book, ensuring the correct identity, reducing friction between processes and systems and

keeping an accurate and exact record of diagnoses and treatments are all important for healthcare systems and litigation risk management
- **Transparency requirements**: healthcare software and data is on the frontline of requirements for data access and controls over transparency, namely, who can see what patient data. The same is also true for pharmaceutical research and testing. Reliable transparency meets these requirements directly and thereby enables and enhances the trust of patient and practitioner engagement in healthcare software and data
- **Data portability needs**: in patient terms, "data portability" means ownership and control of an individual patient's data by the patient themselves. Healthcare data portability and ownership for patients and practitioners means that power and control over healthcare data now resides in the hands of individuals not systems, which, in itself drives far greater adoption and engagement.

Figure 10.1 shows how data is passed verbally from patient to GP and other healthcare professionals, and how disparate databases hinder the sharing of vital information.

10.1.4 The Role of Blockchain in Healthcare

Blockchains – distributed ledgers – are already used in healthcare software and the wider healthcare industry for the purposes of clinical research; the capturing and auditing of medical qualifications; and for specialist record-keeping. Blockchain's

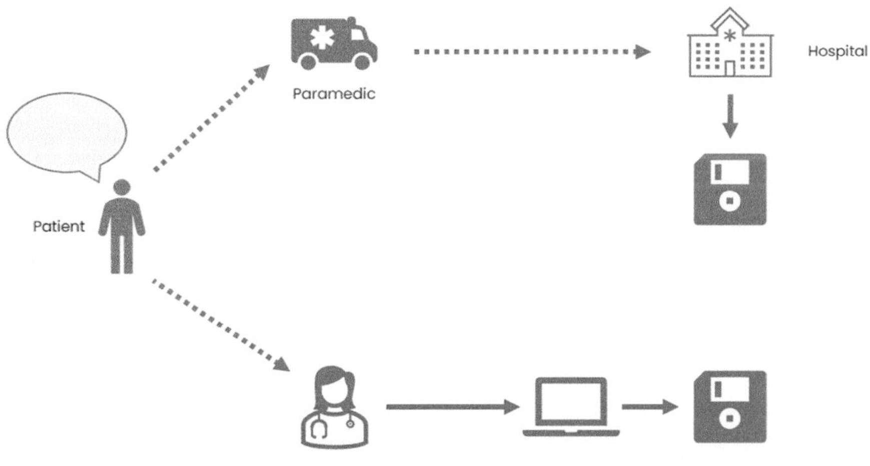

Figure 10.1 Healthcare before Tokenisation.

value compared to existing database and application stacks in healthcare lies in the efficiency it offers certain specialised healthcare functions through its attributes of trust, immutability, security, and access.

Tokenisation could transform healthcare software by addressing the three key pre-conditions for any potential adoption of distributed ledger technology that we have discussed in earlier chapters, for example:

- Can healthcare data be transparent?
- Do patients and practitioners need to trust healthcare data?
- Should there be equitable access to the healthcare data?

As we have discovered in earlier chapters, distributed ledgers offer transparency, immutability, access, and decentralisation, creating conditions for greater efficiency, improved operational processing, fewer integration requirements and reduced error rates.

And tokens in healthcare software have a potentially beneficial purpose in the ways set out in detail in Part 1 of this book. Tokens are deployed on blockchains, and rely on smart contracts, distributed data, distributed applications, on-chain and off-chain data, trustworthy identity and network interoperability. We'll discuss these later in more detail at the end of this chapter.

10.1.5 Healthcare Comparison

The current healthcare software model involves various enterprise systems and legal entities, each deployed via their own software systems, applications, integrations and operating models, often creating a silo of data and functionality. Each of these silos must be maintained, upgraded, added to, edited, archived, secured, and potentially reconciled with all other entities and parts of a highly fragmented healthcare software infrastructure.

Compare that to a blockchain-enabled future state for healthcare. In a distributed ledger infrastructure, healthcare data would be updated synchronously for all parties at all stages and statuses. This would make information about healthcare in any part of the patient or practitioner diagnosis and treatment lifecycle transparent, synchronous, immutable, and fully reconciled.

So blockchain brings potential key benefits to healthcare software and data, adding trust, equitable access, and transparency to existing medical and research records.

Figure 10.2 shows how a shared database across the distributed ledger can help both the patient and a variety of healthcare professionals to see the most up to date version of the patient's critical health information.

Let's explore the differences between the current state of healthcare software and data versus a potential distributed-ledger future state by means of an illustration.

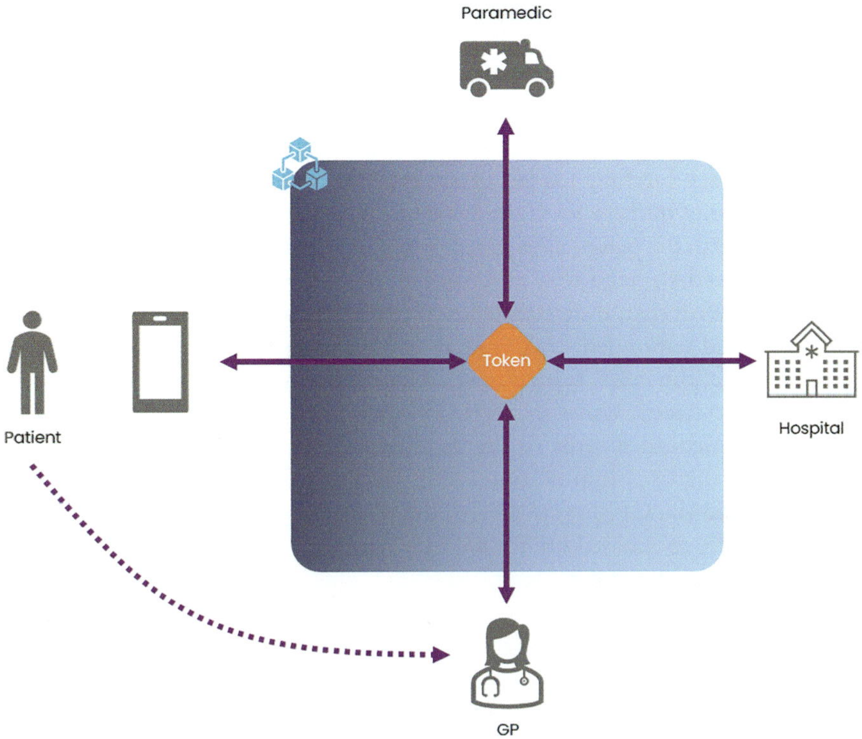

Figure 10.2 Healthcare Tokenised.

10.2 Healthcare Use Case

This chapter section illustrates how blockchain technology and tokenisation might be deployed as use cases – two real-world imagined scenarios. These examples demonstrate the practical benefits of blockchain in emergency care and preventative health management.

10.2.1 Emergency Care Transformation: From Traditional to Blockchain-Enabled

10.2.1.1 The Current State: Harry's Emergency

It was just past nine in the evening when Harry collapsed at a restaurant on Shaftesbury Avenue in London. Fellow diners watched anxiously as a staff member called emergency services. Within minutes, sirens announced the arrival of an ambulance.

The paramedics worked quickly, assessing Harry's condition while asking for his personal details. Harry, drifting in and out of consciousness, managed to indicate his NHS number was stored in his phone's ICE (In Case of Emergency) contact.

"We need to get him to University College Hospital immediately," one paramedic said. They carefully loaded Harry into the ambulance and raced through London's evening traffic toward the hospital's emergency department.

Upon arrival, the paramedics transferred Harry to the A&E team via a hurried professional (verbal) handover, promising to fill out and complete detailed paper reports later. With that, the paramedics rushed back to their ambulance, wrote up their notes, and responded straight away to another emergency call.

Meanwhile, the A&E team struggled to communicate with Harry, who was now barely conscious. Using the NHS number from his phone, they attempted to locate his medical records in the hospital's software and systems, but found only partially digitised information. With Harry's General Practice (GP) doctor unavailable and the GP surgery closed, the emergency team had to make critical decisions on the spot based on limited information.

"It looks like a cardiac arrest," the lead physician diagnosed. "Let's start treatment for that immediately."

Harry responded well to the emergency interventions and was eventually moved to a recovery ward alongside the A&E department for monitoring. Hours later, his worried family arrived from outside London, relieved to hear from the care team that Harry had a good chance of recovery thanks to the rapid response.

After two days of monitoring, Harry was discharged into his family's care. The hospital prepared two letters – one for Harry's GP and another for the hospital's outpatient department – to ensure continuity of care. This paper trail and email communication represented the fragmented information flow that characterised his treatment journey.

10.2.1.2 The Future State: Holly's Emergency

The scene at a Covent Garden theatre was similar when Holly suddenly felt crushing chest pain during an evening performance. A theatre attendant called the emergency services while others tried to keep Holly calm and comfortable.

When the paramedics arrived, Holly was conscious but clearly in distress. "Can I access your NHS app?" one paramedic asked her gently. Holly nodded, unlocking her phone and sharing access to her healthcare token on the NHS blockchain and wider systems.

Within seconds of her unlocking her healthcare token, Holly's complete medical history appeared on the paramedics' devices. "I see you've had a previous heart attack," one paramedic noted, immediately adjusting the emergency treatment approach. "Your blood type is AB negative, and you're allergic to some types of penicillin."

While administering initial treatment on the floor of the theatre, the paramedic team transmitted Holly's medical history and their real-time location to University College Hospital's A&E department with a single tap. At the hospital, the emergency team reviewed Holly's healthcare token software records on wider NHS systems and began preparing specifically for her arrival.

"Patient with previous cardiac history arriving in approximately seven minutes," the A&E coordinator announced. "Prepare the cardiac response unit and alert Dr. Matthews, who treated her last time."

When the ambulance arrived, there was no need for a lengthy verbal handover. The A&E team had already reviewed Holly's records, including the paramedics' in-transit treatment notes and vital signs, which had been continuously uploaded to the blockchain-based system.

"Holly, we're already familiar with your case," the attending physician reassured her. "We've contacted your cardiologist as well."

Simultaneously, Holly's family members received secure notifications about Holly (that didn't divulge personal information) through their own NHS apps, providing them with her location and a carefully edited status report that balanced privacy with essential information. "Mum's had another cardiac event but is stable and at UCLH," her daughter read to her father as they prepared to drive to London straightaway.

Throughout Holly's treatment, each intervention was recorded on the blockchain, creating an immutable record accessible to all authorised healthcare providers. When she was ready for discharge, her complete case history was updated on both blockchain (on-chain) and more traditional systems (off-chain) and thereby automatically shared with her GP and the outpatient clinic, ensuring seamless continuation of care.

The underlying hospital systems remained unchanged, but the blockchain-based tokenised patient records transformed the experience for everyone involved – providing faster, more personalised care for Holly while keeping her support network informed and enabling more efficient follow-up care.

10.2.2 Preventative Healthcare: The Power of Continuous Monitoring

The Current State: Paper-Based Prevention

Dr. Sharma's busy London practice was concerned about the rising number of lifestyle-related health issues among their patients. "We need to be more proactive," she told her colleagues during a staff meeting. "Treatment isn't enough; we need prevention."

The surgery launched a "Live Better" campaign, sending information to patients' homes with guidance on diet, exercise, and healthy habits. The practice used a combination of paper forms and basic spreadsheets to track patient participation and outcomes.

Initially, the results seemed promising. During the first six months, the practice observed fewer appointments related to preventable conditions and a slight decrease in certain prescriptions. However, as the year progressed, these improvements began to fade.

"The data suggests early improvement, but it's within our margin of error," Dr. Sharma explained to her team. "We'll need a more sustained approach over multiple months and years to determine if we're making a real difference."

The practice planned another, more intensive campaign for the following year, hoping that with enough data points they could better assess the effectiveness of their preventative health initiatives. But the disconnect between patient activities and medical records meant they were relying on delayed, fragmented information.

10.2.1.3 The Future State: Token-Based Prevention

When Dr. Sharma's practice decided to modernise their preventative health approach, they invited a cohort of patients to participate in a new blockchain-based healthcare token and monitoring program.

"Instead of just telling you what might help, we want to work with you to discover what actually does help," Dr. Sharma explained to the participant patients at the launch meeting. Each patient received a simple electronic blood pressure monitor and instructions for downloading the new NHS blockchain-enabled health app and minting their individual healthcare token.

James, a 50 year-old driving school instructor with borderline hypertension, was initially sceptical. "Another app to forget about," he thought. But the system's daily reminders were gentle yet persistent, and the interface made logging his diet, exercise, and vital signs remarkably simple.

"I just checked your readings from yesterday," Dr. Sharma told James during his next check-up. "I notice your blood pressure drops significantly on days when you walk more than 8,000 steps. That's valuable information we can use to customise your health plan."

The blockchain system and healthcare token allowed the practice to receive aggregated data about patients in real-time, enabling them to identify trends and adjust recommendations accordingly. When several patients showed improved readings after participating in morning (rather than evening) exercise, the app was updated to suggest this timing to others with similar profiles.

For participating patients, the app provided personalised insights based on their individual data combined with their medical history. "Your prescription for Simvastatin and your recent cholesterol readings suggest you might benefit from reducing your intake of refined carbohydrates," the app advised one patient, with a note that the suggestion had been reviewed by their GP and an update made on the patient's personalised healthcare token.

As the programme continued, word spread among patients about the benefits. "My app noticed I was having higher blood pressure readings on Mondays after weekend social events," explained Rita, a 62-year-old participant, to her friend in the waiting room. "It suggested spreading my social activities throughout the week, and it's actually made a difference"

The practice found that patients were more engaged in their health management when they could see the direct correlations between their behaviours and the health metrics saved on their healthcare token and in off-chain systems and databases. The transparency of the data (under each patient's control), combined with the security and privacy of the blockchain, created a foundation of trust in the information that encouraged continued patient participation.

What began as a limited trial evolved into a standard feature of the practice's care model, with more patients requesting to join and to own healthcare tokens as they saw the positive outcomes among their peers.

10.2.3 The Transformative Impact of Blockchain in Healthcare

Creating trust in healthcare data is a key benefit of distributed ledgers and tokenised data. The personalised healthcare tokens described in the scenarios above also mean that, alongside ownership of their own data, patients can start to understand their own health profile and behaviours – and how health is an individual responsibility, not just top-down care from a medical practitioner.

In Part 1 of this book we looked in great detail at some of the attributes and features of blockchains, or distributed ledgers. Let's consider healthcare in the context of these:

- Smart contracts could automate and personalise healthcare to a greater extent than is possible with currently available fragmented and siloed healthcare data. When "external" healthcare events or information triggers are experienced, such as changes to weight, diet or prescriptions, then personalised healthcare tokens and smart contracts can interact with other tokenised data, for example health or life insurance, prescriptions and so on in a trustworthy, transparent and equally accessible way rewarding "good" patient behaviour financially and enabling insurance and care providers to trust in the underlying data

- **Distributed data**: without the need for complex and expensive system and data integrations, distributed ledgers remove the requirement for healthcare systems to integrate different systems that are often using the same underlying patient data
- **Distributed application**: a healthcare dApp has some obvious and immediate potential benefits: a community of healthcare professional, practitioners, patients and pharmaceutical researchers might, for example, create a distributed application for statistical research into medical symptoms and treatments, where equal access, transparency and trust means that it's patients and practitioners who "own" their own data, rather than this being at arm's length inside commercial research projects
- **On-chain and off-chain data**: careful and ongoing consideration must be applied to define what's "on-chain" and what's not in the context of healthcare software and data. Public blockchains, as we have seen in earlier chapters, have different privacy features compared to private networks. The requirement for healthcare data is not always for total transparency, but ownership and control of data will be in the hands of the patient in a tokenised world, and that is an important benefit
- **Trustworthy identity**: at the heart of healthcare are us: individual human beings with our own identities. Proving, trusting, owning and controlling our identities in the healthcare context is mandatory; and a tokenised healthcare software and data solution will offer that in the form of encryption and control
- **Network interoperability**: if healthcare software and data were tokenised, it is highly likely that more than one blockchain network would be deployed as different token solutions are designed and launched in what is a busy and commercial global healthcare marketplace. Network interoperability will be a key consideration, therefore.

The scenario examples illustrate the possible and likely benefits blockchain technology can bring to healthcare software and data as explained below.

For medical practitioners, distributed ledgers can enhance the foundation of trust in the doctor-patient relationship. Dr. Sharma found that patients were more forthcoming with information when they understood how the secure system protected their privacy and their ownership of their own healthcare data while providing better care outcomes.

For patients like Holly and James, blockchain creates a decentralised repository of immutable, transparent health data that follows them through every healthcare interaction, leading to more personalised and effective diagnoses and treatments.

For healthcare suppliers – hospitals, pharmaceutical companies, and research organisations – blockchain provides reliable, decentralised data that can be securely and accessibly shared across institutions while maintaining patient privacy, creating opportunities for better research and development.

10.3 How has Tokenisation been Applied?

For the healthcare industry as a whole, blockchain technology offers improved planning accuracy, data security, and transparency.

The comparison between current systems and blockchain-enabled futures reveals significant advantages in distributed ledgers versus existing infrastructures.

When healthcare information is fragmented across distributed systems, as in Harry's case, care delivery suffers from gaps that require time-consuming and potentially error-prone manual intervention. Blockchain's decentralised architecture enables healthcare software and data to interact more seamlessly, without the need for manual reconciliation and improving patient outcomes without replacing existing specialised medical systems.

Similarly, when clinical research relies on centralised, non-synchronous data collection methods, which are common in the current state of healthcare software and data, valuable patient or cohort insights may be delayed or missed entirely. Blockchain enables secure, equitable access to verified data, making clinical research more trustworthy and efficient.

These transformations aren't merely technological. Tokenisation represents fundamental potential improvements in how healthcare might be delivered, experienced, and measured. As these examples demonstrate, blockchain technology offers practical solutions to longstanding healthcare challenges, creating a future where medical information flows securely and efficiently to benefit everyone involved in the healthcare journey and where patients own and control their own data.

Software and data for healthcare is vital for our wellbeing as people but also prone to creating an artificial and unwanted barrier between medical practitioners and their patients. It has also become, in some cases, monolithic and difficult to innovate in healthcare technology.

Distributed ledger technology, or blockchains, offer a less intensive route to cutting the size and "siloisation" of healthcare technology, software and data without "throwing the baby out with the bathwater", namely, allowing us to keep the benefits.

Careful assessment of current healthcare software and data will mean that gradual change can take place avoiding putting at risk those who most need good healthcare: us.

We have looked carefully throughout this chapter at how tokens and tokenisation might fit into the global multi-trillion dollar healthcare industry.

In simple terms, the following are benefits that tokenisation might bring to healthcare:

- Ownership and control of medical data at patient level, rather than in hospitals, doctors' surgeries or insurance companies as is the case today
- Programmability of medical information and outcome suggestions via smart contracts
- Process-level automation that might track prescriptions, treatments and care
- Less friction, latency, cost, complexity for healthcare providers, meaning a far greater return on investment than current healthcare software and data infrastructure.

10.4 Legal Considerations for Healthcare and Tokenisation

The healthcare industry is centred around a wealth of sensitive personal data, including names, medical history, and payment information. As a result, institutions such as research labs and hospitals have been faced with the threat of ransomware attacks. The attacks cause disruption to the daily operations of the hospitals, but they also threaten the security of patient data. Tokenisation could offer a secure solution to this risk for medical institutions. The sensitive patient data is replaced by unique, non-sensitive tokens, which authorised systems can track back to the sensitive data. This would ensure that even if the data was intercepted, it would remain meaningless without the correct access or decryption.

Data in the healthcare industry is governed by the General Data Protection Regulation (GDPR), which sets the rules for the processing and use of personal and sensitive data. GDPR regulates the transparency required around the use and retention of personal data, purpose limitation for the use of such data and the necessity for security and confidentiality for personal and sensitive data. Medical researchers often rely on medical data for their work and therefore must be compliant with GDPR. Tokenisation of sensitive data provides for a high level of data security, greatly reducing the risk of data breaches and associated penalties.

An example of pioneering this technology in the healthcare industry can be seen in the LexisNexis® Gravitas® smart contract-powered token. The use case highlighted by this example of tokenisation is the need for the use of Real-World Assets (RWA) data in medical research as this leads to more accurate results. The risk of using RWA for research is that use of personal data is highly regulated due to its sensitive nature. Using de-identification technology and encryption, medical records are anonymised to a standard compliant with GDPR so that RWA can be utilised by researchers without risk to patient privacy. Tokenisation can therefore be used to facilitate a greater level of research into medicines, treatments and patient behaviours, leading to more accurate results.

The healthcare industry can greatly benefit from the data privacy and security enhancements that tokenisation can provide. The necessity for regulatory compliance and the threat of cyberattacks have been a catalyst for the emergency of new use cases and pilot programs for tokenisation in healthcare. Of course, due to the level of sensitivity in this area, it will be essential that all new technologies are tried, tested and reliable before they are implemented.

Chapter 11

Wealth and Fund Management

The management (and growth) of investor wealth comes in a number of guises, each with its own label. Private banking, wealth management, fund management, financial advice, retail savings and investments: all perform the same broad function, namely the buying, holding and selling of financial instruments on behalf of the retail investor. These investments are usually held in an electronic portfolio in the form of a portfolio register or database. Consumers usually have access to financial and investment advice and portfolio management services as part of their wealth management service. Wealth management, fund management and retail investments together form a global industry with some c.US$ 145 trillion in "assets under management" or AUM, as at the time of writing.

Fund management is the business of mutual funds. Mutual funds are a primary investment instrument in the financial advice industry and in retail savings and investing. The advent of mutual funds some 100+ years ago enabled ordinary consumers, many with limited wealth, to be able to access fractionally a regulated, professionally managed portfolio of underlying fixed income bonds, stocks and shares, commodities and more complex derivative-type instruments that were previously inaccessible to them due to ticket size, access to markets and so on. Mutual funds have become very commonplace and popular since their creation

DOI: 10.4324/9781003571421-13

and there have been further evolutionary steps since the creation of the industry too, such as Exchange-Traded Funds (ETF).

Mutual funds are legally established and regulated retail investment entities created to buy, sell, and administer portfolios of third-party underlying investments. Funds vary in style (closed-ended, open-ended, exchange traded, private equity, alternatives, hedge (long/short) funds and so on) and may be managed on a passive or active basis. Each fund has different objectives, specialising in different markets or investment approaches.

Understanding retail savings and investments and fund management is central to gaining knowledge of how the wealth and financial advice industry operates worldwide. The industry has strict rules of governance, price controls, and obligations on the professionals working in it such as "Know Your Client" (KYC) and Anti-Money Laundering (AML) procedures.

Wealth manager, financial advice and fund management fees for professional and administration services provided in the wealth industry and the fund management sector in the course of lengthy (sometime over decades) advisory engagements have a significant impact on investment performance. Studies have shown that high fees (1.5%, or 150 basis points) substantially reduce the overall size and performance of a retail savings and investments portfolio over long periods.

This chapter will look at how the wealth and fund management industries work today and how blockchain and tokenisation could improve them in the future.

11.1 Wealth and Fund Management Overview

The software and data used to power the wealth management and fund management industries has evolved since the early days of informal financial advice and investment records on written ledgers with paper and ink and then spreadsheets, but it is true to say that wealth management, financial advice and fund management remain relatively technologically conservative to this day. And for good reason: advice is personal and based on trust. Investment performance is unpredictable and although all practitioners would acknowledge the useful and important role played by technology, it cannot get in the way of trusted and long-standing professional relationships, skill and experience.

Early wealth management and fund management industry systems partially automated these manual processes but maintained traditional approaches. The industry's slow pace of change over time is due to the ingrained incumbency of reliable (if less than modern) technology, layered fee structures, the costs of risks of migrating data, consumers and instruments between systems and databases and the challenge of handling sometimes complex consumer circumstances and requirements and their associated investments at different technology levels.

The core technology "stack" of the wealth and fund management industry practitioner includes:

- **The front-end user experience layer (app and website)**: where consumers and their financial advisers or wealth managers can log on and access advice, customer relationship management and investment data in a single online location
- **The portfolio and cash administration layer**: where the "nuts and bolts" of a wealth management (retail savings and investments) portfolio and the transactions associated with that, like buying and selling and settlement, are reconciled and safely logged
- **The nominee, depository and custody layer**: where the administration, storage, ownership and safe custody of retail savings and investments are managed. In the case of fiat cash, for example, the safe custody is a regulated bank account and in the case of securities and investment instruments that make up the underlying components of a mutual fund, these are with a specialist custodian bank or depository
- **The brokerage, trading, market and counterparty infrastructure**: where there is a marketplace for the buying, selling, settlement and reconciliation of the underlying instruments in the retail savings and investments industry
- **The fund accountant, transfer agent, asset servicing and fund administration layer**: where the fund manager runs and operates their mutual fund and where processes such as the daily pricing (net asset value, or NAV), unit or share creation and dissolution, corporate actions relating to the fund and other specific actions take place.

The future of technology in the wealth and fund management industries looks somewhat different. The same demand for advice and supply of professional services for advice and investment performance ("alpha") will continue as it is – human beings change little in our habits and customs – but the way that wealth management advice is created and distributed will change to address the more cumbersome, frictional and costly elements by using better technology – in this case, blockchains and tokenisation.

Because of the cost savings available, tokenisation and blockchains provide an almost perfect use case for lowering consumer and adviser costs of, and access to, wealth management and financial advice technology and services. The truth is that many of the repetitive, low value but mandatory (from a regulatory perspective) activities that wealth managers and financial advisers carry out could be done with greater access, transparency and trust in a distributed ledger. The benefits of immutability, trust, and equitable access mean that financial advice is likely to grow in size and scale.

11.1.1 Retail Savings and Investments Policy and Challenges

The primary driver for retail savings and investments policy is the well-reported "advice gap" which stands for the minimum amount of liquid investible cash and assets required for a consumer to "qualify" for quality financial advice, given that most wealth managers and financial advisers charge their fees by means of an ad valorem percentage charge deducted from their clients' assets undermanagement.

The minimum required varies from adviser to marketplace, but as a general rule of thumb it is usually around the $100,000/size.

Government policy on financial advice, in particular, and wealth management in general is that, like health advice, it is of great benefit to both individuals and whole cohorts of the population. Happy voters are an outcome sought on all sides of the political street. So, closing the advice gap (meaning lowering the barriers to accessing quality and personalised financial advice) is a key government policy in all parts of the developed world.

How to do that, however, is another question altogether. In this chapter we'll explore the capacity of tokenisation and blockchains to lower the access point by materially lowering costs, friction, latency and complexity.

11.1.2 Key Entities and Actors

In the real world, retail savings and investments operate through a mixture of mechanical and human processes and operations. Professional staff known as wealth managers or Independent Financial Advisers (IFAs) or RIAs in the USA manage portfolios for a fee. Typical activities include:

- **Investor onboarding (KYC, AML, risk assessment)**: where new and existing consumers ("clients") are checked for identities, authorisations, powers of attorney, suitability and so on initially at onboarding and thereafter annually for regulatory reasons
- **Portfolio construction (setting up, buying/selling, cash management)**: where new and existing clients have a personalised and/or risk-assessed portfolio created and administered for them

- **Portfolio maintenance (administration, settlement, reconciliations)**: the complicated and important exercise of maintaining portfolio asset allocation and risk-rating and reconciling transactions and errors, and so forth
- **Investor maintenance (handling life events, beneficiary maintenance)**: the process whereby investors have their "life events" (such as marriage and divorce/separation, bereavement, and the like), managed by their financial adviser and wealth manager. These can be complicated areas where each case is a bespoke solution as ordered by third parties such as a court order.

Many retail savings and investment managers offer "delegated" services where investors grant power of attorney over their investments. In these arrangements, advisers charge higher fees for the additional work and risk.
The retail investments value chain involves multiple actors:

- **The Investor**: the natural person (or persons, in the case of couples or families) who owns the underlying investments and cash
- **The Adviser**: a natural and/or legal person professionally qualified individual or automated service that collects personal data on consumers and – using an approved mechanism – provides specific financial and sometimes also tax advice in retail savings and investments
- **The Portfolio Manager**: a technical role managing investment distribution and the construction, maintenance and performance of a portfolio of retail savings and investments
- **The Investment Manager**: specialising in specific investment requirements such as the design and construction of a portfolio and how that performs, administered against a benchmark or other scale of measurement.

11.1.3 Retail Savings and Investment Types and Models

The retail savings and investments value chain is complex, often full of manual and cumbersome processes, subject to friction, cost, complexity and latency. Wealth managers and financial advisers commit and invest considerable resources to setting up and operating technology platforms for the administration of consumers and investments that are often expensive and cumbersome and difficult to keep up to date.

There are some standard types and models in the wealth management industry and these are usually defined by the type of wealth manager or financial advisory firm involved in giving the advice. Some typical examples of wealth management and financial advisory firms are:

- **Paraplanners**: qualified, professional individuals and firms who can assist consumers with advice and planning about their financial investments, lifestyle goals and outcomes sought as well as giving advice on retails savings and investments in a tax-efficient way over the medium to long term
- **Independent Financial Adviser (IFA) or Regulated Investment Advisor (RIA)**: usually independent or self-employed, these are small to medium-sized firms of financial advisers who give consumers a range of advice from tax-deferred/tax-efficient retail savings and investment accounts to life insurance and pensions
- **Discretionary Fund Managers (DFMs)**: highly qualified advisers who can assist on a full decisions-making basis with their clients' long-term portfolio requirements, usually involving the control of clients' savings and investments and making all investment and portfolio allocation decisions on their behalf
- **Networks/nationals (in the UK) and TAMPs in the USA**: these are collaborations of advisers with a transversal operations infrastructure that take care of cash management, regulatory alignment and reporting, insurance and, in some instances, also branding and digital services too
- **Wealth Managers**: the distinction between a high-end financial adviser and a "wealth manager" is often not easily identifiable, but wealth management (as a phrase) is often appealing and appropriate for a certain cohort of retail savings and investment customers, who seek to preserve their wealth from tax, disputes and investment downsides and will pay for the privilege
- **Private Banks**: usually reserved for the very wealthy, private banks offer wealth management and advisory services to those with often millions of dollars, pounds and euros to save and invest. The quality of their professional advice is usually very high as are their fees compared to other professional financial advice services
- **Family Offices:** when a family becomes wealthy it can often make sense for a "family office", dedicated financial advice and wealth management adviser(s), to be created to look after inter-generational and often international matters on their behalf.

In terms of what underpins the types and models in the wealth and fund management industries, the following "stack" or orchestration of data and applications applies:

- **UX layer**: where wealth managers differentiate their offerings by providing a compelling and useful digital website or app for consumers and advisors to service their advice needs and portfolio requirements

- **Individual account and advice layer**: managing personal wealth management accounts and recording and assessing financial advice given to consumers taking place within the account and advice components
- **Portfolio administration layer**: in terms of wealth management, offering an integrated portfolio setup, maintenance and administration layer is a crucial part of the wealth management service. This is a technical area that focuses on transactions, performance and investment capability
- **Nominee layer**: in wealth management, in certain jurisdictions, the legal ownership of funds, exchange-traded instruments and cash is arranged through the use of nominees, non-trading private limited liability companies that exist to pool or segregate consumer holdings. These are historical arrangements for wealth holdings, and exist to eliminate friction for individual consumers' holdings
- **Custody layer**: in the wealth management industry, a custodian is a regulated function set out and defined in the fund manager's prospectus where the safekeeping of investments is arranged and managed. Cash is custodied in regulated deposit-taking bank accounts. Exchange-traded instruments (fixed income, exchange-traded funds, investment trusts and stocks and shares) are custodied with a custodian bank or provider
- **Depository layer**: part of the infrastructure of the wealth and fund management industries, a depository (for example, a Central Securities Depository, or CSD) is a ledger and store of investment instruments and information
- **Cash layer**: consumer fiat cash, or "client money", in the wealth industry, is managed separately to both the cash of the wealth manager and the corporate cash of the fund manager. In wealth management, client money is cash on deposit, cash for investments and cash that is generated by investments ("natural income"). In fund management, mutual funds have their own cash allocations and also hold and transfer cash for the purposes of investment transactions
- **Transaction/counterparty layer**: this is the part of the wealth and fund management infrastructure that deals with transactions for the buying and selling of investments.

Figure 11.1 shows how the chain of data stretches from the end investor to the custody or fund accounting layer for their holdings. Each link in the chain must be rigorously reconciled on a (usually) daily basis to meet regulatory requirements designed to protect the end investor. Although it looks complex, this is in fact a simplified and idealised representation – in reality there can be even more layers and actors involved.

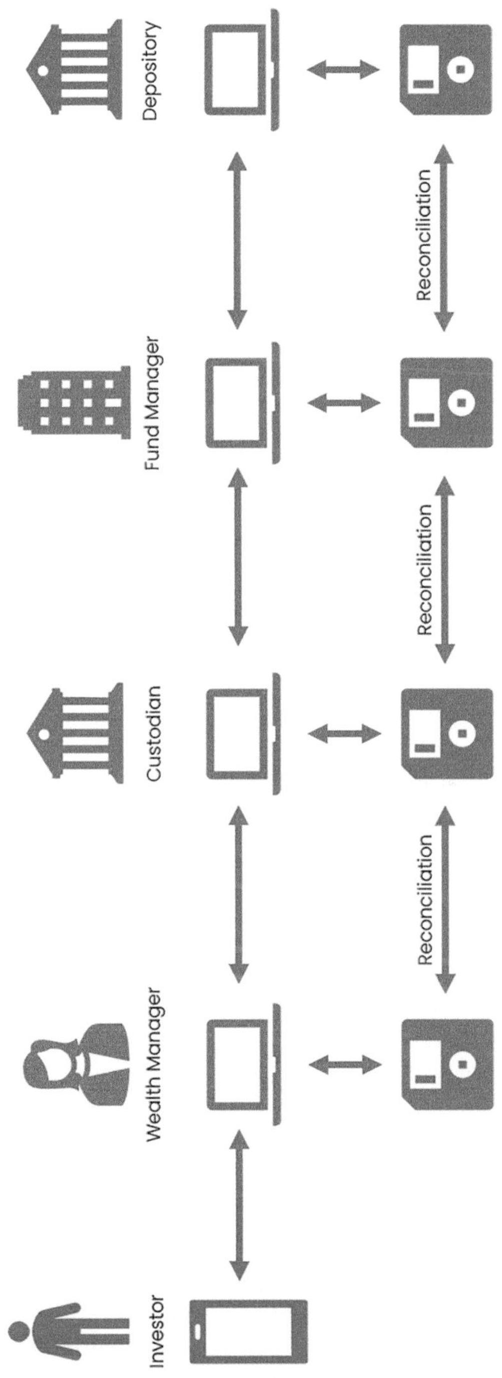

Figure 11.1 Wealth before Tokenisation.

11.1.4 Challenges in Wealth and Fund Management

The industry faces challenges from specialised trends like the rise of algorithmic trading, which is common in corporate banking but less so in wealth and fund management due to latency in legacy systems. Similarly, predictive analysis, AI, and automated advice have potential but face obstacles when interoperating with the complex legacy systems alive and kicking in the wealth and fund management industries.

At a lower level of detail, the wealth and fund management industries experience daily issues with reconciliation breaks usually involving cash (unreconciled client money positions), stock breaks from unreconciled security positions, and the cumbersome and frictional resolutions required to reverse erroneous transactions, which often have consequential dependencies requiring reassessment of portfolios.

More general challenges in the wealth and fund management industries include system speed and latency limitations, entrenched or incumbent infrastructure that is often resistant to change, and the limited portability of data and solutions between providers.

The retail investments industry stands at a technological crossroads, with blockchain offering a path to greater efficiency, transparency, and reduced costs for investors.

11.2 Role of Blockchain in Wealth and Fund Management

The wealth and fund management industries represent an excellent use case for a tokenisation solution. The core attributes of distributed ledger technology – providing trust, access, security, and immutability – will drive efficiency, reduce errors, and improve transparency, all but eliminating the need for reconciliation between multiple databases (very much the bane of operational managers throughout the financial industry).

The multiple databases of the typical mutual fund stack can be replaced with a single decentralised database, with access granted to the fund manager, the wealth manager and even, potentially, the end investor.

Revisiting our three standard tests for blockchain and token relevance for the wealth and fund management industry, we can see:

- **Transparency**: all parties can see the current state of all holdings, ensuring their systems are aligned
- **Requirement for trust:** mutual funds are exchanged and held for vast sums of money: trust is critical

- **Equitable access**: although the fund manager will want to retain control of the distribution of the fund units themselves, all parties need to be able to see and influence those positions through trading interfaces.

Figure 11.2 shows the same mutual funds ownership represented as a tokenised fund. All parties can see the fund at all times, obviating the need for separate reconciliation processes.

11.2.1 Benefits for consumers

Distributed ledger technology enhances trust in the wealth manager-consumer relationship through the removal of friction and by improving trust, which is the major single determinant factor in the success of any advice relationship.

Cost is a barrier to access for many consumers. Historically the wealth and fund management industry, although working hard to reduce costs, has struggled

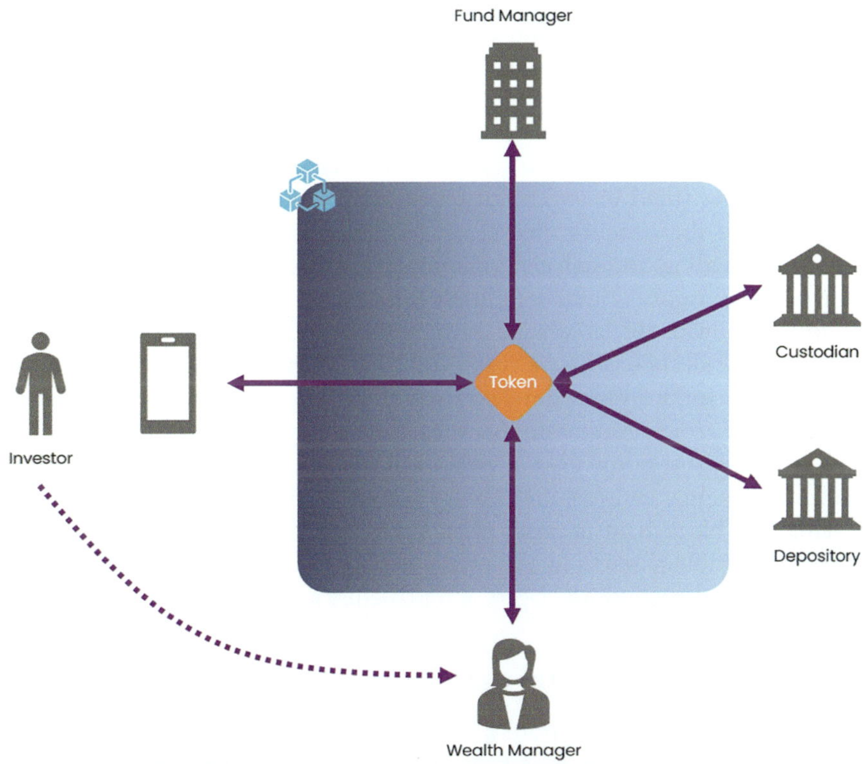

Figure 11.2 Wealth Tokenised.

with cumbersome technology infrastructure, manual processes and incumbent systems and interests. Tokenisation will ultimately result in faster and better wealth and fund management service delivery. Fewer reconciliations (and the associated costs of resolving breaks) will lead to reduced fees for transactions and account management. This reduced cost to serve can be passed on to the consumer, leading to improved investment performance.

Furthermore, with more accurate (client-owned) data at their fingertips, the wealth manager will be able to provide more suitable investment recommendations to the client.

And with their assets held on the blockchain, it is conceivable that the consumer (through a non-branded app on their phone) is able to view their holdings directly rather than needing to always ask the wealth manager for a valuation.

Personalisation, ownership and access – these three features of a tokenised wealth and fund management industry are compelling attractions for consumers.

11.2.2 Cost advantages for wealth managers

Trustworthy wealth management, advice and personal data on distributed ledgers (versus the current technology stack) would considerably reduce wealth managers' back office and operational expenses.

Daily reconciliation of balances and transactions (mandated by the regulatory body in most markets) is a significant overhead to the operations of all involved parties (fund managers, custodians and wealth managers). The task is greater due to the complex lifecycle of most investment transactions (starting from initial trading, through the pricing point applied by the fund manager to settlement against cash, often in multiple legs), meaning that not all the databases are up to date with the latest state of the transaction. A distributed ledger is, in effect, offering all those who use it the same data at the same time. Everyone can instantly agree on the transaction's state and there is nothing to reconcile when all parties see the same information that they agree is correct.

Fewer data and reconciliation errors will in turn lead to a decreased risk of regulatory penalties and customer compensation payments.

Finally, a blockchain network offers direct access to the data held on it to its users. Technology stacks like the types outlined earlier in this chapter are not required, reducing wealth managers' infrastructure costs significantly.

11.2.3 Benefits for fund managers

Fund managers will benefit from a streamlined supply chain with fewer intermediaries. Many fund managers have become disintermediated from their own consumers and distributors (wealth managers) over time as the complexity of the wealth industry infrastructure proliferated. A distributed ledger means that fund managers, if desired, can have a "re-intermediated" relationship with consumers and wealth managers, cutting out intermediaries like platforms, depositories, nominees and so on

As for wealth managers, the fund management industry will always look for reduced compliance overheads (subject to regulatory approval) and less operational complexity.

With every technological innovation of the past (telephone, fax, email, internet and apps), fund managers have adopted the tech to widen and broaden their distribution capability. Tokenisation, and public blockchains in particular, will be the same: more funds sold to more people than before, providing the ability to focus resources on value-added services rather than administration.

Fund managers will benefit from enhanced data security and reduced fraud risk through cryptographically sealed tokens representing both securities and the personal data of consumers which offer uncrackable and unhackable stores of information.

Drivers that make tokenisation using distributed ledgers an industry-wide advantage are:

- **Improved planning accuracy through better data quality**: distributed ledgers are accurate all of the time – as all of the users of it agree, by definition. Therefore, there are fewer errors and activities required to maintain accuracy, and equally importantly, the data that is on a blockchain can be relied upon for planning
- **Greater transparency across all transactions**: wealth management consumers' priorities are almost always about preserving wealth, rather than injecting risk to increase it. By definition, distributed ledgers provide far great transparency for consumers, wealth managers and fund managers alike, and where there is transparency there is trust
- **Enhanced security of sensitive financial information**: tokens are owned by their issuers. In the case of wealth managers, this enhances security means enhanced ownership – and greater engagement with wealth management advice and outcomes
- **Potential for broader access to quality financial advice**: above all, where there is less friction in the wealth and fund management industries, there is lower cost to its participants: providers such as wealth and fund managers; and consumers. Lower cost also lowers barriers to entry, and the overall growth of the industries too.

11.2.1 The Transformation Challenge

The wealth and fund management industry faces significant challenges in adopting blockchain technology despite its clear benefits:

- **Incumbency resistance**: established firms face potential revenue disruption and cultural resistance to fundamental operational changes
- **Technology transition**: most wealth and fund managers currently use legacy systems developed incrementally over decades rather than purpose-built solutions
- **Opportunity for innovation**: the wealth management sector is primed for a technological "species jump" that could eliminate inefficient processes and free advisors to focus on service quality
- **Customer experience**: by reducing administrative complexity, both advisors and clients can concentrate on improved investment outcomes and relationship management.

Through these realistic scenarios, we can see how blockchain technology offers more than incremental improvements to the wealth and fund management industry. Tokenisation presents an opportunity to reimagine the entire issuance, distribution and financial advisory model, creating more efficient, transparent, and accessible financial services for a broader range of consumers while maintaining the essential human elements of quality financial advice.

11.2.2 Case Study: Some Practical Aspects of Mutual Fund Tokenisation

Co-authored with Igor Natanzon.

11.2.2.1 Maturity

One of the core issues that challenge adoption of blockchain technology in legacy financial institutions such as wealth and fund managers is a lack of technical and business maturity of their respective ecosystems. The importance of adherence to regulatory and internal compliance, funding and monetary policy, separation of duties, and other best practices adopted by financial firms in the wealth and fund management industries over the past few decades creates obstacles to blockchain integration and tokenisation adoption. The barriers to adoption are not unsurmountable, but they do require a different approach to be taken.

11.2.2.2 Testing

Testing of distributed applications – especially distributed financial applications – brings new issues to an already complex endeavour. Here, we look at three such issues:

- The need for test money to execute test transactions
- The transparency of test blockchains
- Testnet resets.

Testing of fund management blockchain activity on a public test blockchain requires test money to power the transactions (gas). Thorough testing, which includes stress tests of internal frameworks, requires a lot of test money. Unfortunately, the majority of publicly accessible test coin sources for use on blockchain ("faucets") make this a difficult process. Most faucets that might be adopted by the fund management industry for the provision of test money require either community contributions (requested through social media) or an equivalent amount of "real" cash at the related live network ("mainnet") for the test network.

Using social media to initiate a request may work for a startup or an individual, but established financial institutions invariably have social media policies preventing the use of such strategies. And while it is possible for project team members to take it upon themselves to request test tokens from a public blockchain network, not all are active on social media, do not have nor do they want to have accounts there. Plus, acting on social media for work-related activity may still breach social media policies placed on employees.

Requiring real cash at the equivalent mainnet wallet address creates its own challenges. For example the fact that test wallets on blockchain networks are, by design, (or should be) easily discardable, so having to constantly provide cash for new test wallets on the related mainnet is impractical, often time consuming, and may end up being cost prohibitive if live tokens increase in price.

An alternative approach might be to make private funding requests directly to a public blockchain's governing body or technical team. This approach is considerably more practical for established institutions to utilise, but is not always available as an option depending on the network.

Transparency of testnets may also be an issue for the testing organisation.

Constant, repeated testing of tokenised fund management transactions on public blockchains may create additional concerns as this may expose an ongoing project to outside sources before an individual fund management or fund infrastructure company is ready to make the fact of the project public. There are several ways to mitigate this risk:

- **Obfuscate**: as much as reasonably possible, the testing organisation could obscure any data that is being stored on-chain, to make it hard or impossible to identify the nature of the project until the fund manager is ready to make it public

- **Run testing on a custom/private blockchain**: this is a reasonable strategy for fund managers looking to experiment in tokenisation and blockchains as it alleviates need for test tokens, a need for anonymity, and allows for more consistent stress testing (since it eliminates external factors such as network load). But this approach is not without drawbacks. It requires additional infrastructure resources to run the private blockchain, increasing the costs of the project and possibly extending its timelines. It may also make testing less accurate as it avoids public blockchain considerations, such as block closing times and possible network overload. It also prevents testing with partners and other external entities.

From experience, a blended approach of the above (obfuscation and privacy) may be the most ideal. When possible, running a private blockchain at the start of a fund manager's tokenisation project will allow for more reliable stress testing of internal infrastructure, services, and components, while keeping the project largely out of the public eye. But at some point, the tokenisation team must switch to a public blockchain, to test more realistic scenarios, and to perform proper integration testing.

Some blockchains such as Stellar and XRP, perform a reset of their testnet environments, either on a fixed schedule, or ad-hoc. These resets are important as they reduce the cost of maintaining such a test environment, but this has an impact on fund managers running experimental tokenisation projects, as test data is periodically erased. A project team then has to adapt to such networks by the following means, for example:

- Preserve private keys of test accounts to allow them to be recreated post-reset (if needed).
- Create scripts that snapshot blockchain data (accounts, balances, etc), then use stored data during recovery to recreate the test environment. While transaction history would be lost, state data will be available for continued testing.

This scenario can also be avoided by using private blockchains, with the various benefits and drawbacks as mentioned above.

Also problematic for the purposes of testing is the requirement of having to identify a private key owner and storing/securing this key for completely unnecessary wallets increases burden on the project team.

11.2.2.3 Spam

On blockchain networks that fund managers and others can use for tokenisation projects, spam appears in multiple ways.

Often it takes the form of a low-cost transfer sent to the customer's wallet address, usually with some advertising text. And sometimes this spam consists of a custom token or asset, whose asset code/description itself carries information in it.

Effectively dealing with spam is a challenge for everyone operating on-chain, but it is even more important for traditional financial firms such as wealth and fund managers, which may want to distance themselves from it. Some of the issues that may arise from spam in wealth and fund management tokenisation projects are:

- Public perception of the fund or wealth manager, especially if the wallets managed by the manager are full of spam assets
- Issues with transaction audit and reporting, requiring means of filtering out such assets from various reports.

Unfortunately, dealing with spam in a tokenisation project is tricky, due to volume and identification issues. The best fund managers can do is create rules for identifying spam assets and building filters to prevent them from being included in reports and data analytics.

Blockchain networks have struggled in dealing with spam, due to their decentralised nature and disagreement in how to approach the issue, so this is unlikely to be solved any time soon.

11.3 Retail Savings and Investments Use Cases

Aside from the challenges facing fund managers described above, which at a practical level restrict or generally reduce the accessibility of tokenisation experimentation for fund managers in particular, blockchain technology and tokenisation can revolutionise wealth and fund management through the following two illustrative scenarios, both of which highlight potential improvements in efficiency, cost, and quality of investment advice.

11.3.1 Streamlining Peter's Portfolio Consolidation

11.3.1.1 Current Ways of Working

Peter, a client of St Paul's Investment Advisors (SPIA) in London, decides to consolidate his investment accounts from three different providers (two UK-based and one Swiss). The current process is fraught with inefficiencies.

Each provider follows different procedures based on their terms and national regulations. Peter must provide separate written confirmations to two of the providers. The portfolios exist on entirely different platforms with various custody arrangements across multiple currencies. When SPIA receives the transferred assets, they must reconcile all transaction histories, risk profiles, and open positions into Peter's new consolidated account.

This process takes several weeks, results in cash and stock discrepancies requiring additional resolution work, and ultimately leads to significant transfer fees being charged to Peter from all parties involved.

11.3.1.2 Tokenisation and Blockchain-enabled Solution

In the blockchain-based scenario, Peter's experience is dramatically improved.

All of Peter's investments are tokenised, with each provider (including SPIA) using compatible blockchain databases to manage client portfolios. SPIA's system uses smart contracts to identify Peter's wallets with former providers, requiring only his app-based approval. The "transfer" becomes a simple wallet re-registration process that happens immediately without discrepancies. Peter can instantly see all his assets in the SPIA app and approve the consolidated positions.

This blockchain approach eliminates transfer fees entirely while providing perfect accuracy and security. SPIA can then gradually align Peter's holdings with their recommended portfolio construction over time, charging only their standard management fees.

11.3.2 Aggregating Wealth and Fund Tokens with Tokenbridge

11.3.2.1 Current Wealth and Fund Distribution

Today, Natasha, a career accountant and a busy consumer living in St Paul, Minnesota, employs the services of a local wealth manager, a member of a national network of US-based financial advisory firms, to give her financial and planning advice on her inherited wealth of approximately $5m.

Natasha is a single mom to two children with her ex-partner and her primary instruction to her wealth manager is to preserve her wealth for her own income needs during her lifetime (as a middle-aged person, Natasha will likely live a long time yet) but also to ensure the needs and income of her kids, as her inheritors, are also met in the future.

Natasha owns a portfolio of stocks, bonds, commodities (like gold), exchange-traded funds and mutual funds that her wealth manager selects and maintains for her on her behalf for an annual fee of 1% (100 basis points).

Each year, Natahsa's wealth manager asks her to reconfirm her preferences, attitudes to risk, authorisation for the wealth manager to act on her behalf and to carry out, periodically, checks such as "Know Your Customer" (KYC), anti-money laundering and so on. Whilst not especially onerous, Natasha finds these processes frustrating and bureaucratic and they do not always result in the most personalised outcome for her investments and the performance of these in any case.

11.3.2.2 Tokenised Wealth and Advice: Natasha gets Ownership

Just before her wealth manager's next scheduled annual review, Natasha receives an email saying that things are changing in the way that her wealth manager will run their service going forwards. Natahsa is offered the change by her wealth manager with the stated aim to get better quality advice, more personalisation of her investment portfolio and lower costs if she agrees to take the new version of the wealth manager's app.

Curious, and instinctively drawn to anything that reduces the considerable cost of the wealth management service as well as increasing personalisation and hopefully better investment performance, Natasha agrees.

The next day she notices the wealth manager's app that she has on her phone shows an alert to advise here that there is an update available. Without any interruption save for an app update approval, Natahsa accepts the update and opens the newly refreshed app.

It's hard to determine what has changed at first glance, except that several of the mutual funds and exchange-traded instruments she previously owned in her portfolio are now represented as "tokens". Also, what was before a repetitive task for her and her wealth manager to update her personal data now has become far easier and done just once – by Natasha herself – and then stored as her own personal tokens.

Over time, Natasha realises that a significant change has in fact occurred, where her investments and wealth have become cheaper to own and transact on and that most of her personal data relating to her finances are now owned and controlled by Natasha herself, directly.

Natasha's wealth manager's app is powered by a new type of wealth and fund management technology company – Tokenbridge. Like other services, for example Spotify and Uber, Tokenbridge provides software that works as an aggregator of wealth and fund management tokens, so that consumers like Natasha and her wealth manager can use one single token aggregation software service, like a token supermarket, to create a single view of each consumer's asset and personal data tokens that are issued by firms in the wealth and fund management industry.

11.4 How has Tokenisation been Applied

The fund management industry has been "token curious" for several years now, as at the time of writing. This isn't due to an inherent love of technology, nor is there a strong desire to upend decades of legacy technology and infrastructure for the sake of it. Fund managers are always interested in improving their bottom line and evidence from early tokenisation adopters shows material cost savings (60% and greater) in running basic mutual funds (for example, money market) on distributed ledger technology when compared with legacy systems.

Franklin Templeton, Wisdom Tree, Ondo, Blackrock, Janus Henderson, Aberdeen – some of the world's largest fund managers are already launched in the public domain with regulated mutual funds for institutional and retail consumers alike.

Tokenisation of other types of securities, such as government and corporate bonds, American Depository Receipts (ADRs), real estate bonds and more are also well on the way to tokenisation too. Cost is a primary driver, but the other attributes of tokenisation and blockchains such as equitable access, transparency and trust, score highly in issuers' motivations to tokenise.

The wealth management industry has lagged in the shift to tokenisation. Although consumers are asking for advice on cryptocurrency holdings such as BTC and ETH, there is less understanding and awareness of the cost-to-serve benefits of tokenising personal and wealth data such as KYC, letters of authority, Anti-Money Laundering (AML), powers of attorney and model portfolios.

Further adoption of tokenisation in the wealth and fund management industries will gather pace over the next few years. When more advanced features of tokenisation are adopted in these industries, such as programmability via smart contract, token ownership and product-level process-level automation the speed and penetration of tokenisation adoption will accelerate too.

11.5 Legal Considerations for Wealth Management

Tokenisation can be used to digitise traditional financial assets into blockchain based tokens. The asset is represented by the token which is maintained on a blockchain. This revolutionary approach to traditional assets is granting access to new markets and opportunities for investors. Not only this, but tokenisation offers the opportunity for global access and round the clock trading. It could also be utilised for improved transparency and compliance.

Tokenisation of commodities such as oil and gold can allow for fractionalised ownership which can allow for greater accessibility to new investors. Investing in a fraction of the asset allows for a new investor to pay only a fraction of the full price, creating new opportunities for investors to benefit. The same concept of tokenisation of commodities can be applied to tokenisation of property. Real estate is a common market for retail investors. If a property is tokenised, then fractional ownership is possible, which would expand market access to new participants. Other high-value investments such as private equity and infrastructure projects can also be tokenised. This fractionalisation of historically illiquid assets democratises access to high-value investments.

The challenges facing the tokenisation of assets include the legal foundation for the ownership of digital assets. The laws surrounding the definition of these assets are essential to provide clarity and comfort before ownership of digital assets becomes commonplace. The definition of digital assets in the UK is pioneering, and similar approaches are being taken in other jurisdictions, which is encouraging for the uptake of tokenisation. Legal clarity on the status of tokenised assets and the enforceability of smart contracts is critical to ensure investor confidence and market stability.

A further challenge is the regulatory landscape for tokenised assets. In the UK, the FCA has repeatedly shown a willingness to support tokenisation. This is evidenced in their approach to innovations in the market, but also through their exploration of the use of tokenisation to enhance data transparency and streamline regulatory reporting in fund management. The FCA has also participated in Project Guardian, alongside the Monetary Authority of Singapore. This program aims to explore cross-border tokenised fund transactions which would greatly enhance global market connectivity.

There is a myriad of exciting possibilities for tokenisation in fund management. It is poised to transform the fund management industry through the creation of new asset classes, reduction of barriers to entry for investors and improving liquidity. As tokenisation is adopted in the industry, the opportunities continue to grow. An investment ecosystem could be cultivated which holds client, unit and asset registers on blockchain platforms allowing for seamless transactions and greater transparency.

Chapter 12

Real Estate and Land Registry

Land registration describes the legal, court, procedural and financial systems by which matters concerning property or real estate ownership, possession or other rights in land can be recorded (usually via a national or local government agency or department) to provide evidence of title, to facilitate transactions and to prevent unlawful disposal. A cadastre is normally a parcel based, up-to-date land information system containing a record of interests in land including rights, restrictions and responsibilities.

Land registries and cadastres provide a secure and validated store of property and ownership data for use by buyers, sellers, lawyers, surveyors and governments in the administration and management of real estate. Land registries are more typical in common law countries while cadastres usually appear in territories with Napoleonic codes of administration.

12.1 Land Registry Overview

A land registry is a public database of property and real estate ownership data connected with geographical records, paper archives, the legal system, the taxation system and industry, government policy and political oversight. Most land registries globally still function primarily with paper records. Legal deeds, inheritance

DOI: 10.4324/9781003571421-14

documents, taxation records and court orders form the predominant information source, some dating back centuries.

Many jurisdictions now recognise the need to modernise their land registries. Making a direct leap from legacy paper or relational databases to distributed ledgers and a tokenised solution offers both a technical upgrade to the registry itself as well as making it easier for third-party software (maps, financial calculators, tax systems) to integrate with the newly digitised register.

Policy development towards better land registry systems focuses on security, transparency, and accessibility through digitisation of records and process automation. Those same three attributes, (1) transparency, (2) equitable access and (3) trust in the data are, as we have seen elsewhere in this book, also markers for a distributed ledger use case. Widening access to accurate land registry information benefits democratic institutions and professionals who use these registries daily.

In the developing world, enhanced land registry systems can strengthen democracy by increasing trust and access to underlying real estate information. With high smartphone penetration but lower banking access, digitisation of land registries becomes a must-have policy for financial inclusion.

12.1.1 Key Entities and Actors

Key legal entities in land registries include:

- **The land registry itself**: operating under charter from local and national democratic institutions, government and government agencies. Land registry data must be trusted and accessible to all equally, in order for the population at large to have faith in using it and relying on its records and decisions
- **Owners/sellers/landlords** and **buyers/tenants**: both natural and legal persons, real estate buyers and sellers must be able to rely on the land registry in order to carry out their transactions
- **Realtors/real estate agents**: who represent owners in transactions. Agents are indirect users of land registries, but will often be asked to validate the legal status of a property or real estate in preparation for a sale or lease
- **Banks and finance providers**: often the legal owners of property titles through mortgages, financial institutions must have access to land registry data and be able to validate, update and interact with its records for posting information on debt and registering their own interests in mortgages, for example
- **Surveyors**: independent experts offering quality assurance, surveyors are professionals in assessing the condition and status of real estate and property

- **Local or national government**: the ultimate owner of the land registry, the local and/or national government is the body responsible to the electorate for the integrity and functioning of the land registry.

Important other actors in the system include land registry administrators who manage updates from real estate and property transactions to major system and operations changes like new developments, and auditors who independently verify the registry's accounts and records.

12.1.2 Land Registry Types and Models

Different models exist globally, including the following examples:

- **The UK's His Majesty's Land Registry**: a government agency which guarantees title to registered estates, operates without government funding through registration fees, and covers 88% of the real estate and property in England and Wales
- **The German cadastral system**: developed from taxation legislation and systems to a multipurpose land information system with computerised maps and property registers.

Banks use land registries extensively to record real estate transactions, mortgages, charges, liens, and tenancy information. The integrity of registry data is vital for banks, as better data enables faster, more accurate lending decisions. Potential tokenisation of real estate through blockchain could create a more liquid and accessible market for real estate finance.
Three common scenarios for land registries include:

- **Administering existing plots of land**: which form the majority of cases, involving legacy documentation and complex histories
- **Setting up new builds**: requiring detailed record-keeping of plans and eventual registration of new plots
- **Managing large-scale infrastructure projects**: involving mandatory purchases, clearances, redevelopment and potential disputes.

12.1.3 Challenges for Land Registries

Modern land registries face several significant challenges:

- **Taxation**: over time, land registries (often established to facilitate the measurement and collection of real estate and property taxes) are seeing a continual shift of focus away from pure real estate and property tax collection towards other roles such as planning and development, dispute resolution and reporting for the government, industry and consumers alike

- **Paper legacy**: real estate and property often goes back over many decades and – in many cases – centuries. Paper (or even parchment) deeds, handwritten agreements, long-term leases and leaseholds all include complex, physical documentation. There is a major challenge in digitising land registry information in converting these extensive paper records into digital formats. Not only does this process require significant resources, time and cost: there are also risks in preserving old archives and the potential for errors of proper categorisation and so on
- **Tokenisation**: both a challenge and a benefit, distributed ledgers and tokenisation enable real estate and property owners to fractionalise their ownership. This is of obvious benefit to new-build planners and owners but less useful where there are ancient deeds and reams of paper records. Fractionalising modern apartment blocks, warehouses, data centres and so on facilitates access to ownership for retail and institutional investors, but this may simply create a "two tier" system of land registry data.

12.1.4 Role of Blockchain in Land Registries

Land rights are an obvious use case for blockchain, distributed ledger and tokenisation technology. However, adoption varies according to local and national government capacity to invest in, test and deploy new technology. Blockchain isn't simply a technology upgrade. It requires a fundamental change in how land registries operate.

Developed economies currently lead in blockchain-based registry implementation, but developing economies show potential for significant progress in a "second wave" of adoption.

Blockchain, distributed ledger and tokenisation technology offers several advantages over the use of current paper and relational databases for land registries:

- **Security**: immutable records eliminate the risk of fraud, lower the likelihood of contentious disputes and litigation, and enable real estate and property owners to gain better reassurance over their ownership
- **Transparency**: in a distributed ledger, all real estate and property transactions are visible to authorised parties
- **Efficiency**: with a distributed ledger, when all parties can see all of the data at the same time and agree its integrity, there is potentially a reduced need for system or data intermediaries. Legal functions like conveyancer, mortgage broker, bank and so on of course remain, but it is less likely with a

distributed ledger that these intermediaries will require their own database, reconciliations and integrations, for example

- **Cost-effectiveness**: tokenisation offers lower operating costs through automation. Smart contracts, for example, in relation to tenancy agreements, service charges and so on, provide process-level automation that would remove some (but not all) manual processing
- **Tokenisation potential**: enabling fractional ownership and greater liquidity. As we have already discussed, fractional ownership of property and real estate through tokenisation means that access to ownership can increase without necessarily increasing concentration risks in retail consumer portfolios.

Land registries are evolving from paper-based systems towards more useful and relevant digital platforms for modern societies. This evolution requires balancing technological advances through blockchain with the need to maintain accurate legacy records.

The future land registry must be independent, trusted, authoritative, reliable, and publicly accessible while remaining accountable. Local expertise remains essential for maintaining accuracy and relevance, as land decisions are typically made locally.

For blockchain implementation to succeed, land registries must ensure secure, equitable, transparent access to all users while maintaining the integrity of historical records and accommodating the varying needs of all stakeholders – from individual property owners to government agencies, financial institutions, and real estate professionals.

12.2 Land Registry Use Cases

12.2.1 The United Kingdom: Martina's Flat Sale

In the historic market town of Hereford, nestled near the England-Wales border, agricultural scientist Martina Mendes is finalising the sale of her Bath Street flat. Working abroad on a two-year assignment, she's ready to complete this chapter of her life.

12.2.1.1 The Traditional Process

Martina's flat sale exemplifies the cumbersome nature of traditional property transactions. Despite finding a buyer, Tonya Wilmot, through a modern property app, the process remains firmly anchored in outdated systems.

The cast of characters expands beyond seller and buyer. Martina's Birmingham solicitors coordinate with HSBC (her mortgage provider), while Tonya's legal team carefully scrutinises every document. The estate agents hover in the background, awaiting their commission.

While Tonya's money sits ready for transfer, her solicitors demand verification from HM Land Registry first. Martina's legal team initiates the request, setting in motion a fragmented process where registry staff cobble together information from paper files, spreadsheets, image libraries, and databases.

The resulting report, transmitted via email, reveals a technical issue. With cautious formality, both legal teams jointly appoint local surveyor Natalie Bowden to inspect the property. Her professional assessment eventually satisfies Tonya's concerns, allowing the transaction to proceed.

Some weeks later, after numerous confirmations between banks and solicitors, the sale completes. Martina receives her funds (minus the mortgage balance), while Tonya's name replaces Martina's in the official records. Each participant updates their separate systems, and the case is marked "closed" – a process that took months rather than days.

12.2.1.2 The Blockchain Alternative

In the reimagined scenario, HM Land Registry has launched a blockchain-powered proof of concept that transforms this tedious process. Martina's newly-built flat qualifies for this innovative approach, with its records already migrated to the blockchain system.

Each participant – seller, buyer, banks, solicitors, surveyor, and registry – functions as a node in this secure network. Their smartphone apps connect them to a system governed by smart contracts that automate and validate each step.

When Tonya's solicitors request a survey, surveyor Natalie Bowden receives an immediate alert. After inspection, she updates her approval directly through her phone app, triggering the next stage automatically.

All parties receive simultaneous notification that exchange and completion can proceed. As each confirms their component – title transfer, money exchanges, mortgage settlement – the system creates a new block containing these verified transactions. The property's updated status appears on public record instantly, without the reconciliation headaches of the traditional process.

12.2.2 Bangladesh: Nazrul's Development Plot

In Bangladesh, property developer Nazrul Islam is exploring investment opportunities in Titas, an administrative region in the Chittagong Division established in 2004.

12.2.1.3 The Traditional System

Bangladesh's current land registry typifies challenges faced in developing nations – fragmented paper records scattered across tax offices and local authorities with no centralised database.

When Nazrul approaches Ahmed A. Jamal about selling his land, Ahmed agrees readily, eager to fund his return to Dhaka to care for his elderly mother. However, locating the paper title deeds requires an arduous search through the Sub Registry archives.

The outdated deeds need administrative updates to reflect changes since the formation of Titas Upazila. After a cash transaction, Nazrul takes responsibility for updating the registry records. Meanwhile, facing planning approval complexities, he leaves the land undeveloped as its value slowly rises.

12.2.1.4 The Blockchain Revolution

In the alternative scenario, Bangladesh has created the Bangladesh Blockchain Land Rights Service (BBLRS), with Titas Upazila among the first regions digitised. All plots within its boundaries have been mapped digitally, with paper records consolidated, scanned, and categorised.

Local property owners receive education on using the new BBLRS smartphone app and verify their ownership details directly. Nazrul, as a potential buyer, can instantly view specific plot details, ownership status, and administrative information through the same application.

After negotiating terms, both Nazrul and Ahmed submit their transaction through the app, confirming their new statuses as "owner" and "former owner" respectively, along with price and tax information. Nazrul then submits his development plans digitally to local authorities, who update the blockchain with their approval.

12.2.3 How has Tokenisation been Applied?

Blockchain-powered land registries using tokenisation offer benefits extending far beyond simple property transfers:

- **Property development and planning**: the digital system enables more efficient, transparent planning applications. Neighbours can participate in the process, while updated valuations facilitate infrastructure planning for utilities and transportation.
- **Simplified taxation**: when tax authorities participate as blockchain nodes, property sales, inheritance matters, and estate management become more

straightforward. Estate planners face fewer surprises and contentious issues diminish.

- **Population and planning analysis**: comprehensive digital land records assist with immigration planning and infrastructure development. Schools, healthcare facilities, and other public services can be allocated based on accurate land use data.

While no universal standard exists for land registries due to Earth's infinite geographic variations, blockchain technology offers common benefits: trust, security, immutability, equitable access, and transparency. Secondary advantages include improved planning processes, potential for tokenisation of land rights, and more democratic approaches to contentious matters like zoning laws.

The digitisation journey may never reach 100% completion – dusty paper records or completely undocumented properties will likely remain outside digital systems. Nevertheless, blockchain technology, distributed ledgers and tokenisation represents a transformative step forward in how we record, transfer, and verify our most fundamental asset: land.

12.3 Legal Considerations for Trade Finance and Tokenisation: The Chain

A common scenario, particularly in domestic property transactions, is that of the chain.

The commuter-belt town of Greenbridge Common, in rural England, is seeing a rise in popularity as it is perfectly placed for the hybrid worker. Property sales are booming and three local estate agents, Meadow and Marsh, Greenfield Property Partners, and Elm and Alder are doing good business.

Unfortunately, three separate transactions are locked in a mutually-dependent chain. All the parties are hoping that their purchases will complete today – as soon as possible as they all have removal vans lined up in the town's narrow lanes.

Daniel Ofori is buying 12 Willow Way for £450,000 from Aisha Patel who is moving away from the area. But Daniel first needs to sell his own house, 27 Oak Terrace, for £375,000, enabling him to redeem his existing mortgage with Barclays Bank. Michelle Hughes is in turn looking to move into 27 Oak Terrace, but only once she's sold her own property at 45 Chestnut Lane to Priya Singh for £500,000.

Figure 12.1 shows this chain and the separate silos of data involved.

Today, resolving the chain requires a fraught, complex dance orchestrated by the lawyers involved. The process relies on each stage completing without issue to ensure that each buyer and seller can complete the transaction on the same day,

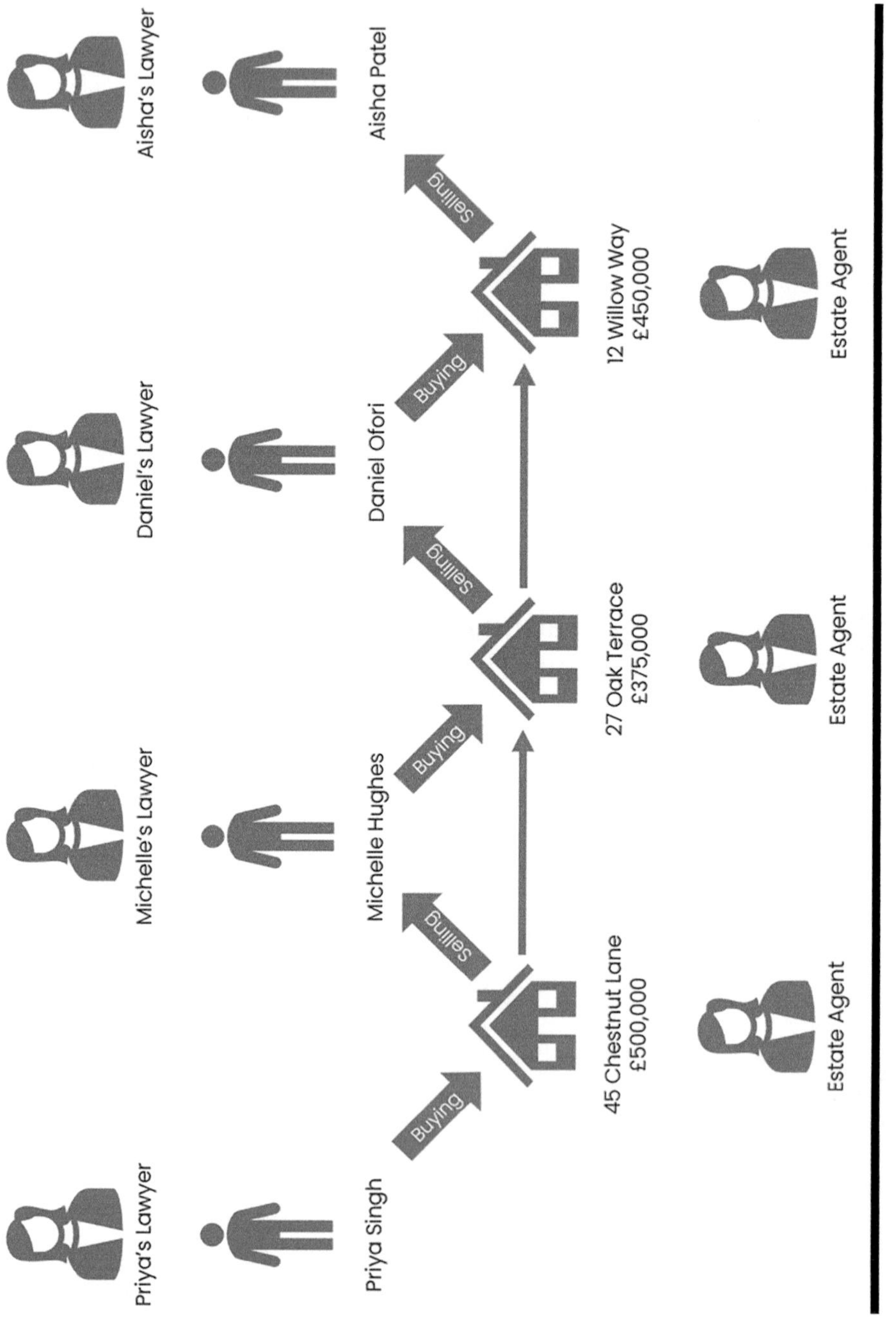

Figure 12.1 Real Estate before Tokenisation.

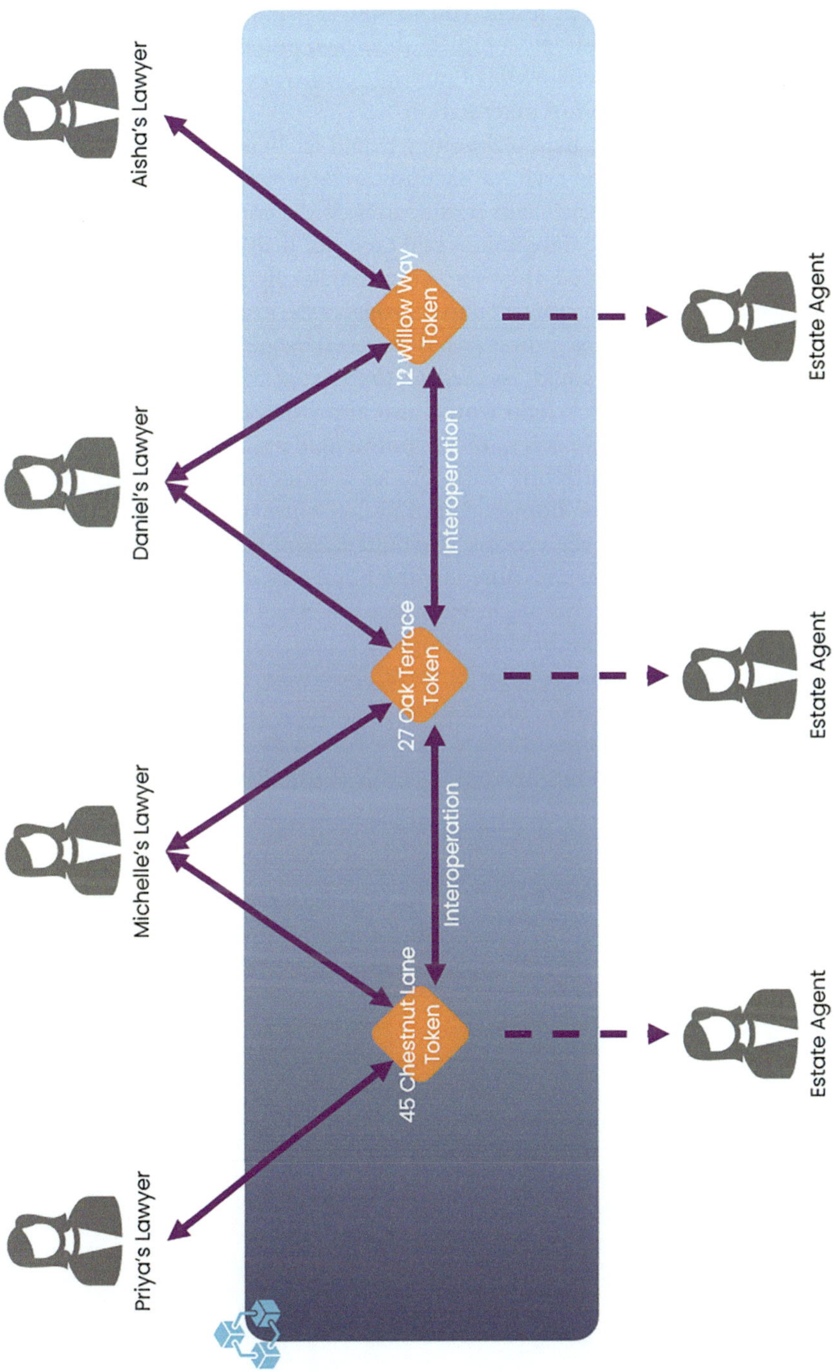

Figure 12.2 Real Estate Tokenised.

in fact simultaneously, with each seller-turned-buyer gaining the capital from the sale of their property, so they can complete their own purchase.

With tokenisation, the chain sale of multiple properties would be streamlined through the implementation of tokenisation.

Tokenisation and blockchain technology would facilitate this process because the pre-defined conditions of each transaction can be programmed into the smart contract. Applying this to the chain transactions, if the conditions of one transaction fail, then none of the transactions will proceed. If all transactions are ready and the conditions are satisfied, they execute automatically. Once the condition is fulfilled, the algorithm in the smart contract triggers the events specified, namely, once the money for the first property has been exchanged, the smart contract would be satisfied, and it could proceed to the next sale in the chain. Storing the information on the blockchain would also improve the process, because the necessary parties would have access to the immutable data throughout the process. Chain transactions currently occur under a strict timeline which can be delayed by the necessity for human action and confirmation. With the introduction of tokenisation to the process, it would streamline the chain and vastly reduce any delays and any errors caused by the human element.

Figure 12.2 shows how this might work in a tokenised landscape.

Adoption of tokenisation for chain property transactions remains in a proof-of-concept stage, with multiple pilot projects underway. There are examples of the foundational infrastructure for tokenisation being tested as well, such as blockchain networks that connect estate agents, conveyancers and banks. If there is a successful implementation, this could provide the framework for tokenisation of the chain sale process.

Conclusion

So where does all this leave the case for tokenisation?

Has it been made?

The question, to a certain extent, is moot. The great thing about business is that eventually it finds the optimum platform for effective execution. If tokenisation is the right answer for a multi-party business process, it will happen. Maybe not yet, but soon.

In the meantime, let's revisit our key criteria.

Transparency:

- In Part 1, we saw how transparency is achieved through participation as a node in a blockchain network. Data is available to all parties, without the need for a trusted operator to store and reveal the data as required. We also saw how important it is that the right amount of data is shared, with private data held securely off-chain and confirmed through zero-knowledge validation.
- In Part 2, we saw valid use cases where all parties need to share data, such as the case of the missing concrete (trade finance), or during Holly's emergency (health). In all the scenarios, we have seen how parties need access to reliable data, in some cases without wanting other external agents to be involved.

Equitable Access:

- Part 1 demonstrated that equitable access and blockchains go hand in hand. It is precisely the absence of a trusted third party that both enables blockchain's value and defines many of its operating paradigms: cryptographic security, distributed data, and identity management.
- Part 2 outlined a number of use cases where multiple parties require equitable access to data. Core banking and finance, wealth management, as well as real estate and health industries all share a need for the reliable transport and availability of large amounts of data.

Trust:

- Part 1 showed us that blockchain is all about trust. First, how to transfer and hold items of value (cryptocurrencies or tokens) in a trustless environment, and second how that trust is achieved through cryptographic keys.
- In every use case outlined in Part 2, trust is key. Whether it's Martina selling her flat in Hereford or consolidating Peter's investment portfolio, the need for trust is clear.

So, from a purely theoretical perspective, it looks as though the case for tokenisation is solid.

There are clearly some issues to work through. Identity management is a hot topic, and we've seen that the legal certainty of transferring and holding tokens is a work in progress. Then there are some technical and operational aspects: scalability, the throughput of transactions and speed of finality, as well as the cost of each transaction – these can all vary quite dramatically from one network to the other.

We've also seen some of the problems faced by tokenisation projects such as difficulties during testing and dealing with spam.

The authors, though, do not doubt that the global technical and business communities have the ambition, acumen and wherewithal to address and overcome these issues. There are such riches on offer, in terms of streamlined processes, faster and more reliable communication, more profitable partnerships and better outcomes for the end consumer. The businesses that adapt to Web3 and all it has to offer will quickly gain ascendancy over those that do not.

Tokenisation is ready to become a major component in the industrial and commercial landscape – a springboard for those who are ready to jump into the unknown.

Index

For Product Safety Concerns and Information please contact our EU representative GPSR@taylorandfrancis.com Taylor & Francis Verlag GmbH, Kaufingerstraße 24, 80331 München, Germany